STUDY GUIDE

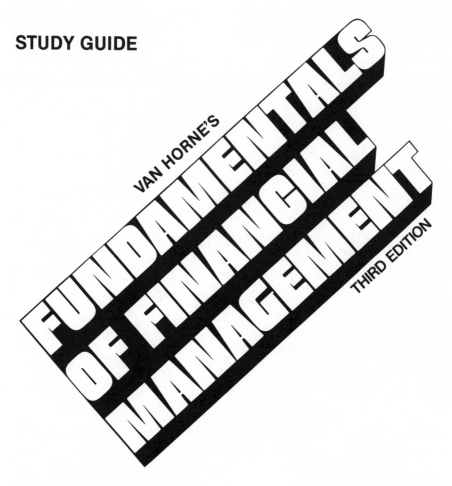

VAN HORNE'S
FUNDAMENTALS OF FINANCIAL MANAGEMENT
THIRD EDITION

DAVID SCOTT, JR.
Texas Tech University

J. WILLIAM PETTY
Texas Tech University

JOHN D. MARTIN
Virginia Polytechnic Institute and State University

ARTHUR J. KEOWN
Virginia Polytechnic Institute and State University

PRENTICE-HALL, INC., *Englewood Cliffs, New Jersey 07632*

Library of Congress Cataloging in Publication Data
Main entry under title:

Study guide, Van Horne's Fundamentals of financial management.

1. Corporations--Finance. 2. Corporations--Finance--Problems, exercises, etc. I. Scott, David F.,(date) II. Van Horne, James C. Fundamentals of financial management. HG4011.V36 1977 Suppl. 658.1'5 76-56367 ISBN 0-13-339366-6

© 1977 by Prentice-Hall, Inc., Englewood Cliffs, New Jersey 07632

10 9 8 7 6 5 4 3 2

Printed in the United States of America

ISBN 0-13-339366-6

PRENTICE-HALL INTERNATIONAL, INC., *London*
PRENTICE-HALL OF AUSTRALIA PTY. LIMITED, *Sydney*
PRENTICE-HALL OF CANADA, LTD., *Toronto*
PRENTICE-HALL OF INDIA PRIVATE LIMITED, *New Delhi*
PRENTICE-HALL OF JAPAN, INC., *Tokyo*
PRENTICE-HALL OF SOUTHEAST ASIA PTE. LTD., *Singapore*
WHITEHALL BOOKS LIMITED, *Wellington, New Zealand*

Contents

Preface

The objective of this *Study Guide* is to provide a student-oriented
supplement to the third edition of *Fundamentals of Financial Management* by
James C. Van Horne. There are two basic ways in which we have attempted to
accomplish that end. The first involves providing a condensation of each
chapter in the form of a detailed sentence outline. This overview of the key
points of the chapter can serve both as a preview and quick survey of the
chapter content and as a review. A second way in which we have attempted to
accomplish our overall objective is through providing problems (with detailed
solutions) and self-tests which can be used to aid in the preparation of
outside assignments and in studying for examinations. The problems were
keyed to the end-of-chapter problems in the text in order to provide a direct
and meaningful student aid. Both multiple-choice and true-false questions
are used to provide a self-test over the descriptive chapter material. The outline,
problems and solutions, and self-tests combined provide what we believe is a
valuable learning tool for the student of financial management.

The Role of Financial Management

Orientation: The financial executive is responsible for the management of the firm's flow of funds, the objective being to maximize the shareholders' wealth. However, toward this end, a conflict could potentially develop between the shareholders and management. Also, in striving to maximize the shareholders' position, "social responsibility" may have to be recognized.

I. Introductory comments

    A. The business entity may be viewed as representing a pool of funds, with these funds originating from a variety of sources and being committed to a number of uses.

    B. During an elapse of time, this pool of funds is subject to change, with the modifications being defined as *funds flows.*

    C. Financial management is directly involved with the management of the funds flows, particular responsibilities being as follows:

        1. The determination of the proper amounts of funds to be employed in the firm.

        2. The efficient allocation of the respective sources to the various uses.

        3. The determination of a financial mix offering the most favorable terms feasible.

D. Historically, the financial manager was concerned only with the raising of funds; however, in more recent times, financial executives have become involved in all three of the responsibilities listed.

E. The effectiveness of the financial decision maker has an impact not only upon the success of the company but also on the economy overall.

II. The goal of the firm

A. To evaluate management's performance in overseeing the flow of funds, a guideline must be provided as the basis for decisions.

B. For the purposes of financial decisions, maximization of the present owner's wealth will be used as the basic criterion against which all decisions are to be evaluated.

C. Although the market price may not necessarily be a precise measure of wealth, this surrogate represents the best estimate available.

D. Wealth maximization is a superior goal to profit maximization, in that profit maximization is not as inclusive a goal. The advantage of wealth maximization comes through the recognition of a number of important factors, these being:

1. Recognition of the timing of expected returns.

2. The means for the inclusion of the riskiness of the prospective earning streams.

3. Recognition of the impact of the financial mix upon the return on equity.

4. Treatment of the impact of the dividend policy upon the stock-holders' position.

E. In summary, the market price represents the evaluation of the marketplace of management's performance, thereby representing an overall performance index or report card of the company's progress.

III. In a large corporation, the stockholders may only have limited control or influence over the operations of the company, the principal control being maintained by management.

A. In such a situation, management is thought at times to be *satisficers* rather than *maximizers,* as they are concerned primarily with survival.

B. On the other hand, survival in the long run may require management to perform in a fashion reasonably consistent with the maximization of shareholder wealth.

IV. The objective of shareholder maximization represents a normative or ideal goal, indicating how the firm *should* act, not necessarily how it *does* act.

    A. Justification for the wealth-maximization objective on a normative basis comes from its contribution to allocate savings in an economy in an efficient manner, based upon expected return and risk.

    B. An alternative objective may result in the suboptimal allocation of funds, thereby resulting in less growth and capital formation in the economy.

    C. Social responsibility has to be recognized by management.

        1. Some individuals would contend that the corporation's existence depends upon the firm being socially responsible.

        2. Social responsibility may create problems for the company.

            a. Social responsibility may fall unevenly on different corporations.

            b. The responsibility may also be in conflict with the objective of wealth maximization, which could cause a less efficient allocation of resources in society.

    D. Other individuals would contend that management should not be called upon to resolve the conflict between wealth maximization and social responsibility.

        1. Society should be offered the opportunity to make these decisions.

        2. With such decisions being made by society, the corporation could then engage in wealth maximization subject to certain constraints.

V. Functions of the financial manager

    A. In the context of wealth maximization, the function of the financial decision maker may be subdivided into two areas:

        1. Efficient allocation of funds within the enterprise.

        2. Acquisition of funds on as favorable a basis as possible.

    B. In the allocation of funds to the various uses within the firm, the analysis may be segmented into two classifications of assets:

        1. The management of current assets: The objective in this instance is the determination of a proper level of current assets, which depends upon the profitability and flexibility associated with a

given liquidity level relative to the costs of maintaining such a level.

2. The allocation of fixed assets: Fixed-asset management (capital budgeting) involves making investment decisions offering benefits in future years.

   a. Since expected future returns are uncertain, risk must be recognized.

   b. An acceptance criteria for an investment project must be developed in accordance with the objective of maximizing shareholder wealth.

C. In the raising of funds, the financial manager must determine the best mix of financing for the company, being aware of the implications of any decision upon the shareholders' wealth.

SELF-TESTS

True-False

___F___ 1. Profit maximization is considered to be a more appropriate goal than wealth maximization because it considers the timing of the expected returns of the firm.

___T___ 2. Wealth maximization considers the effects of the riskiness of a prospective earnings stream.

___F___ 3. Originally, the role of the financial manager of a firm was quite extensive (covering many areas of the firm); recently, however, his responsibilities have been narrowed so that he might devote more time to the raising of funds.

___T___ 4. By efficient allocation of funds, we mean that funds are allocated to those assets in such a manner that the shareholders' wealth is maximized.

___T___ 5. The efficient management of the flow of funds within the firm implies that management must have a goal by which efficiency can be measured.

___F___ 6. No conflict is possible between the goals of management and those of the shareholders.

___T___ 7. The purpose of capital markets is to channel funds from savers to investors.

___F___ 8. Whenever management contemplates investing in a particular asset, its acceptability is evaluated solely upon the basis of its rate of return to the company.

_T_   9. The optimal level of a *current* asset depends on the profitability and flexibility associated with that level in relation to the cost involved in maintaining it.

_F_   10. The allocation of funds among current assets is known as capital budgeting.

Multiple Choice

1. The long-run objective of financial management is to:
   a. Hold large quantities of cash.
   b. Increase sales regularly.
   c. Maximize earnings per share.
   d. Maximize the value of the firm.

2. Maximizing the value of the firm means maximizing the value of the firm's:
   a. Assets.
   b. Cash.
   c. Investments.
   d. Profits.
   e. Market price of its stock.

3. Important functions of financial management are:
   a. To provide for adequate financing.
   b. Long-range planning.
   c. To control costs.
   d. To identify desirable investment projects.
   e. All of the above.

4. The financial manager is concerned with which of the following responsibilities?
   a. The proper amount of funds to employ in the firm.
   b. Seeing that the financial statements of the firm are properly presented.
   c. Raising funds for the firm on the most favorable terms possible.
   d. a and b.
   e. a and c.

5. Profit maximization is not the proper objective of a firm because:
   a. It is not as inclusive a goal as the maximization of shareholder wealth.
   b. It does not consider the risk of the prospective earnings stream.
   c. It does not allow for the effect of dividend policy on the market price of the stock.
   d. All of the above.
   e. None of the above.

6. The market price of a share of stock is determined by:
   a. The New York Stock Exchange.
   b. The company's management.
   c. All shareholders in the company.

    d. Individuals buying and selling the stock.
    e. None of the above.
7. Which of the following represents a problem that social responsibility creates for a firm?
    a. It falls unevenly upon different corporations.
    b. It could potentially conflict with the objective of wealth maximization.
    c. Neither of the above.
    d. a and b.
8. Which of the following would a company do if its objective was to maximize profits?
    a. Never pay a dividend.
    b. Become more socially responsible.
    c. Analyze investments as to both their risk and return.
    d. None of the above.
    e. a and c.

Organizational Form and Taxes 2

Orientation: The objective of this chapter is to afford the student a familiarity with the legal setting in which the firm operates. In this regard, the basic forms of business organization are reviewed. Also, a highlight of the basic tax implications relating to financial decisions is given consideration.

I. Legal forms of business organizations

    A. Sole proprietorship: A single person owns the business.

        1. Advantages:

            a. Easily established with few complications.

            b. Flexible.

            c. Minimal organizational costs.

            d. Does not have to share profits or control with others.

        2. Disadvantages:

            a. Unlimited liability for the owner.

            b. Difficult to raise capital.

            c. Certain tax disadvantages.

            d. Transfer of ownership is more difficult than other forms.

    B. Partnership: Similar to proprietorship except that there is more than one owner.

1. There are a number of types of a partnership, with the two basic classifications being as follows:

   a. General partnership

      (1) All partners have unlimited liability.

      (2) Usually agreement exists stating how profits, losses, and responsibilities are to be divided among the partners.

   b. Limited partnership

      (1) A limited partner contributes capital but the liability is limited to the amount of capital invested.

      (2) There must be at least one general partner who has unlimited liability in the partnership.

2. Advantages:

   a. Ease of formation.

   b. Modest organizational expense.

   c. Do not have to share profits or control with outsiders.

3. Disadvantages:

   a. Unlimited liability of the partners.

   b. Difficult to raise large sums of money.

   c. Death of any partner causes dissolution of the business.

C. The corporation: an "impersonal" legal entity, having the power to own assets and incur liabilities while existing separately and apart from its owners.

1. Ownership is evidenced by shares of stock.

2. A corporation is incorporated in a specific state by filing an application with the appropriate state official.

3. If approved, a charter is issued which establishes the corporation as a legal entity and sets forth the conditions under which it is to exist.

4. Advantages:

   a. Limited liability of owners.

   b. Ease of transferability of ownership.

   c. The death of individual owners does not result in the discontinuity of the firm's life.

        d. Ability of the corporation to raise capital apart from its owners.

    5. Disadvantages:

        a. Possible tax disadvantages.

        b. More difficult and expensive to establish.

II. Corporate income taxes

    A. The majority of business decisions are directly or indirectly impacted by taxes.

    B. A corporation's taxable income is found by deducting all expenses, including depreciation and interest from revenues.

    C. Involves a graduated tax schedule: The first $25,000 in taxable income is taxed at a 22% rate, with any additional income being taxed at 48%.[1]

    D. Corporations usually file quarterly tax payments each year on April 15, June 15, September 15, and December 15, with the final settlement for taxes being on April 15 of the following year (assuming that the tax year ends on December 31).

    E. Depreciation

        1. Three methods may be used for tax purposes:

            a. Double-declining balance.

            b. Sum-of-the-years' digits.

            c. Straight line.

        2. The Internal Revenue Service has established depreciable-value and depreciable-life guidelines for most types of assets.

        3. The method of depreciation employed does not affect the total amount of depreciation charges, only the timing of those charges.

    F. Interest expenses

        1. Interest charges on debt issued by a corporation are deductible for tax purposes.

        2. Dividends paid to preferred and common shareholders are not tax deductible.

---

[1] A temporary measure was enacted by Congress beginning in 1975 in which the first $25,000 in taxable income is taxed at a rate of 20%; the next $25,000 is taxed at a rate of 22%; and all amounts in excess of $50,000 are taxed at a 48% rate.

3. Use of debt by the firm may result in significant tax advantages.

G. Dividend income: If a corporation receives dividends on stock owned in another company, only 15% of the dividends are taxed.

H. Carry-back and carry-forward: Operating losses of a corporation may be carried back 3 years and forward 5 years to offset taxable income in these years.

I. Capital gains and losses

   1. A capital asset is defined as any asset not held for sale in a normal course of business.

   2. When a capital asset is sold, a capital gain or loss is incurred.

   3. If the asset is held for 6 months or less, the gain or loss is defined as short-term; otherwise, the gain is long-term.

   4. Short-term capital losses are subtracted from short-term capital gains, with any net gain being added to the corporation's ordinary income.

   5. Any net long-term capital gains (long-term gains less long-term losses) in excess of net short-term capital losses are taxed at a rate not to exceed 30%.

   6. If a depreciable capital asset is sold at a price in excess of the depreciated book value but for less than the original cost, the gain is deemed to be *recapture of depreciation* and is taxed as ordinary income.

   7. A capital loss may not be deducted from ordinary income for tax purposes, but may only be used to offset capital gains.

   8. If after deducting all capital gains and capital losses the company has a net capital loss, such loss may be carried back for 3 years and forward for 5 years to offset any capital gains occurring during those periods.

J. If a company has installment sales, a special tax provision exists by which the profits from the sale are spread over the years in which payments are received.

K. Investment tax credit is available to corporations and individuals who invest in certain types of qualified assets.

   1. Currently up to 10% of the total cost of a qualified asset may be used to offset taxes to be paid by the taxpayer.

   2. A maximum 10% credit is available on qualified property with a

useful life of 7 or more years, with a lesser credit being available for shorter-lived assets.

III. Personal income tax

   A.   Individual income tax rates are graduated from a marginal tax rate of 14% to 70%.

   B.   Dividend income is taxed as ordinary income, with an exemption for the first $100 for a single return and $200 if the stock is jointly owned and a joint return is being filed.

   C.   Short-term capital gains are taxed as ordinary income.

   D.   Long-term capital gains not exceeding $50,000 are taxed at the lesser of (1) a 25% tax rate or (2) one-half of the individual's marginal tax rate on ordinary income.

   E.   Individuals are required to net long-term and short-term capital gains and losses.

   F.   A net short-term capital loss may be deducted against ordinary income up to a maximum of $1,000 per year, with any remaining loss being carried forward into future years.

   G.   One-half of the excess of net long-term capital losses may be deducted from ordinary income up to a maximum of $1,000 in a taxable year, with any unused loss being carried forward into future periods.

IV. Subchapter S

   A.   Subchapter S of the Internal Revenue Code permits the owners of a small corporation with 10 or fewer stockholders to use the corporate organizational form but be taxed as though the firm was a partnership.

   B.   This treatment eliminates the double taxation normally associated with dividend income.

STUDY PROBLEMS

1. Mr. Smith had ordinary income of $100,000 for 1976. He also sold some stock, resulting in a long-term capital gain of $100,000. If his average tax rate is 35% and long-term capital gains are taxed at a rate not to exceed 25% or one-half his ordinary average tax rate, what would he be required to pay in taxes?

Solution:

(1) Tax on ordinary income: (0.35) ($100,000) = $35,000

(2) Tax on capital gain: (0.175) ($50,000) =   8,750
                                        + (0.35) ($50,000) =   17,500
                                                                          $61,250

(*Note:* Long-term capital gains in excess of $50,000 are taxed as
ordinary income—hence, only one-half of the capital gain
is subject to the preferential tax treatment.)

2. (a) Mr. Jones had $10,000 of ordinary income in 1976. He had a net long-
term capital loss on the sale of securities of $5,000, and a net short-term capital
loss of $300. What is his taxable income?

(b) What amounts of short-term and long-term capital losses will he carry
forward?

Solution:

(a) $9,000 ($10,000 ordinary income less the $1,000 capital-loss
limitation).

(b) $0 short-term loss and $3,600 long-term loss. Short-term losses
were taken in 1976, and $1,400 of the long-term loss was used in
order to receive credit for $700 (1/2 of $1,400). Thus, $3,600
($5,000 − $1,400) is carried forward.

3. A corporation had $63,500 in taxable earnings in 1976. What is the tax bill
related to this income?

Solution:

$23,980: (22% X $25,000) + (48% X $38,500)

4. (a) A corporation has earnings before interest and taxes of $50,000, an
interest charge of $9,000, and dividend income of $5,000. What is the taxable
income related to this income?

(b) How much taxes would be paid?[1]

Solution:

(a) $41,750: [50,000 + (0.15)($5,000) − $9,000]

(b) $13,540: (22% X $25,000) + (48% X 16,750)

---

[1] The solution uses the 22%-48% schedule rather than the current "temporary" legislation,
which gives the corporation a 20%-22%-48% scale.

5. The taxable income of Gilmore Corporation is as follows (losses are shown in parentheses):

1970	$(200,000)
1971	100,000
1972	150,000
1973	300,000
1974	(150,000)

What is Gilmore's tax payment or tax refund in each year after carry-forwards and carry-backs are recognized?

Solution:

Year	Taxable Income	Tax Payment	Tax Refund
1970	$ 0	$ 0	$ 0
1971	0	0	0
1972	50,000	17,500	0
1973	300,000	137,500	0
1974	0	0	65,500*

*Refund of 1972 taxes plus refund of $48,000 of 1973 taxes.

6. In 1970, the James Company purchased a lathe for $25,000 that had a depreciable life of 10 years and an expected salvage value of zero. Five years later the firm sold the machine for $27,500. If the firm uses straight-line depreciation, how much taxes would result as a consequence of the sale, assuming that the firm has a marginal tax rate of 48% and a capital gains rate of 30%?

Solution:

Sale value	$27,500
Book value	12,500
Gain	$15,000

Sale price over original cost	2,500	(capital gain)
Recapture of depreciation	$12,500	(ordinary income)

Taxes = $(0.48)($12,500) + (0.3)($2,500) = \underline{\$6,750}$

7. Bill Smith is currently self-employed and operates his business as a sole proprietorship. The business earns $75,000 in annual income. Mr. Smith is considering whether or not to incorporate, but before doing so, he wants to consider the tax consequences. If he incorporates, he will receive $20,000 in salary from the corporation, plus $15,000 in yearly dividends. With an average tax rate of 35% on personal income, what should he do?

Solution:

Tax payments if incorporated:

Corporate taxable income	$55,000 ($75,000 − $20,000)
Taxes	$19,900 (22% × $25,000 + 48% × $30,000)
Individual income	$34,900 (after deducting $100 for dividend exclusion)
Taxes	$12,215 (35% × $34,900)
Total tax after incorporation	= $19,900 + $12,215 = $32,115

Tax payments if not incorporated:

Taxable income prior to incorporation	$75,000
Taxes	$26,250 (35% of $75,000)

Decision: If tax considerations were the only decision variable, he should not incorporate, in that he would pay additional taxes of $5,865 if incorporation is chosen.

8. Smith Brothers, a small implement company, sells lawn mowers. The firm has a marginal tax rate of 50%. The lawn mowers retail for $700, which includes a gross profit margin of 30%. It sells the mowers on both a cash basis and on an installment basis. For installment sales, payments are spread over a period of 6 years, with $100 being paid as a down payment, and $100 due at the end of each of the next 6 years. With a cash sale, the full purchase price is due at the time of sale.

(a) Which method results in more taxes being paid?

(b) Which method is more favorable with respect to taxes?

Solution:

Installment Sales

	Installment Receipt	Gross Profit	Taxes
Year of sale	$100	$30	$ 15
Year 1	100	30	15
Year 2	100	30	15
Year 3	100	30	15
Year 4	100	30	15
Year 5	100	30	15
Year 6	100	30	15
			$105

Cash Sales

	Receipt	Gross Profit	Taxes
Year of sale	$700	$210	$105

(a) Both methods result in the same taxes being paid.

(b) The installment sale is better in that the tax payments are spread over the 6-year period.

SELF-TESTS

True-False

         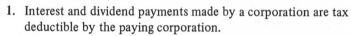

F   1. Interest and dividend payments made by a corporation are tax deductible by the paying corporation.

T F   2. For corporations, capital losses are deductible against ordinary income.

F   3. In a limited partnership, all the partners have limited liability.

T F   4. Many businesses are formed as corporations to avoid the double taxation of income.

T F   5. By using the sum-of-years'-digits form of depreciation, the asset is never fully depreciated.

T   6. If a capital asset is held for more than 6 months and then sold for a gain, the gain is classified as a long-term capital gain.

T F   7. If a capital asset is sold for a price in excess of its depreciated book value but for less than its original cost, the excess is subject to a capital-gains tax.

T F   8. The Tax Reduction Act of 1975 increased the investment tax credit from 7% to 10% for all assets having a useful life of 7 or more years.

T F   9. Long-term capital gains for individuals are always taxed at one-half of the individual's ordinary income tax rate up to a maximum rate of 25%.

T F   10. Subchapter S of the Internal Revenue Code permits owners of small corporations to use the corporate organizational form but to be taxed as though the firm were a proprietorship or a partnership.

Multiple Choice

1. For corporations, net long-term capital gains are limited to a tax rate of:
   a. 50%.
   b. 48%.
   c. 25%.
   d. 22%.
   e. 30%.

2. A corporation owning stock in another corporation is taxed on what percentage of the dividends received from the owned corporation?
   a. 15%.
   b. 85%.
   c. 48%.
   d. 50%.
   e. 25%.

3. Advantages of the sole proprietorship are:
   a. Ease of formation.
   b. Unlimited liability.
   c. Double taxation.
   d. Nominal organizational costs.
   e. a and d.

4. Disadvantages of the partnership are:
   a. Unlimited liability.
   b. Ease of formation.
   c. No double taxation on income.
   d. Lack of permanence.
   e. a and d.
   f. b and c.

5. The pair containing one advantage and one disadvantage of the corporation is:
   a. Limited liability and perpetual life.
   b. Costly to form and lack of secrecy.
   c. Unlimited liability and ease of transference of shares.
   d. Limited liability and more complex to form.
   e. a and c.
   f. b and c.

6. Which of the following forms of business organization is the largest form with respect to numbers?
   a. Partnership.
   b. Sole proprietorship.
   c. Corporation.

7. Which of the following is not an advantage of the partnership?
   a. Limited liability.
   b. A voice in the management of the partnership.

c. Limited life.
d. a and b.
e. a and c.

8. Advantages of the corporation include:
   a. Unlimited liability.
   b. Transferability of interest.
   c. Ability of the corporation to raise capital.
   d. None of the above.
   e. b and c.

9. If a corporation sustains a net operating loss, this loss may be:
   a. Carried back 5 years and forward 3 years to offset taxable income.
   b. Carried back 3 years and forward 5 years to offset taxable income.
   c. Deducted against long-term capital gains.
   d. Nothing may be done with the loss.

10. An individual's short-term capital gains are taxed:
    a. As ordinary income.
    b. At a rate not to exceed 25% of the gain.
    c. At one-half of the individual's ordinary tax rate.
    d. None of the above.

3 Financial Analysis

Orientation: Financial analysis involves the use of the analytical tools of ratios, source and use statements, financial forecasting, cash budgets, and pro forma financial statements to assess a firm's financial condition and plan for its future condition. Chapter 3 deals specifically with the use of financial ratios, where ratios are discussed in terms of four categories: liquidity, leverage, coverage, and profitability.

I. Framework for financial analysis

    A. The first step in the analysis is to determine the financing needs of the firm. Here we attempt to assess the amount of funds needed, as well as the most suitable plan for obtaining them.

    B. The final consideration in the proposed framework for financial analysis involves negotiating with suppliers of capital for the needed funds. This step in the suggested procedure gives recognition to the fact that the firm's management must consider the necessity for "selling" its financing plan to the suppliers of capital, as well as determining what it considers to be the best financing plan for the firm.

II. Financial ratios can be used to assess both financial condition and performance in terms of two types of ratio comparisons:

    A. *Trend comparisons* can be made for a given firm, whereby ratios based on current information are compared with past and expected ratios to determine whether there has been an improvement or deterioration in the financial condition and/or performance of the firm over time.

B. A second method of comparison involves *comparing* the ratios for the firm *with* those of *similar firms* or *industry norms* so as to gain insight into the relative financial condition and performance of the firm.

III. Types of ratios

A. *Liquidity ratios* are used to assess a firm's ability to meet its short-term financial obligations.

1. Although it is a very crude measure, the most frequently used measure of firm liquidity is the *current ratio.*

a. The current ratio is defined as

$$\frac{\text{current assets}}{\text{current liabilities}}$$

with a higher ratio indicating increased liquidity.

b. Since the current ratio does not take into account the liquidity of the individual current asset accounts, its use as the exclusive measure of firm liquidity can be misleading.

2. The *quick* or *acid-test ratio,* which is defined as

$$\frac{\text{current assets less inventories}}{\text{current liabilities}}$$

provides a more discerning measure of firm liquidity in that it omits inventories from the firm's liquid assets.

3. Liquidity in accounts receivable can be measured in a number of ways.

a. The first of these measures is the *average collection period,* represented by

$$\frac{\text{average accounts receivable} \times 365 \text{ days}}{\text{annual credit sales}}$$

which indicates the average number of days that receivables are outstanding before collection.

b. A second measure of the liquidity of accounts receivable takes the form of the *receivable turnover ratio*

$$\frac{\text{annual credit sales}}{\text{average accounts receivable}}$$

which is directly related to the inverse of the average collection period.

   c. Still another method for analyzing receivable liquidity is through the aging of *accounts receivable*. This tool involves categorizing outstanding accounts at a particular point in time in accordance with the period of time the accounts have gone uncollected since their original creation.

  4. Liquidity in inventories can be measured with the *inventory turnover ratio*, which is defined as

$$\frac{\text{cost of goods sold}}{\text{average inventory}} .$$

B. To determine a firm's ability to meet long-term obligations, two basic leverage ratios are often used:

  1. A general indication as to the credit worthiness and financial risk of a firm is given in the *debt/net worth ratio*, which is equal to

$$\frac{\text{total liabilities}}{\text{net worth}} .$$

  2. A second leverage ratio is given in the *long-term debt/total capitalization ratio*, which measures the relative importance of long-term debt in the firm's capitalization (i.e., the sum of the firm's noncurrent liabilities, preferred stock, and common stockholders' equity).

C. Profitability ratios give an overall indication as to the firm's efficiency of operation and can be categorized into two groups of ratios:

  1. The first group includes those profitability ratios based on sales.

   a. The *gross profit margin* is defined as

$$\frac{\text{sales less cost of goods sold}}{\text{sales}}$$

and indicates both the efficiency of the firm's operations and the pricing policies of the firm.

b. Still another widely used profitability ratio is the *net profit margin,* which equals

$$\frac{\text{net profits after taxes}}{\text{sales}}$$

and provides a measure of the net result of the firm's operations for a period of study based on the sales generated for that period.

2. The second group of profitability ratios relate profits to investment.

a. *The rate of return on common stock equity* is defined as

$$\frac{\text{net profits after taxes less preferred stock dividends}}{\text{net worth less par value of preferred stock}}$$

and indicates to the analyst the earnings of the firm on the book value of the common stockholders' equity.

b. An important measure of the firm's efficient use of its assets, which in turn influences the profitability of the firm, is given in the *total-tangible-asset turnover ratio,* which is defined as

$$\frac{\text{sales}}{\text{total tangible assets}}.$$

c. A very informative profitability ratio is found in the *return on total assets* or *earning power ratio,* which is defined as the product of the net profit margin and the total-tangible-asset turnover ratios:

$$\frac{\text{sales}}{\text{total tangible assets}} \times \frac{\text{net profit after taxes}}{\text{sales}}$$

D. Coverage ratios have as their purpose the measurement of the firm's ability to meet its financial charges when due.

1. A traditional coverage ratio is found in the *interest coverage measure,* which is simply defined as

$$\frac{\text{earnings before interest and taxes}}{\text{interest}}.$$

2. A refined measure of the firm's ability to meet its fixed finance charges is given in the *cash-flow coverage ratio,* which can be defined as

$$\frac{\text{annual cash flow before interest and taxes}}{\text{interest} + \text{principal payments } \frac{1}{1-t}}$$

where t refers to the firm's marginal federal income tax rate.

STUDY PROBLEMS

1.   J.P.G. Paint Company
                                            Balance Sheet
                                        December 31 (millions)

	1976	1977		1976	1977
Cash	$ 4	$ 3	Accounts payable	$ 8	$10
Accounts receivable	7	7	Notes payable	5	5
Inventory	12	20	Accrued wages	2	3
Total current assets	23	30	Accrued taxes	3	2
Net plant	40	40	Total liabilities	18	20
			Long-term debt	20	20
			Common stock equity	25	30
Total	$63	$70	Total	$63	$70

J.P.G. Paint Company
Income Statement
1977 (millions)

Sales	$	$100
Cost of goods sold	(50)	
Selling, general, and administrative expenses	(15)	
Depreciation	(3)	
Interest	(2)	
Net income before taxes		(70)
Taxes		30
Net income		(15)
		$ 15

Assume that you are a commercial loan officer for the MBC National Bank, and J.P.G. representatives approach you concerning a $1,000,000, 6-month loan. The loan will be used to finance needed additional inventories for spring sales. Analyze J.P.G.'s loan request in light of the following ratios:

	J.P.G. 1976	J.P.G. 1977	Industry Norm (1977)
Current ratio	–	–	2.0 ×
Acid-test ratio	–	–	0.7 ×
Long-term debt/total capitalization	–	–	0.5 ×
Inventory turnover*	4.2 ×	–	6.0 ×
Average collection period†	7 days	–	30 days
Return on total assets	21%	–	24%

*Based on cost of goods sold and ending inventory.
†Based on ending accounts receivable and using 360-day year.

Solution:

	J.P.G. 1976	J.P.G. 1977	Industry Norm (1977)
Current ratio	1.3 X	1.5 X	2.0 X
Acid-test ratio	0.6 X	0.5 X	0.7 X
Long-term debt/total capitalization	0.44 X	0.4 X	0.5 X
Inventory turnover	4.2 X	2.5 X	6.0 X
Average collection period	7 days	7 days	30 days
Return on total assets	21%	21%	24%

Based on the information conveyed in the above ratios, it would appear that J.P.G. is in the grips of a liquidity problem (based on the current ratio, acid-test ratio, and inventory turnover), which would argue against extending the 6-month loan. Also, the low inventory turnover ratio indicates an excessive investment in inventory at the present time relative to the industry norm (the need for additional inventory may have resulted from poor buying practices in the past). The only bright spots for the firm relate to their very rapid collection of accounts receivable, which suggests that the firm may have a very different set of credit terms than the industry (which may be costing the firm sales), and the profitability on invested assets, which is very close to the industry norm of 24%.

Any decision to extend the credit would probably carry some very restrictive covenants relating to the improvement in overall liquidity, controls over inventory purchases, and limits on the ability of the firm to incur any additional short-term debt. The decision to extend the requested loan is certainly a questionable one based on the financial data presented and analyzed here.

2. A company has total annual sales (all credit) of $1,000,000 and a gross profit of $200,000. The firm's current assets are $200,000; current liabilities are $120,000; inventories are $80,000; and cash is $40,000.

(a) How long should the average collection period be if the firm wants to maintain an average level of accounts receivable of $100,000?

Solution:

$$\text{average collection period} = \frac{\text{average accounts receivable} \times 360}{\text{credit sales}}$$

$$ACP = \frac{100,000 \times 360}{1,000,000}$$

$$= \underline{\underline{36 \text{ days}}}$$

(b) How much inventory should the firm have on hand (on average) so as to maintain an inventory turnover of 8?

Solution:

$$\text{Inventory turnover} = \frac{\text{cost of goods sold}}{\text{average inventory}}$$

$$8 = \frac{800,000}{\text{inventory}}$$

$$\text{inventory} = \frac{800,000}{8} = \$100,000$$

3. Using the following information, complete the balance sheet:

Long-term debt/net worth	0.6 X
Total asset turnover	1.0 X
Average collection period*	22.0 days
Inventory turnover	10 X
Gross profit margin	20%
Acid-test ratio	1 X

*Assume a 360-day year and that all sales are credit sales.

Cash		Notes and payables	$ 80,000
Accounts receivable		Long-term debt	
Inventory	$80,000	Common stock	400,000
Plant and equipment	_____	Retained earnings	
Total	======	Total	_____ ======

Solution:

Cash	$ 18,889	Notes and payables	$ 80,000
Accounts receivable	61,111	Long-term debt	345,000
Inventory	80,000	Common stock	400,000
Plant and equipment	840,000	Retained earnings	175,000
	$1,000,000		$1,000,000

SELF-TESTS

True-False

1. The net profit margin ignores the utilization of assets.
2. The turnover ratio ignores profitability on sales.
3. The business risk characteristic of a firm can best be assessed by analyzing the variability of earnings before interest and taxes.
4. The current ratio is more accurate than the quick test.
5. A firm should attempt to have as low an average collection period as possible.

_____F_____ 6. When the inventory turnover is relatively high, it indicates slow-moving inventory.

_____T_____ 7. Preferred stock is always included in net worth.

_____F_____ 8. The cumulative deduction method is the most widely used method of computing interest coverage.

_____T_____ 9. The financial risk characteristic of a firm can be assessed by analyzing the debt/net worth relationship.

_____T_____ 10. Ratio analysis provides information reflecting such economic parameters as risk and profitability.

Multiple Choice

1. Financial ratios can best be used by:
   a. Comparing them with the ratios of the industry of which the firm is a member.
   b. Comparing them with the historical ratios of the firm.
   c. Comparing them with both the historical and industry ratios of the firm.
   d. None of the above.

2. All the following are measures of profitability with the exception of:
   a. Net operating income divided by sales.
   b. Net income divided by sales.
   c. Rate of return on total assets.
   d. Debt divided by common equity.
   e. Gross profit margin.

3. Which of the following changes could not possibly bring about an apparent improvement in the current ratio for a firm (if everything else is held constant)?
   a. Selling fixed assets and reducing current liabilities with the released funds.
   b. Issuing long-term debt and increasing current assets with the acquired funds.
   c. Using current assets to reduce current liabilities outstanding.
   d. Increasing current liabilities to finance increased fixed assets.
   e. Issuing equity securities and increasing the level of inventory with the funds.

4. The gross profit margin ratio tells us:
   a. The relative efficiency of the firm after taking into account all expenses and income taxes but no extraordinary charges.
   b. The profit of the firm relative to sales after we deduct the cost of producing the goods sold.
   c. The earning power on the book value of the shareholder's investment.
   d. None of the above.
   e. a and b only.

5. Liquidity ratios are used to:
   a. Judge a firm's ability to meet short-term obligations.
   b. Obtain insight into the present cash solvency of a firm.
   c. Judge a firm's ability to remain solvent in the event of adversities.
   d. All of the above.
   e. Both a and b.
   f. Both a and c.

6. Aging of accounts can be used to obtain insight when examining the firm's:
   a. Liquidity.
   b. Leverage.
   c. profitability.
   d. Coverage.
   e. None of the above.

7. If the gross profit margin is essentially unchanged over a period of several years, but the net profit margin has declined over the same period, the cause is:
   a. Higher expenses relative to sales.
   b. Increased sales.
   c. A higher tax rate.
   d. All of the above.
   e. Both a and b.
   f. Both a and c.

Source and Use Statements and Financial Forecasting

4

Orientation: This, the second chapter in our examination of the tools of financial analysis and control, deals with the analysis of fund flows and financial forecasting. Specifically, in this chapter the discussion centers around source and use-of-fund statements, cash budgets, and pro forma statements.

I. The source and use-of-funds statements give the financial manager insight into a firm's uses and corresponding sources of funds for a specific time interval. Funds statements are prepared on either a cash basis or a working-capital basis.

    A. A funds statement on a cash basis consists of an enumeration of both sources and uses of funds that affect cash over a particular time interval.

        1. Sources of funds that increase cash are as follows:

           a. A net decrease in any asset other than cash or fixed assets.

           b. A decrease in gross fixed assets.

           c. A net increase in any liability.

           d. Proceeds from the sale of either preferred or common stock.

           e. Funds provided by operations.

        2. Uses of funds that decrease cash are as follows:

           a. A net increase in any asset other than cash or fixed assets.

      b. An increase in gross fixed assets.

      c. A net decrease in any liability.

      d. A retirement or repurchase of stock.

      e. The payment of cash dividends.

  B. A funds statement on a working-capital basis consists of an enumeration of the sources and uses of working capital instead of cash. The only difference in this and the funds statement on a cash basis is the omission of changes in the various components of current assets and current liabilities.

II. A cash budget involves a projection of future cash receipts and disbursements of the firm over a future time period. It reveals to the financial manager the timing and amount of expected cash needs of the firm such that he can exercise effective control over the firm's cash and liquidity.

  A. The basis for the cash-receipt projection is the sales forecast followed by an analysis of the firm's collection policies and expectations.

  B. Cash-disbursement projections are tied to projected sales and corresponding operating expenses along with planned expenditures for plant and equipment, federal and local taxes, and cash dividends.

  C. Once all foreseeable cash flows have been projected, the cash disbursements are netted against cash receipts to determine the expected net change in cash for the period. Where deficits are expected, additional financing must be sought.

  D. Since a cash budget represents a point estimate of future cash flows, it is better to work with a whole range of possible cash flows, thus adding flexibility to the procedure.

III. Still another useful tool in financial planning is the pro forma financial statement.

  A. Pro forma statements embody forecasts of all asset and liability changes, as well as income statement items for the relevant planning period.

  B. Financial ratios can be computed from these pro forma statements to assess the direction of change in the financial condition and performance of the firm.

STUDY PROBLEMS

1. Prepare a statement of sources and uses of funds for Carlton Corp. for 1977 using the appropriate balance sheets and the income statement given.

Carlton Corporation
Balance Sheets

	1975	1976	1977
Cash	$ 25,500	$ 11,900	$ 8,500
Accounts receivable	102,000	115,600	161,500
Inventory	127,500	212,500	344,250
Total current assets	$225,000	$340,000	$514,250
Land and building	20,400	54,400	51,000
Machinery	62,900	49,300	42,500
Other assets	11,900	3,400	2,550
Total assets	$350,200	$447,100	$610,300
Notes payable, bank		42,500	119,000
Accounts and notes payable	40,800	64,600	127,500
Accruals	20,400	23,800	32,300
Total current liabilities	$ 61,200	$130,900	$278,800
Mortgage	18,700	17,000	15,300
Common stock	85,000	85,000	85,000
Paid in capital	68,000	68,000	68,000
Earned surplus	117,300	146,200	163,200
Total liability and equity	$350,200	$447,100	$610,300

Carlton Corporation
Income Statement
1977

Net sales	$1,190,000
Cost of goods sold	952,000
Gross operating profit	$ 238,000
General administration and selling	102,000
Depreciation	51,000
Miscellaneous	51,000
Net income before taxes	$ 34,000
Taxes (50%)	17,000
Net income	$ 17,000

Solution:

Carlton Corporation
Statement of Sources and Uses of Funds
1977

Sources			Uses		
Funds provided by operations			Dividends	0	
Net income	17,000		Additions to fixed assets		$ 40,800
Depreciation	51,000	$68,000	Increase in assets		
Decrease in assets			Accounts receivable	45,900	
Other Assets	850	850	Inventory	131,750	177,650

Sources			*Uses*		
Increase in liabilities			Decrease in liabilities		
Notes payable,			Mortgage		1,700
bank	76,500				$220,150
Accounts payable					
and notes					
payable	62,900				
Accruals	8,500	147,900			
Decrease in cash position		3,400			
		$220,150			

2. Techland Manufacturing Company is attempting to estimate its needs for funds during each of the months covering the third quarter of 1977. Pertinent information is given in the table.

(1) Past and estimated future sales:

	Actual		*Estimated*
Apr.	$100,000	July	$100,000
May	80,000	Aug.	110,000
June	90,000	Sept.	120,000
		Oct.	100,000

(2) Rent expense is $4,000 per month.

(3) A quarterly interest payment on $100,000 in 5% notes payable is paid during September 1977.

(4) Wages and salaries are estimated as follows:

July	$10,000
August	11,000
September	12,000

Payment is made within the month in which the wages are earned.

(5) Fifty percent of sales are for cash, with the remaining 50% collected in the month following the sale. (Bad debts are negligible.)

(6) Techland pays 80% of the sales price for merchandise and makes payment in the same month in which the sales occur, although purchases are made in the month prior to the anticipated sales.

(7) Techland plans to pay $10,000 in cash for a new forklift truck in July 1977.

(8) Short-term loans can be obtained at 12% annual interest with interest paid during each month for which the loan is outstanding.

(9) Techland's ending cash balance for June 30, 1977, is $55,000, and the minimum balance they wish to have in any month is $45,000.

(a) Set up, in a logical and easy-to-follow format, a cash budget for Techland for the quarter ended September 30, 1977.

Solution

Worksheet

	June	July	August	September
Sales	$90,000	$100,000	$110,000	$120,000
Cash sales		50,000	55,000	60,000
Collections (50% 1 month later)		45,000	50,000	55,000
Total cash collections		$ 95,000	$105,000	$115,000

Cash Budget

	July	August	September
Cash receipts			
From sales	$ 95,000	$105,000	$115,000
Cash disbursements			
Payments on purchases	(80,000)	(88,000)	(96,000)
Rent	(4,000)	(4,000)	(4,000)
Wages and salaries	(10,000)	(11,000)	(12,000)
Interest (0.05 × 100,000 × 1/4)			(1,250)
Purchase of forklift truck	(10,000)		
Short-term-borrowing interest (0.12)			
Total cash disbursements	(104,000)	(103,000)	(113,250)
Net	(9,000)	2,000	1,750
Beginning cash balance	55,000	46,000	48,000
Borrowing (repayment)	0	0	0
Ending balance	$ 46,000	$ 48,000	$ 49,750

(b) Prepare a pro forma income statement for Techland covering the quarter ended September 30, 1977. You may assume that Techland's marginal tax rate is 22%. Also, Techland has $110,000 in fixed assets with an average expected useful life of 10 years. (Techland uses straight-line depreciation.)

Solution:

Techland Mfg. Co.
Pro Forma Income Statement
for the Quarter Ended
September 30, 1977

Sales	$330,000
Cost of goods sold	(264,000)
Gross profit	66,000
Operating expenses:	
Wages and salaries	(33,000)
Rent	(12,000)
Depreciation	(2,750)
Total operating expenses	(47,750)

Earnings before interest and taxes	$ 18,250
Interest expense	(1,250)
Earnings before taxes	17,000
Taxes (22%)	(3,740)
Net profit after taxes	$ 13,260

(c) Given the following balance sheet for Techland (dated June 30, 1977) and the results of parts (a) and (b), construct a pro forma balance sheet as of September 30, 1977:

Techland Mfg. Co.
Balance Sheet
June 30, 1977

Cash	$ 55,000	Accounts payable	$100,000
Accounts receivable	45,000	Accrued taxes	0
Inventories	100,000	Notes payable	100,000
Fixed assets, net	100,000	Common equity	100,000
	$300,000		$300,000

Solution:

Techland Mfg. Co.
Pro Forma Balance Sheet
September 30, 1977

Cash	$ 49,750	Accounts payable	$100,000 §
Accounts receivable	60,000*	Accrued taxes	3,740
Inventory	100,000†	Notes payable	100,000
Fixed assets, net	107,250‡	Common equity	113,260η
	$317,000		$317,000

*Accounts receivable (beginning balance)	$ 45,000
+ credit sales	165,000
– collections	$(150,000)
Ending balance	60,000

‡Fixed assets (beginning balance)	$100,000
+ purchases	10,000
– depreciation	(2,750)
Ending balance	$107,250

ηCommon equity (beginning balance)	$100,000
+ net income	13,260
– cash dividends	0
Ending balance	$113,260

†Inventories (beginning balance)	$ 100,000
+ purchases	264,000
– cost of goods sold	$(264,000)
Ending balance	100,000

§ Accounts payable	$ 100,000
+ purchases	264,000
– payments	(264,000)
Ending balance	$ 100,000

SELF-TESTS

True-False

_T_   1. An analysis of gross funds flow is more revealing than an analysis of net funds flow.

_T_   2. Funds provided by operations include noncash expenses such as depreciation.

_F_   3. When total uses of funds is subtracted from the total sources, the difference should equal the change in net worth.

_T_   4. The only difference between a funds statement on a working-capital basis and one on a cash basis is the omission of changes in the various components of current assets and current liabilities.

_T_   5. The cash budget is only as useful as the accuracy of the forecasts that are used in its preparation.

_F_   6. Steady production usually results in lower inventory carrying costs.

_T_   7. Cash budgets represent estimates of future cash flows.

_F_   8. Future net fixed assets are estimated for the pro forma balance sheet by adding planned expenditures to existing net fixed assets and adding to this sum depreciation for the period.

_F_   9. The pro forma balance sheet and pro forma income statement are audited and certified by CPA firms.

_F_ 10. A credit sale represents a source and a use of working capital.

Multiple Choice

1. Sources of funds that increase cash include:
   a. Cash dividends.
   b. A net increase in any liability.
   c. Proceeds from sale of common stock.
   d. A gross increase in fixed assets.
   e. b and c.
   f. a, d, and e.

2. The key(s) to the accuracy of most cash budgets is the:
   a. Forecast of cash disbursements.
   b. Forecast of collection schedule.
   c. Forecast of sales.
   d. None of the above.
   e. b and c.

3. Pro forma statements embody:
   a. Forecasts of prospective future cash positions of the firm.
   b. Forecasts of all assets and liabilities.
   c. Forecasts of the firm's long-range goals and objectives.
   d. All of the above.
   e. a and b.
4. Which of the following items would be included in a cash budget?
   a. Depreciation charges.
   b. Goodwill.
   c. Patent amortization.
   d. All of the above.
   e. None of the above.
5. The cash budget provides the financial manager with the following information:
   a. The exact amount of borrowing needed for the budget interval.
   b. The type of loan which should be obtained to meet the cash needs for the time interval.
   c. A point estimate of the borrowing needs for the budget interval.
   d. An estimate of the cash needed for depreciation charges.
   e. A point estimate of the expected funds provided by operations.
6. Funds statements can be used to:
   a. Detect an imbalance in uses of funds.
   b. Analyze past and future expansion plans.
   c. Evaluate a firm's financing plan.
   d. All of the above.
   e. a and b.
7. Sales forecasts are based on:
   a. Internal analysis.
   b. External analysis.
   c. Cash receipts.
   d. Regression analysis made between the industry sales and the economy in general.
   e. a and b.
   f. a, b, and d.
8. Sources of the funds that increase cash include:
   a. Cash dividends.
   b. Net increase in any liability.
   c. Proceeds from sale of common stock.
   d. Gross increase in fixed assets.
   e. b and c.
   f. a, d, and e.

Working- 5
Capital
Management

Orientation: The optimal level of liquid assets is determined by examining the relationship between risk and expected returns. Risk in this context is defined as the probability of insolvency. In analyzing the problem, management should consider the level of liquid assets and the maturity structure of the firm's debt. However, these two factors must be studied concurrently in order to recognize the interdependence which exists.

I. Introduction

    A. Current assets, by accounting definition, represent those assets normally converted into cash within 1 year.

    B. Working-capital management involves the administration of current assets and current liabilities.

    C. The administration of fixed assets (capital budgeting), in contrast to working-capital management, involves the management of long-term investments.

    D. Working-capital management relates to decisions involving the firm's liquidity and the maturity composition of its debts, which in turn involves a trade-off between profitability and risk.

    E. Decisions affecting the asset liquidity of the firm include the following:

        1. Management of cash and marketable securities.

    2. Credit policy and procedures.

    3. Inventory management and control.

    4. Administration of fixed assets.

F. Assuming that cash and marketable securities yield a return lower than the return on investment in other assets, the lower the proportion of liquid assets to total assets, the greater the firm's return on total investments.

G. Profitability with respect to the level of current liabilities is a function of (1) the variation in costs between various methods of financing, and (2) having money borrowed during a period when funds are not needed.

    1. Generally, short-term financing is less expensive than long-term financing.

    2. The employment of short-term debt as opposed to long-term liabilities typically permits greater profitability as a result of the short-term debt being paid off when seasonal funds are not needed.

H. As a consequence of the foregoing relationships:

    1. A low proportion of current assets to total assets and a high degree of current liabilities to total liabilities would provide greater *expected* return on investment.

    2. However, the benefit of increased profitability by the preceding strategy produces increased risk to the firm.

I. Risk is defined as the probability of technical insolvency.

    1. Legal insolvency occurs when the assets of a firm are less than the liabilities.

    2. Technical insolvency arises when the corporation is unable to meet the cash obligations.

J. Liquidity may be defined as the ability to realize value in money from an asset, and has two dimensions.

    1. The time necessary to convert an asset into money.

    2. The certainty of the conversion.

K. The risk involved with various levels of current assets and current liabilities must be examined in terms of the profitability associated with the respective levels.

II. Financing current assets.

    A. The financing of current assets involves a trade-off between risk and profitability.

    B. A portion of the company's current liabilities may be expected to fluctuate spontaneously with the level of current assets.

    C. The primary interest of the chapter relates to the current assets, which are not automatically financed by accounts payable and accruals.

    D. A firm may adopt a "hedging approach" by financing a current asset with an indebtedness having the same approximate maturity.

        1. Short-term or seasonal variations in current assets should be financed with short-term debt.

        2. The permanent component of current assets and fixed assets should be financed with long-term debt or equity.

        3. Financing short-term requirements with long-term debt necessitates the payment of interest for the use of funds during times when these funds are not needed.

        4. In a growth situation, permanent financing will increase in keeping with the growth in permanent fund requirements, both for current assets and fixed assets.

        5. The exact synchronization of the expected future cash inflows with the debt payments is not possible in a world of uncertainty.

            a. In matching cash inflows and cash outflows, a margin of safety should be built in to the analysis to allow for adverse fluctuations in cash flows.

            b. The shorter the maturity schedule of a debt, the greater the probability that the firm will be unable to meet maturing obligations.

            c. The maturity structure of debt will depend upon management's risk-return preferences.

                (1) Lengthening the maturity structure of debt relative to expected net cash flow reduces the risk of being unable to meet principal and interest payments.

                (2) However, the longer the maturity schedule, the more costly the financing will generally prove to be, both in

terms of the explicit cost of long-term financing and in maintaining long-term debt when funds are not needed.

    d. To provide a safety margin, a portion of the expected seasonal fund requirements less payables and accruals would be financed on a long-term basis.

III. The level of current liquid assets

    A. A relationship exists, although not linear, between the organization's output and the current-asset level.

    B. The specific relationship between output and current assets within a particular enterprise ensues from the risk-return trade-off.

        1. Increasing the proportion of current assets to fixed assets lowers the rate of return on assets but increases the liquidity cushion to meet unexpected needs for funds.

        2. Decreasing the percentage of current assets to fixed assets increases the return on assets but provides a lesser amount of liquidity to meet unexpected needs for capital.

    C. The risk-return relationship in working-capital management is a function of the profits foregone by maintaining assets which generate less cash flow than fixed assets, but provide increased liquidity.

IV. Interdependence of the two facets.

    A. The financing of current assets and the proportion of liquid assets relative to total assets are interdependent.

        1. A firm with a high level of liquid assets is better able to finance the current assets on a short-term basis.

        2. However, a firm financing current assets entirely with equity will have less requirements for liquidity.

    B. As a result of the interdependence, these two facets of working capital must be considered jointly.

    C. A margin of safety may be developed by (1) increasing the level of liquid assets and (2) lengthening the maturity schedule of financing.

        1. The appropriate margin of safety is a function of the risk, the profitability, and the utility preferences of management with respect to the risk-return trade-off.

        2. The optimal margin of safety can theoretically be determined in one of two fashions:

a. Compare the expected cost of running out of cash with the profits foregone as a result of having to maintain a liquid balance. The optimal solution is at the point where the marginal opportunity cost of carrying liquid assets equals the marginal expected cost for cash stockout.

b. Devise a strategy which satisfies a risk-tolerance level while minimizing the cost associated with this risk level.

STUDY PROBLEMS

1. The Marriott Corporation has a net sales level of $550,000 with an 8% profit margin before interest and taxes. The firm currently has $250,000 in total assets, which includes $100,000 in current assets.

(a) Compute the total-asset turnover and the return on investment at (1) the existing level of working capital and (2) if the current assets were reduced by $30,000.

(b) What are the implications of your solution?

Solution:

(1) Asset turnover = $\dfrac{\$550,000}{250,000}$ = 2.2

   Return on investment = $\dfrac{44,000}{250,000}$ = 17.6%

(2) Asset turnover = $\dfrac{550,000}{220,000}$ = 2.44

   Return on investment = $\dfrac{44,000}{220,000}$ = 20%

(c) The problem indicates that a reduction in working capital, which is typically a low-income-producing asset, permits the firm to increase the expected return on assets through more efficient utilization of assets. However, to do so increases the company's risk in terms of the probability of insolvency. Also, the solution assumes *complete* independence between revenues and the level of working capital, which may not be realistic.

2. The managers of the Schmitt Corporation have projected current assets and fixed assets for the next 5 years as shown. The business is currently financed by $75 million in equity, with the remainder being in long-term bonds and payables.

Date	Current Assets	Fixed Assets
1/1/77 (now)	$18,000,000	$75,000,000
6/30/77	26,000,000	77,000,000
1/1/78	20,000,000	80,000,000
6/30/78	30,000,000	80,000,000
1/1/79	24,000,000	81,000,000
6/30/79	32,000,000	83,000,000
1/1/80	24,000,000	86,000,000
6/30/80	37,000,000	88,000,000
1/1/81	26,000,000	90,000,000
6/30/81	34,000,000	93,000,000

(a) Graph the growth of current assets and fixed assets over time.

(b) Using the hedging approach, devise a financing plan.

Solution:

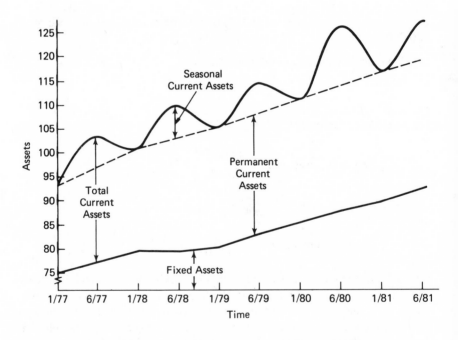

(1) Finance permanent current assets and fixed assets with long-term debt and equity.

(2) Finance seasonal current assets with short-term debt.

3. Jackson Incorporated, a petroleum company, is currently involved in off-shore drilling in the Gulf of Mexico. To continue such drilling, it has become

necessary for the firm to obtain additional financing. At the present time, only two alternatives seem viable.

(1) The company can pursue its present policy which has been a gradual stretching of the maturity of its payables. Simmon Sharp, vice-president of finance, has estimated that such a practice costs the firm approximately 25% per year. The current financial structure of Jackson is as follows:

Accounts payable	$ 30,000*
Short-term debt	50,000
Net worth	120,000
	$200,000

*$20,000 of the payables are current.

Jackson has a seasonal element to its business, with sales rising to a peak in April. By October, the demand for its products declines by 40%. Mr. Sharp has estimated Jackson's requirements for payables and debt for next April depending upon three possible states of the economy:

State	Requirements	Probability
Boom	$200,000	0.30
Normal	150,000	0.40
Recession	100,000	0.30

(2) A second financial alternative available to the firm is a term loan. The First National Bank of Houston has agreed to loan no more or less than $100,000 at a rate of 15%. Any additional needs may be financed through Fleecem Finance Company at a rate of 25%. Mr. Sharp has asked you to evaluate the 6-month interest costs of the term loan in relation to the present policy of stretching payables at two times: April 30 and October 31 of this year. The analysis should recognize the three possible states of the economy. Which alternative should be selected?

Solution:

(a) Cost of stretching accounts payable:

Recession	April	October
Funds required	$100,000	$60,000
Normal payables	20,000	12,000
Stretched payables	80,000	48,000
Six-month cost	10,000	6,000

Normal		
Funds required	$150,000	$90,000
Normal payables	20,000	12,000
Stretched payables	130,000	78,000
Six-month cost	16,250	9,750

Boom	April	October
Funds required	$200,000	$120,000
Normal payables	20,000	12,000
Stretched payables	180,000	108,000
Six-month cost	22,500	13,500

(b) Cost of term-loan alternative:

Recession	April	October
Funds required	$100,000	$ 60,000
Normal payables	0	0
Term loan	100,000	100,000
Six-month cost	7,500	7,500

Normal		
Funds required	$150,000	$ 90,000
Normal payables	20,000	0
Term loan	100,000	100,000
Finance company loan	30,000	0
Six-month cost	11,250	7,500

Boom		
Funds required	$200,000	$120,000
Normal payables	20,000	12,000
Term loan	100,000	100,000
Finance company loan	80,000	8,000
Six-month cost	17,500	8,500

Total Interest Costs for Both Methods

	Recession	Normal	Boom
Current financing alternative	$16,000	$24,000	$36,000
Term-loan alternative	15,000	18,750	26,000

The firm should borrow via the term loan, since it results in lower interest costs in all three states.

SELF-TESTS

True-False

1. Working-capital management involves a trade-off between the firm's profitability and risk.

2. Technical insolvency occurs whenever a firm is unable to meet its lease obligations.

F   3. Expected cash flows are usually known for certain by the firm, making the management of working capital considerably easier.

T   4. The lower the proportion of liquid assets to total assets, the greater the firm's return on total investment.

F   5. If a firm adopts a hedging approach to financing, each asset would be offset with some form of long-term debt.

F   6. The longer the maturity schedule of debt is in relation to net cash flows, the greater the risk of being unable to meet principal and interest payments.

T   7. The longer the maturity schedule, the more costly the financing is likely to be.

F   8. The use of short-term debt as opposed to long-term debt will usually result in lower profits for the firm.

T   9. One of the risks associated with short-term debt is that the firm may be unable to refinance when the debt comes due.

F   10. A firm may reduce the risk of cash insolvency either by decreasing the maturity schedule of its debt or by decreasing the relative maturity of its assets.

Multiple Choice

1. Which of the following accounts would not be a prime consideration in working-capital management?
   a. Cash.
   b. Accounts payable.
   c. Bonds payable.
   d. Marketable securities.
   e. Accounts receivable.

2. Which asset-liability combination would result in the firm having the greatest risk of technical insolvency?
   a. More current assets and less current liabilities.
   b. More current assets and more current liabilities.
   c. Less current assets and more current liabilities.
   d. Less current assets and less current liabilities.

3. The greatest margin of safety would be provided by:
   a. More current assets and less current liabilities.
   b. More current assets and more current liabilities.
   c. Less current assets and more current liabilities.
   d. Less current assets and less current liabilities.

4. Which of the following statements is true?
   a. The shorter the maturity schedule of the debt, the smaller the risk.
   b. The longer the maturity schedule of the debt, the greater the risk.

    c. The shorter the maturity schedule of the debt, the greater the risk.
    d. None of the above.

5. Which of the following are dimensions of liquidity?
    a. The rate of return on an investment.
    b. The time necessary to convert an asset into money.
    c. The cost of an asset, and how the asset is to be financed.
    d. None of the above.

6. Which of the following illustrates the use of a hedging approach?
    a. Short-term assets financed with long-term liabilities.
    b. Permanent assets financed with long-term liabilities.
    c. Short-term assets financed with short-term liabilities.
    d. All of the above.
    e. b and c.

7. Which of the following represents a way in which management can provide a margin of safety to meet unexpected cash drains?
    a. Decrease the proportion of liquid assets.
    b. Shorten the maturity schedule of financing.
    c. Increase the proportion of fixed assets.
    d. Lengthen the maturity schedule of financing.

Cash and Marketable Securities 6

Orientation: The intent of this chapter is (1) to determine the appropriate division of funds between cash and marketable securities; (2) to examine methods for improving the efficiency of cash management; and (3) to study the investment of excess funds in marketable securities.

I. Transactions and precautionary balances

    A. Three motives for holding cash have been provided.

        1. The *transactions motive* is the need for cash to meet payments arising in the ordinary course of business.

        2. The *precautionary motive* for holding cash relates to maintaining a cushion or buffer to meet unexpected contingencies.

        3. The *speculative motive* is concerned with holding cash to take advantage of expected changes in securities prices as a result of interest-rate changes; however, most companies do not hold cash for this reason.

    B. Key factors having an influence upon the amount of transactions and precautionary balances include the following:

        1. The expected net cash flows of the firm as determined by the cash budget.

        2. Possible deviations from expected net cash flows.

3. The maturity structure of the firm's debt.

4. The firm's borrowing capacity to meet emergency needs.

5. The utility preferences of management with respect to the risk of cash insolvency.

6. The efficiency of cash management.

C. As the efficiency of cash management is improved, smaller transactions and precautionary balances will be required.

II. The efficiency of cash management

A. Efficient cash management comes as a result of improving methods in collections and disbursements.

B. The acceleration of collections.

1. Objective: Reduce the delay between the time a customer pays the bill and the time the check becomes usable funds for the company.

2. Methods in accomplishing this objective include the following:

a. Shorten the mailing time of payments from customers to the corporation.

b. Reduce the time during which payments received by the company remain uncollected funds.

c. Accelerate the movement of funds to disbursement banks.

C. Concentration banking

1. Objective: Shorten the period between the time a customer mails a payment and the date by which the company has the use of the funds.

2. Method

a. Establish multiple collection centers based upon the geographic areas served and the volume of billings in a particular area.

b. Deposit receipts in the collection center's local bank.

c. Transfer surplus funds from the local bank to a concentration bank either by a wire transfer or a depository transfer check.

3. The advantage of the system is the reduction in time required for mailing and collecting the checks.

D. Lock-box system

1. Objective: Eliminate the time between the receipt of remittances and the date of deposit in the bank.

2. Method

   a. Select regional banks in accordance with the experienced billing patterns.

   b. Rent a local post office box, authorizing the local bank to pick up remittances in the box.

   c. Customers are instructed to forward their remittance to the lock box.

   d. The bank deposits the checks received in the lock box on behalf of the company.

3. Evaluation

   a. Advantage: The lag time between the receipt of a check and the time the check is deposited in the bank is eliminated.

   b. Disadvantage: The cost of a lock-box arrangement may not be economically feasible if the average remittance is small.

   c. Rule of adoption: Compare the added cost of the more efficient system with the marginal income that may be generated from released funds.

E. Other procedures which might be implemented to minimize the collection time.

   1. Special handling of large accounts.

   2. Avoid excessive funds being tied up in various divisions within the firm.

   3. Avoid establishing too many bank accounts.

F. Control of disbursements

   1. Objective: Maximize the balances in the disbursements bank accounts by slowing down outflows as much as possible.

   2. Operating procedures

      a. Minimize the loss of discounts due to clerical inefficiencies.

      b. Make payments on due dates, not before or after.

   3. Techniques for delaying disbursements

      a. The use of drafts.

      b. "Playing the float."

        c. Maintaining separate accounts for special disbursements which have a high degree of predictability (e.g., payroll).

    4. In controlling disbursements, the company should be aware of the potential damage to the firm's credit standings by delaying payments too extensively.

III. The optimal split between cash and marketable securities

    A. Assuming that the proper level of transactions and precautionary balances has been determined, identification of the split between cash and marketable securities must be made, with the criteria being twofold:

        1. Compensating balance requirements.

        2. A self-imposed constraint relating to the following:

            a. Expected cash-flow levels.

            b. Possible deviations in the cash flows.

            c. The interest rate on marketable securities.

            d. The fixed cost associated with a security transaction.

    B. Compensating balances

        1. Compensating requirements are a function of the profitability of a given bank account.

            a. The profitability is related to the amount by which the average balance of the checking account exceeds the amount the bank is required to place at the Federal Reserve, that being 17%.

            b. The actual earnings capability of an account to the banker is determined by multiplying the "excess" cash flows by the earnings rate of the bank less the cost incurred in servicing the account.

            c. The minimum average level of cash balances required by the bank is the point at which the account is just profitable.

        2. A firm borrowing money from a bank may be required to maintain compensating balances in order to compensate the bank for the activity of the account.

        3. In contrast to requiring compensating balances, a trend toward paying cash for services rendered by a bank is developing.

    C. Models for determining an optimal split between cash and marketable securities

1. Economic-order-quantity formula (inventory model)

   a. Purpose: Find the optimal average level of transactions balances to be maintained.

   b. Assumptions

      (1) Demand for cash during the planning period is known.

      (2) Uniform usage of cash over time.

   c. Strategy: Minimize the total costs of maintaining the cash balance, where costs include:

      (1) Carrying cost of holding cash.

      (2) Fixed cost of transferring marketable securities to cash.

   d. Computation

      (1) Definition of notations:

         C = amount to be transferred from marketable securities to cash per transfer

         b = fixed cost of a transfer from marketable securities to cash, regardless of the amount transferred

         T = total expected cash needs for the planning period

         i = interest rate on marketable securities that would be sold to replenish cash

      (2) Computation of costs:

         T/C = number of transfers during the period

         $C/2$ = average cash balance

         Accordingly, the *total* costs (TC) for maintaining a particular cash balance would be

$$TC = \underbrace{b\left(\frac{T}{C}\right)}_{\substack{\text{total} \\ \text{ordering} \\ \text{costs}}} + \underbrace{i\left(\frac{C}{2}\right)}_{\substack{\text{total} \\ \text{carrying} \\ \text{costs}}} \qquad (1)$$

      (3) Minimization of total costs

         (a) Methodology: Using calculus, solve for the first derivative of the total cost curve and set equal to zero, that being the minimal point of the curve.

    (b) Result: When the first derivative of the total cost curve is taken, the result is

$$C^* = \sqrt{\frac{2bt}{i}} \qquad (2)$$

where C^* = optimal level of C, the amount to be transferred to cash

Thus, the optimal level of cash is $C^*/2$.

  e. Example: Management estimates the total cash needs for the next month to be \$10,000. The cost of transferring marketable securities to cash is \$25, and the yield on marketable securities is 9% (0.0075 per month). Thus, the optimal transaction size would be

$$C^* = \sqrt{\frac{2bt}{i}} = \sqrt{\frac{2(25)(10,000)}{0.0075}} = \$8,164.97$$

and the optimal average cash balance is \$4,082.48 (8,164.97/2).

  f. Difficulties in applying the model

    (1) The fixed costs associated with the transaction are difficult to measure.

    (2) The two assumptions, uniform usage of cash and known demand, may not hold.

  g. The economic-order-quantity (EOQ) model is not a precise rule, only an indication of the optimal cash balance.

2. Stochastic models

  a. Objective: Satisfy the demand for cash at the lowest possible total cost.

  b. Appropriateness of the model: The model should be used when the demand for cash is stochastic (random) and unknown in advance.

  c. Strategy: Apply control theory by setting upper and lower bounds beyond which the cash balance is not permitted to reach.

    (1) When the cash level touches the upper limit, a transfer of cash to marketable securities is transacted.

    (2) When the cash balance reaches the lower limit, a transfer from marketable securities to cash is enacted.

d. Factors determining the limits

(1) The fixed cost associated with a securities transaction.

(2) The opportunity cost of holding cash.

(3) The degree of likely fluctuations in cash balances.

e. Results: Without becoming involved in mathematics, the resulting equation for determining the amount of cash to remain in the checking account (z) after the correction from an upper or lower limit would be as follows:

$$z = \sqrt[3]{\frac{3b\sigma^2}{4i}}$$

where b = fixed cost associated with a securities transfer

σ^2 = "variance" (square of the standard deviation) of daily cash flows, a statistical measure of variation

i = daily interest rate on marketable securities

3. Relationship of the models: For most firms, the EOQ model is more applicable than the control-limit model, in that near-term cash flows are relatively predictable.

D. The optimal average cash balance will be the higher of (1) the compensating-balance requirements for the bank, and (2) the amount of cash suggested by a cash-marketable securities model.

IV. Investment in marketable securities

A. Types of investments

1. *Treasury securities,* comprising the largest segment of the money markets, include treasury bills, treasury notes, and treasury bonds. These securities offer the greatest safety and marketability but provide the lowest yield relative to other marketable securities.

2. *Agencies' securities* represent obligations of federal government agencies.

a. These securities are guaranteed by the agency involved and offer a higher yield than treasury securities.

b. The maturities extend up to 15 years, but generally mature in less than 1 year.

3. *Bankers' acceptances* are drafts that are accepted by banks and used in the financing of foreign and domestic trade. The rate on this security is slightly higher than treasury bills of like maturity.

4. *Commercial paper*

   a. Consists of short-term unsecured promissory notes issued by large companies.

   b. Rates are slightly higher than the rates on treasury bills of the same maturity and approximate the rates available on bankers' acceptances.

   c. Sold on a discount basis, with maturities ranging from 30 to 270 days.

   d. Sold in relatively large denominations, usually in excess of $25,000.

5. *Repurchase agreements*

   a. Involves a sale of short-term securities by a dealer to an investor, with the dealer agreeing to repurchase the securities at a specified future time.

   b. The maturity is tailored to the needs of the investor, but usually extends for only several days.

   c. Since the instrument involved is a treasury security, there is no default risk.

6. *Negotiable certificates of deposit*

   a. Represents the deposit of funds in a commercial bank for a specified period of time and at a specified rate of interest.

   b. Yields on CDs exceed treasury bills and repurchase agreements and approximate the yields of bankers' acceptances and commercial paper.

   c. The most common denomination of a CD is $100,000.

   d. Original maturities of CDs generally range from 30 to 360 days.

   e. Default risk could be related to the probability of the bank failing, which in most instances is quite low.

B. Portfolio management

   1. The amount and type of marketable securities is interdependent and should be based upon the evaluation of expected net cash flows and the certainty of these cash flows.

   2. If future cash flows are relatively uncertain, the most important characteristic of a security becomes its marketability and risk with respect to fluctuations and market value.

STUDY PROBLEMS

1. Using the inventory model, determine the optimal level of cash the firm should hold if:

(a) The interest rate on marketable securities is 6% for the next year.

(b) The cost of converting from cash to marketable securities is $50.

(c) The firm feels it will need $1,000 in cash over the next period of 1 year.

Solution:

$$\text{Transaction balance} = C^* = \sqrt{\frac{2(50)(1,000)}{0.06}} = \sqrt{1,666,667} = \$1,291$$

$$\text{Optimal level of cash} = \text{transaction balance} \div 2 = \frac{C^*}{2} = \frac{\$1,291}{2} = \underline{\underline{\$645.50}}$$

2. The Phillips Corporation is considering modification of its billing system to a lock-box plan. At present, it takes about 6 days for the customers' payments to reach the company. Two additional days are required before the deposit can be made. The firm has an average daily collection of $700,000, and it is felt that the installation of the lock-box plan would reduce total time of mailing and processing by 5½ days.

(a) How much reduction in cash balances can be achieved through installation of the lock-box plan?

(b) Assuming a 7% return on short-term instruments, what is the opportunity cost of the present system?

(c) If the lock-box system will cost $100,000 to install, should it be initiated?

Solution:

(a) (5 1/2)($7,000) = $3,850,000.

(b) (7%)($3,850,000) = $269,500.

(c) Yes, benefits ($269,500) exceed cost ($100,000).

3. If Mr. Jackson is considering taking out a loan at First National Bank and is given the option of an 8% 1-year loan for $1,000, with interest and principal due at the end of the year, or a 7% 1-year loan for $1,000, in which a 15% compensating balance is required, which should he take?

Solution:

Cost of the 8% loan would actually be 8%.

$$\text{Cost of the 7\% loan} = \frac{\$ \text{ interest}}{\text{funds available}} = \frac{70}{1,000 - 150} = 8.24\%$$

Take the 8% loan.

4. The demand for the Kennedy Brothers Co.'s products has a stochastic nature. The cash balances of the firm also fluctuate randomly, with the standard deviation of daily cash flows being $750. The firm wishes to maximize earnings by utilizing all idle balances of cash in the form of marketable securities. The current interest rate on securities is 8%, with the fixed cost of each transfer being $350. What are the upper and lower bound control limits?

Solution:

The return point, z, may be computed by

$$z = \sqrt[3]{\frac{3b\sigma^2}{4i}}$$

where b = fixed cost associated with a securities transaction
  σ^2 = variance of daily net cash flows
  i = interest rate per day on marketable securities

$$z = \sqrt[3]{\frac{3b\sigma^2}{4i}} = \sqrt[3]{\frac{3(350)(750)^2}{4(0.000222)}} = \$8,729$$

where i = 0.08/360 = 0.000222.

The optimal value of the upper control limit, h, equals 3z or $26,187. The lower-bound control limit is 0.

5. The vice-president in charge of finance has suggested to the board of directors that the company move its $5 million in excess cash from commercial paper, which is yielding 8%, into Boston Edison Common, a stock selling for $22, and paying an annual dividend of $2.44.

(a) Assuming the corporate tax rate is 50% and there is an 85% dividend exclusion, compute the after-tax yield of the two alternatives.

(b) Would you follow the vice-president's suggestion?

Solution:

(a) Commercial paper: $(0.08)(1 - 0.50) = 0.04$ or 4%

   Boston Edison Common: $\frac{2.44}{22} - (0.15)(0.50)\frac{2.44}{22} = 10.26\%$

(b) The decision depends on the firm's financial position and the expectations of future market movements.

6. The Klimate Control Corporation expects $50,000 in cash outlays for the next year. The projected opportunity interest rate is 7%, and the firm expects a cost of $75 each time it borrows. Cash outlays should be evenly distributed throughout the year. Drawing upon the economic-order-quantity formula:

(a) Calculate the transactions demand for cash (C*) for Klimate Control.

(b) What is the total cost (TC) for the use of cash needed for transactions demand?

(c) What would be the average cash balance for the firm?

Solution:

(a) $$C^* = \sqrt{\frac{2bT}{i}}$$

where   b = $75
T = $50,000
i = 0.07

$$C^* = \sqrt{\frac{2(75)(50,000)}{0.07}}$$

$$= \$10,351$$

(b) $$TC = b\left(\frac{T}{C^*}\right) + i\left(\frac{C^*}{2}\right)$$

$$= \frac{75(50,000)}{10,351} + \frac{(0.07)(10,351)}{2}$$

$$= \$362 + \$362$$

$$= \$724$$

(c) Average cash balances = $C^*/2 = \$10,351/2 = \$5,176$.

7. Assume that Klimate Control (problem 6) had $100,000 in cash at the beginning of the year.

(a) What amount would initially be invested in securities?

(b) How much would be invested in securities after 227 days?

Solution:

(a) Since, in problem 6 the optimal level of cash is $10,351 in cash, the firm can invest the difference in securities, or:

$$\$100,000 - \$10,351 = \$89,649$$

(b) The solution of this portion of the problem requires determining how many times during the 227-day period the firm must transfer funds to cash to meet its transaction demand for money. Thus: If T = $50,000 (problem 2) and C* = $10,351, management must transfer funds from marketable securities 4.83 times per year: 50,000/10,351. Thus, the velocity is 75.6 days, 365/4.83; or, in other words, every 75.6 days, Klimate Control must put $10,351 into cash to meet its transactions demand for money. Furthermore, given that the firm has $100,000 in funds to start with, the amount of funds which would be remaining in securities in 227 days would be

$$[\$100,000 - \quad (3+1) \quad (10,351)] = \underline{\$58,596}$$

$$\uparrow \qquad\qquad \uparrow \qquad\qquad \uparrow$$

| beginning securities | number of transfers in a 227-day period, $\dfrac{227}{75.6} + 1$ | amount to be transferred per transfer |

8. Assume that Gitton Industries expects the monthly cash balances shown (net of transaction needs). The precautionary demand for cash is $100,000.

January	$200,000
February	500,000
March	300,000
April	800,000
May	700,000
June	400,000
July	600,000
August	400,000
September	100,000
October	900,000
November	300,000
December	400,000

Develop a maturity schedule which maximizes the profits generated from investments in marketable securities.

Solution:

Management wants to maintain $100,000 to meet the precautionary demands for cash. Remembering that a transfer in a given month reduces the cash balances in subsequent months, the solution may be developed as follows:

(a) January investment: $100,000 of the January cash balance could be invested for 8 months (January through August) but would have to be used in September to satisfy the September precautionary needs.

(b) February investments:
   (1) $100,000 of the February cash flows could be invested for the February through August period. To invest more would reduce the March balance below the $100,000 minimal level.

   (2) $200,000 could be invested for the month of February only.

(c) March investment: No investment could be made from the March cash flows without violating the precautionary balance requirement.

(d) April investments:
   (1) An investment of $100,000 for the period of April through August could be made.

   (2) A $300,000 investment for the period of April through May will bring the cash level of the firm down to the minimum level of of $100,000 for May.

   (3) An additional investment of $100,000 solely for the month of April would still satisfy the minimum requirements.

(e) May and June investments: No investment in either of these months would be permitted, since the minimum cash levels have already been reached as a consequence of prior investments.

(f) July investment: A $200,000 investment for the month of July only could be made.

(g) August and September investments: No investment could be made in these months and still satisfy the minimum desired cash levels.

(h) October investments:
   (1) $200,000 can be invested for the 3-month period October through December.

   (2) Management could invest $600,000 for the month of October.

(i) November investment: No investment will be made in the month of November.

(j) December investment: $100,000 could be invested for the month of December.

SELF-TESTS

True-False

Ø F   1. The basic aim of cash management is to speed up receipts and disbursements.

F   2. Even though the time required for mailing is not reduced by concentration banking, the time required to collect checks is reduced.

F   3. An advantage of the lock-box system is the inexpensive costs of implementation.

T   4. The use of drafts and bank float are two ways by which management can reduce the speed of cash disbursements.

F   5. The optimal average cash balance is the lesser of the compensating-balance requirements of a bank and that which is suggested by a cash-marketable securities model.

F   6. Bankers' acceptances are evidenced by a deposit of funds at a commercial bank for a specified period of time at a specified rate of interest.

T   7. The repurchase agreement allows the purchaser to "lock in" a profit without the risk of market fluctuations in interest rates.

T   8. Agency securities generally carry a somewhat higher yield than treasury securities.

T   9. The transaction motive for holding cash is the need for cash to meet payments arising out of the ordinary course of business.

T   10. The more efficient the cash management of the firm, the less transactions and precautionary balances that will need to be maintained.

Multiple Choice

1. The following item is not a motive for holding cash:
   a. Transactions.
   b. Speculation.
   c. Precautionary.
   d. All of the above are motives.

2. The following item is not a limitation of the inventory model in cash planning:
   a. Cash payments are assumed to be steady over the period of time.
   b. Cash balances can fluctuate randomly.
   c. Cash payments are assumed known with certainty.

3. Identify the determinant(s) of the amount of transactions and precautionary balances held by the firm.
   a. The expected net cash flows of the firm.
   b. The maturity structure of the firm's debt.
   c. The firm's schedule of investment opportunities.
   d. a and b.
   e. a and c.

4. Specify the method(s) by which a firm can speed up its collection process and maximize available cash.
   a. Concentration banking.
   b. Lock-box plan.
   c. Inventory models.
   d. All of the above.
   e. None of the above.

5. Indicate the item which is not an advantage of the lock-box system.
   a. Remittances are collected sooner.
   b. The cost is minimal.
   c. Speeds up the cash flow to the firm.
   d. All of the above are advantages.

6. Which of the following is not a method for controlling disbursements?
   a. Drafts.
   b. Playing the float.
   c. Having a checkless society.
   d. All of the above are methods for control.

7. What is the primary advantage of stochastic models?
   a. Recognize the uncertainty of cash payments.
   b. Handle steady cash flows.
   c. Help the manager determine the correct level of cash to hold.

8. Which of the following U.S. government securities has an original maturity of 1 to 7 years?
   a. Treasury bills.
   b. Treasury bonds.
   c. Treasury notes.
   d. None of the above.

7
Accounts Receivable

Orientation: The policy of investing funds in accounts receivables involves a trade-off between profitability and risk. Both the aggregate as well as the individual accounts of the firm are considered. It is evidenced that the variables affecting accounts receivable are all closely aligned and related. The relationships that exist must be understood so as to contribute to the optimal receivables structure.

I.   Credit and collection policies

    A.   The credit profile the firm assumes may largely determine the success of its marketing effort.

        1.   If credit is too tight, it can dampen the demand for a company's goods.

        2.   If credit standards are too low, the volume of bad debts rises and cuts into the profitability of the firm.

            a.   Costs associated with easy credit also include the expense of running a large credit department and the slower turnover of the accounts receivable.

        3.   Credit should be extended to the point that marginal profitability on additional sales equals the required return on the additional investment in receivables necessary to generate those sales.

B. Credit terms involve both the time period and discount associated with the credit.

    1. The term is usually set by the industry (e.g., "2/10, net 30"); however, a company may increase demand by increasing its time period.

    2. By varying the discount given, the hope is to increase the turnover of receivables.

        a. The length of the discount period also may affect the collection period by enticing more customers to take the discount than before. However, it will also cause those who used to pay early to now wait until the last day allowed.

            (1) The trade-off between those who will now pay earlier and those who will pay later must be determined.

C. Default risk is a function of the ease of receiving credit and the terms under which that credit is to be repaid.

D. Collection policy is a combination of letter sending, telephone calls, personal visits, and legal actions.

    1. The greater the amount spent on collecting, the lower the volume of bad debts.

        a. The relationship is not linear, however, and beyond a point is not helpful.

        b. If sales are independent of collection efforts, then methods of collection should be evaluated with respect to the reduction in bad debts against the cost of lowering those bad debts.

II. Analyzing the credit applicant

A. Several avenues are open to the firm in considering the credit rating of an applicant. Among these are financial statements, independent credit ratings and reports, bank checking, information from other companies, and past experiences.

B. Once the decision to extend credit has been made and if the decision is yes, a maximum credit line is established as a ceiling on the amount of credit to be extended.

III. Additional considerations.

A. The firm will want to establish clear-cut methods for dealing with delinquent accounts so as to provide consistency.

B.   A firm may take out bad-debt insurance to protect against loss.

C.   The use of computers provides for a more orderly and efficient handling of accounts receivable. It also provides rapid access to data.

STUDY PROBLEMS

1. Assume that a firm has annual credit sales of $5 million and an average collection period of 72 days. Presently, sales are net 30 with no discount and the turnover of receivables is 5 times. The average receivables is then $1,000,000. By providing a discount of 2/10, net 30, the collection period is cut to 40 days, and now 60% of the customers use the discount offered. What is the opportunity cost of the new discount and what is the benefit realized by the firm having an increased turnover ratio? Assume that the firm has a 12% opportunity cost of funds.

Solution:

$$\text{Opportunity cost} = (0.02)(0.6)(\$5 \text{ million}) = \$60,000$$

$$\text{Average receivables} = \frac{5,000,000}{9} = \$555,555.55$$

$$\$1,000,000 - \$555,555.55 = \$444,444.45$$

$$\text{Profit from change} = (\$444,444.45)(0.12) = \$53,333.34$$

Thus, they should not make the change.

2. Assume that a company sells its product for $20, out of which $15 is variable cost before taxes, including credit department costs. Annual sales stand at $6 million, represented totally by credit sales. The cost per unit is $17.50. By implementing a new credit system the firm will effect a slowing in receivables collection from 30 days to 45 days, but old customers are expected to continue to pay as before. Increased sales are expected to reach 20%, or a total of $1.2 million, for a sum of $7.2 million. Assume further that the firm enjoys excess capacity and a required return of 20%. Should the firm undertake the proposed change?

Solution:

$$\text{Profit on additional sales} = (\$1,200,000)(1 - 0.75) = \$300,000$$

$$\text{Required return on new investments} = \frac{45}{360}(\$1,200,000 \times 0.75) = \$112,500$$

$$(\$112,500)(0.20) = \$22,500$$

Profit on additional sales exceeds required return, so the credit plan should be undertaken.

SELF-TESTS

True-False

_F_ 1. The objective in credit policy management is to minimize losses.

_T_ 2. An increase in the time period in which credit must be reapid will increase demand.

_T_ 3. Receivables arise from credit sales.

_T_ 4. With the easing of credit standards, there are increased risks associated with the future flow of the earnings stream.

_T_ 5. To speed up the turnover of receivables, a firm may either shorten the discount term or increase the discount offered.

_F_ 6. The expression "5/10, net 30" means that the customers receive a 10% discount if they pay within 5 days; otherwise, they must pay within 30 days.

_T_ 7. As credit standards are tightened, a point is reached where sales revenues will decline at an increasing rate while bad debts and the collection period decrease at a decreasing rate.

_F_ 8. The collection period and accounts receivable turnover provide different information to the credit manager.

_T_ 9. The famous "three Cs" of credit are: character, collateral, and capacity.

_T_ 10. To protect against unusual losses, it is possible for a firm to get credit insurance.

Multiple Choice

1. The major objective of a credit policy is to:
   a. Maximize sales.
   b. Minimize losses.
   c. Maximize profits.
   d. None of the above.

2. Which ratio might you be most concerned with in analyzing a firm's credit position?
   a. Inventory turnover.
   b. Debt/net worth.
   c. Earning power.
   d. Acid-test ratio.

3. An increase in the receivables turnover ratio means that:
   a. They are collecting credit sales more quickly than before.

      b. They are collecting credit sales more slowly than before.

      c. Sales have gone down.

      d. All of the above.

4. Which of the following would be a source of credit information?

      a. Firm's financial statement.

      b. Credit ratings from Dun & Bradstreet.

      c. A credit check through a bank.

      d. The company's past experience.

      (e.) All of the above.

5. Which of the following is not part of the firm's credit and collection policy decisions?

      a. The credit period.

      b. The cash discount given.

      (c.) The dividend decision.

      d. The level of collection expenditures.

      e. The quality of account accepted.

6. Which of the following is a cost associated with relaxed credit standards?

      a. Enlarged credit department.

      b. Increased probability of bad debt.

      c. Additional investment in receivables.

      (d.) All of the above.

      e. None of the above.

Inventory Management and Control

8

Orientation: With the introduction of the computer in the field of inventory control, an increase in the accuracy and availability of information is now at the disposal of the financial manager. Because inventory plays such a major role in the linking of sales and production for a firm, it is vital that it be managed efficiently. Involved in this control is regulation of work in process, in-transit inventories, raw-material inventory, and finished goods. Accurate control of its inventories provides the firm with economies of production and flexibility.

I. Inventory control directly affects the flexibility of the firm regarding its production scheduling, thereby influencing profitability.

    A. The greater the efficiency of the inventory control, the smaller the investment necessary.

    B. The economic order quantity provides the optimum order quantity for a good given its forecasted usage, ordering cost, and carrying cost.

       1. The EOQ is given as

$$Q^* = \sqrt{\frac{2SO}{C}}$$

        where C = carrying costs per period
                  O = ordering costs
                  S = total wage (in units) of an item of inventory for that period
                 Q^* = optimal order quantity

2. A constant lead time does not affect the EOQ.

3. Often an EOQ range, not a point, is used, since depending on the sensitivity of EOQ added flexibility is gained without less economy.

C. Often discounts are made available to a firm for lot sizes that conflict with the EOQ.

1. Where Q' = new order size, the additional carrying cost is

$$\frac{(Q' - Q^*)C}{2}$$

The savings in ordering costs is

$$\frac{SO}{Q^*} - \frac{SO}{Q'}$$

The net difference will determine whether or not to take the quantity discount.

II. Marginal analysis of inventory policy pits incremental benefits against the incremental costs of going from one inventory level to another.

A. To determine this comparison it is necessary to compute the savings from a change in ordering costs against the increased carrying costs of making larger orders, or vice versa.

1. Marginal analysis allows us to see nonlinear relationships not depicted in the EOQ.

III. Modification for safety stocks is necessary since the usage rate of inventory is seldom stable over a given timetable.

A. This safety stock is used to safeguard the firm against changes in order time and receipt of shipped goods.

B. The greater the uncertainty associated with forecasted demand or order time, the larger the safety stock.

1. The costs associated with running out of inventory will also determine the safety stock levels.

2. A point is reached where it is too costly to carry a larger safety stock given the associated risk.

IV. The relationship of inventory control to the financial manager is one of attempting to balance the advantages of additional inventory against the cost of carrying it.

A. The financial manager is directly concerned about the funds invested in the inventory.

   1. The greater the opportunity cost associated with the funds invested in inventory, the lower the optimal average inventory and order quantity.

STUDY PROBLEMS

1. The Johnson Furniture Co. is trying to determine the optimal order quantity for sofas. Annual sales for sofas are 800 at a retail price of $300. The cost of carrying sofas is $1 per month. It costs $35.00 to prepare and receive an order.

(a) Determine the EOQ.

(b) If the monthly sales rate for November-December is 100 and for June-July only 25, what is the EOQ for each period?

(c) The wholesaler's cost of $100 can be reduced to $93 if orders of 100 are made. Assuming steady sales during the year, should the order size be increased to 100?

Solution:

(a) $\text{EOQ} = \sqrt{\dfrac{2(67)(35)}{1}} = \sqrt{4,690} = 68.48 = 68 \text{ sofas}$

(b) $\text{EOQ} = \sqrt{\dfrac{2(100)(35)}{1}} = \sqrt{7,000} = 83.66 \text{ (November-December)}$

$\quad = \sqrt{\dfrac{2(25)(35)}{1}} = \sqrt{1,750} = 41.83 \text{ (June-July)}$

(c) $\text{Additional cost} = \dfrac{(Q' - Q)C}{2} = \dfrac{100 - 68(\$1)}{2} = \dfrac{32}{2} = \$16$

$\quad \text{Order cost savings} = \dfrac{SO}{Q} - \dfrac{SO}{Q'} = \dfrac{67(35)}{68} - \dfrac{67(35)}{100} = 34.45 - 23.45$

$\qquad\qquad = \$11$

Net increase in costs effect = $16 − $11 = $5

Discount savings = 67(7) = $469

Total savings = $469 (discount) − $11 (increased order cost)
$\qquad\quad$ = $458

2. The United Furniture Co. has an annual total demand for chairs of 25,000.

The EOQ is 2,500; therefore, inventory is ordered 10 times per year. The company maintains a safety stock of 2,000 chairs. The average inventory therefore is

$$\frac{2,500}{2} + 2,000 = 3,250$$

The cost of placing an order is $600. Suppose that the United Furniture Company decided to increase its average inventory by increasing its order quantity to 5,000. Compute the savings that United can realize by increasing its order quantity.

Solution:

Total ordering cost at EOQ of 2,500 was $600 × 10 = $6,000

Total ordering cost at order quantity of 5,000 is $600 × 5 = $3,000

Total savings is $6,000 – $3,000 = $3,000

Now, assume that the cost of carrying the additional inventory (warehousing, insurance, etc.) is $2,500 per year. Moreover, suppose that the average investment in inventory is $100 per unit. The required return on investment is 20% before taxes. Compute the new average inventory level and cost of carrying the new inventory in order to determine the net effect of increasing the order quantity from 2,500 to 5,000.

Solution:

$$\text{New average} = 2,000 + \frac{5,000}{2} = 4,500$$

$$4,500 - 3,250 = 1,250 = \text{incremental change in inventory level}$$

1,250 × $100 (per unit investment) = $125,000

$125,000 × 0.20 (required return) = $25,000

Annual costs equal	$25,000	(return)
	2,500	(insurance, etc.)
	$27,500	

Total costs	$27,500
Total benefits	3,000
	$24,500

The firm should not change its order quantity.

SELF-TESTS

True-False

_____ 1. There is no one level of inventory which is efficient for all firms.

_____ 2. While the EOQ and marginal analysis do not follow the same analytic procedure, they do provide approximately the same outcome.

_____ 3. In determining the level of safety stock it is important to evaluate the trade-off between the cost of carrying the additional inventory with the risk of running out of inventory.

_____ 4. Lead time in determining the reorder point refers to the time between the receipt of a customer's order and the shipment of that order.

_____ 5. Order point is determined soley by safety stock.

_____ 6. Large safety stocks tend to reduce the possibility of stockouts.

_____ 7. The marginal analysis of inventory policy assumes that increases in inventory will generate a permanent increase in sales.

_____ 8. The EOQ provides for an optimal safety stock determination.

_____ 9. Given a constant usage rate, the EOQ is easily adjusted to compensate for a new level of optimality.

_____ 10. Quantity discounts always take precedence over EOQ since it represents a savings and not just a cost as in the EOQ.

Multiple Choice

1. Inventory provides a link between:
   a. Production and sales of a product.
   b. Profits and sales.
   c. Raw material and finished goods.
   d. Production and distribution.

2. A major difference between the EOQ and the marginal analysis approach is:
   a. The EOQ deals only with costs while the marginal approach handles only savings.
   b. The marginal approach is nonlinear in nature while the EOQ is linear.
   c. The marginal approach is an optimal solution while the EOQ is not.
   d. The EOQ considers lead time while the marginal-analysis approach does not.

3. Marginal analysis deals specifically with:
    a. Savings derived from varying inventory levels.
    b. Incremental benefits minus incremental costs.
    c. Excess production capacity.
    d. Reduction of carrying costs.

4. All of the following are relationships that exist for safety stock except:
    a. The greater the risk of running out of stock, the larger the safety stock.
    b. The larger the opportunity cost of the funds invested in inventory, the smaller the safety stock.
    c. The greater the uncertainty associated with future forecasts of use, the larger the safety stock.
    d. The higher the profit margin per unit, the lower the safety stock necessary.

Trade *Credit and Commercial Paper* 9

Orientation: Based upon the assumption that a decision has been made regarding the proper proportion of short-term financing in the firm's financial mix, attention in this chapter is directed toward the types and composition of short-term financing. In particular, the chapter reviews the costs and benefits of trade credit and commercial paper, with an emphasis being placed upon determining the appropriate use of these two short-term financing instruments.

I. Trade credit as a source of financing

    A. Trade credit is the largest source of short-term funds for business firms and represents a particular important source of funds for small companies.

    B. Types of trade credit:

        1. Open-account arrangements: The seller ships goods to the buyer along with an invoice indicating the merchandise shipped and the terms of the sale.

        2. Notes payable: The buyer formally acknowledges the debt by signing a promissory note, indicating a commitment for repayment at a specified future date.

        3. Trade acceptance:

            a. The indebtedness of the buyer is formally recognized by payment of the draft at a future date.

    b. The seller does not release the goods until the buyer accepts the time draft.

    c. Depending upon the credit worthiness of the buyer, the trade acceptance may be negotiable. If so, the seller may sell the acceptance at a discount and receive immediate payment for the merchandise.

C. Terms of sale: For open-account trade credit, the following terms of sale become important considerations:

    1. *COD* (cash on delivery of the goods) permits the seller to avoid any risk except that the buyer may refuse the shipment.

    2. *CBD* (cash before delivery) avoids all risks on the part of the seller.

    3. *Net period no cash discount* involves the seller specifying the period of time allowed for payment, with no cash discount arising from early remittance.

    4. *Net period with cash discount* offers a cash discount if the bill is paid during the early part of the net period, thereby offering an incentive to the buyer for early payment.

    5. *Datings,* used frequently in seasonal business, encourages customers to place orders before the heavy selling period.

D. Trade credit as a means of financing:

    1. Trade credit is a built-in source of financing varying to a large extent with the production cycle.

    2. While trade credit is dependent upon the purchasing of inventories by the firm, two items remain at the discretion of the purchaser:

        a. Not taking the cash discount on the last day of the discount period.

        b. Payment being made beyond the final due date.

    3. Payment on the final due date:

        a. Making the remittance on the final due date, thereby foregoing the cash discount, results in a definite opportunity cost.

        b. If a firm does not take a cash discount, its effective percentage cost of trade credit declines the longer the payment is postponed.

4. Stretching accounts payable:

    a. Stretching accounts payable, or "leaning on the trade," carries with it a twofold cost: The cost of the cash discount foregone and the possible deterioration in credit rating.

    b. Periodic and reasonable stretching of payments is not necessarily bad and should be evaluated in relation to its cost and alternative sources of short-term credit. However, in doing so, every effort should be made to keep the suppliers fully informed of the situation.

E. Advantages of trade credit:

    1. A readily available and a continuous form of credit.

    2. Less formality is required, thereby avoiding the negotiation process relating to the terms and restrictions of the loan.

    3. Advantageous to small firms having difficulties in obtaining credit elsewhere.

F. The advantages of using trade credit must be weighted against the cost.

    1. The purchaser should be cognizant that even if the invoice is paid within the discount period, the supplier may pass the cost on to the buyer in the form of higher prices.

    2. The buyer should recognize that the cost of trade credit changes over time, varying with interest rates and the supply of money.

II. The use of commercial paper

A. Commercial paper, sold in the money markets, consists of unsecured short-term negotiable promissory notes of large, well-established, credit-worthy corporations.

B. The phenomenal growth of commercial paper in the past decade has been a function of (1) the growth of the economy as a whole and the growth in installment financing of durable goods, and (2) periods of credit curtailment on the part of banks.

C. The commercial-paper market is composed of two segments: the dealer market and the direct-placement market.

    1. The dealer organization:

        a. This market consists of a limited number of major institutions purchasing commercial paper from the issuer and in turn selling it to investors.

      b. The paper generally ranges from 1 to 6 months in maturity and from $25,000 to several million dollars in size.

  2. Direct-placement markets:

      a. A number of large finance companies issue commercial paper directly to investors, tailoring both the maturity and the amount of the note to the needs of the purchaser.

      b. Maturities on directly placed paper may range from a few days to 9 months.

      c. Finance companies use commercial paper as a permanent source of financing.

      d. Directly placed paper has recently come to account for 60 to 80% of the total commercial paper outstanding.

D. Advantage to borrower:

  1. The cost of commercial paper is normally 0.25% to 2% lower than the prime rate for bank loans, with the differential increasing in periods of tight money.

  2. The use of commercial paper avoids the legal limitations on the size of a loan that a commercial bank may extend.

E. Criteria for use:

  1. In assessing commercial paper as a means of financing, the company should weigh the relative cost and availability of alternative sources of funds.

  2. The firm should be careful not to impair relations with its bank by employing commercial paper exclusively.

STUDY PROBLEMS

1. If the terms of sales are 3/10, net 30, what is the effective annual interest cost?

    Solution:

$$\frac{3}{(100-3)} \times \frac{360}{20} = 55.67\%$$

2. How much additional trade credit will be spontaneously generated if a firm having previously averaged $3,000 of purchases per day on terms of net 30 increases its purchases to $4,000 per day and receives new terms of net 60?

Solution:

$4,000 × 60 days = $240,000 average payables outstanding—new terms
$3,000 × 30 days = $ 90,000 average payables outstanding—existing terms
$150,000 additional trade credit

3.

Thomas Manufacturing
Balance Sheet
December 31, 1976

Cash	$ 5,000	Accounts payable	$ 8,000
Marketable securities	10,000	Bank loans (8%)	12,000
Accounts receivable	25,000	Notes payable	15,000
Inventories	20,000	Total current liabilities	$ 35,000
Total current assets	$ 60,000		
Fixed assets	$ 80,000	Long-term debt	$ 50,000
		Net worth	55,000
Total assets	$140,000	Total liabilities	$140,000

Sales for the year = $560,000

(a) If the asset turnover remains at 4 times, how much new financing will be required if sales increase by 10%?

(b) Thomas' suppliers sell on credit terms of 60 days; however, Thomas currently has payables representing 80 days of purchases. All else being constant, what would the debt-to-total assets ratio be if new short-term financing is used to bring the firm current on its trade obligations?

(c) What would the current ratio be if marketable securities are sold off to generate the funds necessary to become current on trade obligations?

Solution:

(a) ($560,000)(1.10) = $616,000 new sales

$$\frac{\$616,000}{X} = 4$$

X = $154,000 new asset level

New asset financing needed = $14,000 ($154,000 − $140,000)

(b) None. The new short-term financing will be equal to the overdue payables. Thus, the debt ratio is unchanged.

(c) If 80 days' payables are represented in the $8,000 balance-sheet figures and 60 days' payables are considered current, then 1/4 of the payables are overdue. Thus, (1/4) ($8,000) = $2,000 overdue. Accordingly, if $2,000 in marketable securities are sold off, current assets would be reduced to $58,000 ($60,000 − $2,000), and current liabilities would be $33,000 ($35,000 − $2,000).

$$\text{current ratio} = \frac{58,000}{33,000} = 1.76$$

4. Jones Brothers purchases materials on 1/10, net 20 terms. The company has a policy to pay bills within 15 days after purchases are made. The reason given for not taking the discount was that a bank loan would cost 10%, whereas the discount saves only 1%.

(a) Is the company correct in the analysis?

(b) What is the real cost of not taking the discount?

Solution:

(a) Jones Brothers is failing to compare the cost of the bank loan with the *annual* cost of using the funds for the 5-day period from the discount date to final due date.

(b) $$\text{Cost} = \frac{1}{99} \times \frac{360}{5} = 72.73\% \text{ on annual basis}$$

5. McMillan Lumber Company needs to increase its working capital by $25,000. It has two alternatives of financing available:

(a) Forgo cash discounts on accounts payables with terms of 2/10, net 20.

(b) Negotiate a bank loan at 12%, with a 20% compensating balance being required.

Which alternative should be selected?

Solution:

(a) $$\text{Cost of not taking discount} = \frac{2}{98} \times \frac{360}{10} = 73.47\%$$

(b) $$\text{Cost of bank loan} = \frac{\text{quoted interest rate}}{100\text{-percentage compensating balances}} = \frac{0.12}{0.80}$$

$$= 15.00\%$$

The firm should borrow from the bank in order to pay within the discount period.

SELF-TESTS

True-False

_T_ 1. On the whole, trade credit may be an extremely expensive form of short-term financing.

_F_ 2. Commercial paper consists of secured short-term negotiable promissory notes sold in the money market.

_T_ 3. The dealer market occurs if a commercial-paper issuer goes through a dealer for the purpose of issuing the securities.

_T_ 4. Commercial paper usually carries a lower interest rate than bank loan rates.

_F_ 5. Bank credit is the largest source of short-term funds for business firms collectively.

_T_ 6. Under COD terms of sale, the *only* risk that the seller undertakes is that the buyer may refuse the shipment.

_F_ 7. With a trade discount, a customer is given a discount if the shipment is above a certain amount.

_F_ 8. The dealer market for commercial paper is composed of the five largest banks in the country.

_T_ 9. A possible reason why commercial paper is used is that banks have legal limitations on the size of a loan that can be made to any one borrower.

Multiple Choice

1. Spontaneous sources of credit include:
   a. Trade credit.
   b. Commercial paper.
   c. Bank credit.
   d. Accrued wages.
   e. a and b.
   f. a and d.

2. Examples of trade credit would *not* include which of the following:
   a. Open account.
   b. Bank acceptances.
   c. Trade acceptances.
   d. Notes payable.

3. The trade terms 2/15, net 30 indicate:
   a. A 2% discount is permitted if payment is made within 15 days.
   b. A 15% discount is permitted if payment is made within 30 days.
   c. A 2% discount is permitted if payment is made within 30 days.
   d. A 30% discount is permitted if payment is made within 15 days.

4. Advantages of trade credit would *not* include:
   a. Ready availability.
   b. Many negotiations with suppliers.
   c. Not as many restrictions.
   d. A flexible form of financing.

5. A cost to a firm attempting to stretch its accounts payable would *not* include:
   a. The cost of the cash discount forgone.
   b. A possible deterioration in credit rating.
   c. All of the above.
   d. None of the above.

6. Which of the following is *not* a characteristic of the commercial-paper market?
   a. It is a short-term promissory note.
   b. It is issued by credit-worthy companies.
   c. The market is composed of two parts: the dealer market and the direct placement market.
   d. None of the above are characteristics.
   e. All of the above are characteristics.

7. Advantages of the commercial-paper market to the borrower would *not* include:
   a. It is generally cheaper than a short-term business loan from a commercial bank.
   b. The interest rates fluctuate very minimally.
   c. It is quite useful for short-term financing.
   d. All of the above are advantages of commercial paper to the borrower.

8. Which of the following is *not* considered to be a term of sale?
   a. COD.
   b. CBD.
   c. Bill of lading.
   d. Net period with cash discount.
   e. Net period with no cash discount.

Short-Term Loans

10

Orientation: In Chapter 9 we considered two important sources of short-term financing: trade credit and commercial paper. In the present chapter we consider short-term loans. Specifically, we will be concerned with loans from commercial banks and finance companies, which, for expository purposes, are classified as either secured or unsecured loans.

I. Unsecured bank credit

    A. Short-term, unsecured bank loans typically are regarded as *self-liquidating* in that the assets purchased with the proceeds generate sufficient cash flows to repay the loan in less than 1 year.

    B. Unsecured bank credit often takes the form of a line of credit which represents an arrangement between a bank and its customer with respect to the maximum amount of unsecured credit the bank will permit the firm to owe at any one time.

    C. A revolving credit agreement differs from a line of credit in that it represents a legal commitment on the part of the bank to extend credit up to a maximum amount.

    D. When a firm needs short-term financing for only one particular purpose, a transaction loan is generally used.

    E. The terms under which unsecured bank credit is issued can be summarized in terms of the following characteristics of the loan agreement:

1. In addition to charging interest on loans, commercial banks often require the borrower to maintain demand-deposit balances at the bank (known as a compensating balance) in direct proportion to either the amount of funds borrowed or the amount of the commitment.

2. The second key element in an unsecured bank loan agreement is the rate of interest.

    a. Unlike the rates set on money market instruments such as treasury bills or commercial paper, the rate of interest on an unsecured bank loan is determined through personal negotiation between the borrower and the lender.

    b. In some measure, banks do try to vary the interest rate charged in accordance with the credit worthiness of the borrower and, also, in keeping with existing money-market conditions.

    c. Interest can be computed on a collect basis, in which case it is paid at maturity of the loan; or it can be computed on a discount basis, whereby interest is deducted from the initial amount of the loan.

II. Secured credit

   A. Secured loans vary with respect to their source, cost, and specific covenants, but these all are concerned in some way with collateral values and security devices.

       1. Collateral value refers, very simply, to the value of the specific assets pledged as security for the loan.

       2. Security devices are the legal conditions surrounding the rights of the lender in the event of default and are specified in Article 9 of the Uniform Commercial Code.

   B. There are two basic forms of secured loans which are based on accounts receivable: assignment and factoring.

       1. An assignment of accounts receivable involves the pledging of receivables as collateral for a short-term loan from either a bank or a finance company.

       2. When a firm factors its receivables, it actually sells them to a factor, as opposed to an assignment, where the firm retains title to the receivables.

   C. Inventories also represent a reasonably liquid asset, which can be used as security for a short-term loan. We discuss five types of loans secured by inventories.

1. Under the Uniform Commercial Code, a borrower can pledge his inventories "in general" without specifying the specific items of inventory involved, in which case the loan agreement is referred to as a *floating lien.*

2. Where specific items of inventory are identified as collateral, the security agreement is referred to as a *chattel mortgage.*

3. A third form of inventory loan is called a *trust receipt* loan, whereby the borrower holds the inventory and proceeds from the sale of inventory in trust for the lender. This type of financing is commonly used by automobile and equipment dealers to finance their floor stock and thus is referred to as *floor planning.*

4. A borrower secures a *terminal warehouse receipt* loan by storing inventory with a public or terminal warehousing company.

5. A *field warehouse receipt* loan involves making loans which allow the borrower to maintain the inventory on his premise.

D. Collateral other than accounts receivable and inventories may be used as collateral for loans. Examples include stocks, bonds, and the cash surrender value of life insurance policies.

E. Further, cosigning serves as an important source of security for short-term loans.

STUDY PROBLEMS

1. Ratchet, Inc., needs $100,000 to meet a temporary need for working capital during an upcoming seasonal peak in its sales. Ratchet's bank has agreed to loan the funds at a rate of 9% for the necessary 4-month interval provided that a 20% compensating balance is maintained. Ratchet does not ordinarily maintain more than a $10,000 demand deposit balance with the bank. Estimate the annual (effective) cost of the loan to Ratchet.

Solution:

To obtain the needed $100,000 and meet the compensating balance requirement, Ratchet must borrow X dollars, where X is found as follows:

$$
\begin{aligned}
X - 0.20X - 10,000 &= 100,000 \\
0.8X &= 90,000 \\
X &= \$112,500
\end{aligned}
$$

Thus, Ratchet borrows $112,500, for which it must maintain a compensating balance of 0.20 × 112,500 = $22,500, of which $10,000 will come from its normal demand deposit and $12,500 must be borrowed, which leaves the firm the use of $100,000.

The interest cost of the loan is computed as follows:

$$\text{Interest} = 0.09 \times 112{,}500 \div 3 = \$3{,}375$$

We divide by 3 since the loan is for only 4 months, or one-third of a year.

The effective annual cost of the loan is found as follows:

$$\text{Annual rate} = \frac{\$ \text{ loan cost}}{\$ \text{ funds available}} \div \text{loan maturity as a fraction of 1 year}$$

$$= \frac{3{,}375}{100{,}000} \div \frac{4}{12}$$

$$= 0.10125, \text{ or } \underline{\underline{10.125\%}}$$

2. A factor has agreed to buy Alpha Company's receivables ($100,000 per month), which have an average collection period of 60 days. The factor will advance up to 75% of the face value of the receivables for an annual charge of 8% of the funds advanced. The factor also charges a handling fee of 2% of the face value of all accounts purchased. What is the effective annual cost of the factoring arrangement to Alpha if the maximum advance is taken every month?

Solution:

With an average collection period of 60 days and monthly credit sales, Alpha could build up a loan advance over 2 months of 0.75 × 200,000 = $150,000. This loan would be constantly rolling over as accounts were being collected and new credit sales being made.

The 60-day interest cost of the loan would be computed as follows:

$$\text{interest} = 150{,}000 \times 0.08 \div 6 = \$2{,}000$$

The factor's fee would be as follows:

$$\text{fee} = 0.02 \times 200{,}000 = \$4{,}000$$

Thus, the effective annual cost of the 60-day loan would be:

$$\text{Annual rate} = \frac{\$2{,}000 + 4{,}000}{\$150{,}000} \div \frac{2}{12} = \underline{\underline{0.24}}, \text{ or } \underline{\underline{24\%}}$$

3. The Harbor Company has been factoring its accounts receivable for the past 5 years. The factor charges a fee of 2% and will lend up to 80% of the volume of receivables purchased for an additional 3/4% per month. The firm typically has sales of $600,000 per month, 60% of which are on credit. By using the factor, Harbor does not have to maintain a credit department costing approximately $3,200 per month, nor does the firm incur bad-debt losses estimated at 1/2% per month.

The firm's bank has recently offered to lend the firm up to 70% of the face value of the receivables shown on the schedule of accounts. The bank would charge 7% per annum interest plus a 1% processing charge per dollar of receivables lending. The firm extends terms of net 30, and all customers who pay their bills do so by the thirtieth of the month. Should the firm discontinue its factoring arrangement in favor of the bank's offer if the firm borrows, on the average, $150,000 per month on its receivables?

Solution:

The cost of factoring is found as follows:

Fee (0.02 × $600,000 × 0.60)	$7,200
Interest cost (0.0075 × $150,000)	1,125
	$8,325

The cost of the bank loan is found as follows:

Fee (0.01 × $150,000)	$1,500
Interest (0.07 × $150,000 × 1/12)	875
	$2,375

Plus:

Credit department cost per month	$3,200
Bad-debt losses (0.005 × $600,000 × 0.60)	1,800
Total cost	$7,375

Yes, go with the bank loan arrangement.

SELF-TESTS

True-False

__F__ 1. Finance companies almost always will offer unsecured loans.

__T__ 2. Self-liquidating loans are most popular in financing seasonal buildups in accounts receivable and inventories.

___T___ 3. A line of credit does not constitute a legal commitment on the part of the bank to extend credit.

___F___ 4. With a revolving credit agreement, a bank can only extend a maximum of $1 million credit.

___T___ 5. Compensating-balance requirements may increase the liquidity position of the borrower from the bank's point of view.

___F___ 6. The prime rate is the highest rate typically charged on business loans to large well-established companies.

___F___ 7. The effective rate of interest is lower on a discount note than on a collect note.

___F___ 8. When a firm factors its receivables, it retains title to them.

___T___ 9. Line of credit and revolving credit agreements are more flexible than most other forms of short-term financing.

___F___ 10. Field warehouse receipt lending is particularly appropriate when a borrower makes infrequent use of inventory.

Multiple Choice

1. An informal arrangement between a bank and its customer with respect to the maximum amount of unsecured credit the bank will permit the firm to owe at any one time is a:
   a. Line of credit.
   b. Revolving credit agreement.
   c. Transaction loan.
   d. None of the above.

2. When a firm needs short-term funds for only one purpose, a bank will grant a:
   a. Line of credit.
   b. Revolving credit agreement.
   c. Transaction loan.
   d. Compensating balance.
   e. Speculative loan.

3. If a firm borrows $1 million at 8% and is required to maintain $100,000 more in compensating balances, the effective annual interest cost is:
   a. 8%.
   b. 8.88%.
   c. 7.27%.
   d. None of the above.

4. Suppose that a firm has a $10,000 loan at 7% interest for 1 year. The effective rate of interest on a discount basis is:
   a. 6.54%.
   b. 7%.

c. 7.35%.
d. None of the above.

5. With security, the sources of loan payment for the lender are the:
   a. Cash-flow ability of the firm to service the debt.
   b. Collateral value of the security.
   c. Outstanding common stock.
   d. All of the above.
   e. a and b.
   f. b and c.

6. Inventory is in the possession of a third party under which of the following methods?
   a. Floating lien.
   b. Terminal warehouse receipts.
   c. Chattel mortgage.
   d. Trust receipts.
   e. None of the above.

7. The key influencing factor when a firm is deciding upon the most appropriate mix of short-term financing is the:
   a. Cost.
   b. Availability.
   c. Timing.
   d. Flexibility.
   e. Degree to which the assets of the firm are encumbered.

$.08 - 100,000 = 1,000,000$

$X - .10X - 100,000 = 1,000,000$

$.90x = 1,100,000$

$\$1,222,222.222 @ 8\% = 97777.78$

$\dfrac{977.78}{\$1,100,000}$

$.0888 = 8.88\%$

11 *Intermediate-Term Financing*

Orientation: In this chapter we discuss alternative sources of intermediate-term financing which are generally employed to finance fixed assets and underlying buildups of receivables and inventories. Specifically, our interest in this chapter is in describing the nature of and general limitations associated with intermediate-term credit arising from: bank term loans, insurance company loans, equipment loans, government guaranteed loans to small businesses, and lease financing.

I. Types of intermediate-term debt

   A. Term loans made by commercial banks have a final maturity of more than 1 year and represent credit extended under a formal loan agreement.

      1. An ordinary term loan is a business loan with an original, or final, maturity of more than 1 year, repayable according to a specified schedule.

         a. Ordinary term loans are written with a maturity in the 1- to 10-year range.

         b. The interest rate on a term loan is higher than the rate on a short-term loan, and may be set as a fixed or variable rate.

         c. The principal advantage of an ordinary bank term loan is flexibility with convenience and quickness being secondary attractions.

      d. The major limitations of these loans are their short maturities and the restrictive provisions likely to be imposed in the loan agreement.

  2. Revolving credit is a formal commitment by a bank to lend up to a certain amount of money to a company over a specified period of time. Revolving-credit agreements can be set up so that at the maturity of the commitment, the outstanding balance can be converted into a term loan at the option of the borrower.

  3. In order to safeguard itself, the lender will require the borrower to maintain its financial condition at a level at least as favorable as when the commitment was made. The provisions for protection contained in a loan agreement are known as protective covenants.

      a. The formulation of the different restrictive provisions should be tailored to a specific loan situation.

      b. The important procedure covenants of a loan agreement may be classified in the following manner.

          (1) The first type are general provisions used in most loan agreements and are varied to fit the particular situation involved.

          (2) Second are the routine provisions used in most agreements which are not variable.

      c. Although the lender is instrumental in establishing loan restrictions, the restrictiveness of the protective convenants is subject to negotiation between the borrower and the lender.

B. Complementary to bank term loans are insurance company term loans.

  1. The maturities are longer and the interest rates are higher on insurance as opposed to bank term loans.

  2. Often an insurance company and a bank will participate in the same loan.

C. The Small Business Administration, an agency of the federal government, has the authority to make or guarantee loans to small businesses when they are unable to obtain funds elsewhere.

  1. The definition of a small business depends upon its sales in relation to those of the industry, and upon the number of employees.

2. When possible, the SBA prefers to participate with a private lending institution in extending credit.

D. Equipment loans arise where equipment is pledged to secure a loan. Depending upon the quality of the equipment, the lender will make a percentage advance against the equipment's market value.

1. In setting the repayment schedule the lender wants to be sure that the market value of the equipment always exceeds the balance of the loan.

2. Sources of equipment financing include commercial banks, finance companies, and the sellers of equipment.

E. A chattel mortgage is a lien on property other than real property. The borrower signs a security agreement which gives the lender a lien on the equipment specified in the agreement. The lender can then sell the equipment if the borrower defaults in the payment of principal or interest.

II. Lease financing

A. A financial lease is a noncancellable contractual commitment on the part of a lessee to make a series of payments to a lessor for the use of an asset.

B. Three types of lease financing are important:

1. Under a sale and lease-back arrangement a firm sells an asset it owns to another party, and this party leases it back to the firm.

2. Under direct leasing, a company acquires the use of an asset that it did not own previously. In most cases the vendor sells the asset to the lessor, who, in turn, leases it to the lessee. The lessee has use of the asset, along with a contractual obligation to make lease payments to the lessor.

3. Leveraged leasing has developed in conjunction with the financing of assets requiring large capital outlays. The major difference in a leveraged lease and the two forms of leasing already described is that there are three parties involved in leveraged leasing: the lessee, the lessor, and the lender.

C. The accounting treatment of leases has changed over the years toward greater and greater disclosure. Today, there is enough disclosure of leases that the financial statement user now is able to judge the impact of this important source of contractual obligations in the same way in which he is able to analyze the importance of debt payments.

1. Omitting consideration for lease obligations can have a favorable, and deceptive, effect upon the financial condition of a firm.

2. Today, at the very least, the lease obligation must be disclosed in a footnote to the audited financed statements.

3. Presently a proposal is being considered by the Financial Accounting Standards Board which calls for capitalization (annual lease payments to be capitalized at an appropriate discount rate and the capitalized liability shown on the balance sheet, together with the amortized value of the asset) of certain types of leases.

D. A lease payment is deductible as an expense for federal income tax purposes; however, with the passage of the 1954 tax code, which permitted accelerated depreciation, the tax advantage of leasing was largely eliminated.

1. One remaining tax advantage with leasing is that the cost of land can be amortized in the lease payments.

2. A firm may also gain certain tax advantages in a sale and lease-back arrangement when the assets are sold for less than their depreciated value.

3. An important tax consideration is the investment tax credit which is available to corporations and individuals who invest in certain types of assets. The credit itself can be taken by the lessor and can result in lease payments which are lower than they would be in the absence of the credit if (all or a part of) the credit is passed on to the lessee.

III. Leasing versus borrowing

A. Whether lease financing or borrowing is favored will depend upon the patterns of cash outflows for each financing method and upon the opportunity cost of funds.

B. One means for analyzing lease financing in relation to debt financing involves discounting to present value the net cash outflows after taxes under each alternative with the preferred alternative being the one that provides the lower present value.

STUDY PROBLEMS

1. The H & M Mfg. company is seeking an $18,000 loan for the next 10 years. The firm has contacted three sources (two banks and an insurance company) and found that the following terms are available to it:

Bank 1: Annual interest payments of $2,160 plus $18,000 at the end of 10 years.

Bank 2: Annual payments of $3,185.72 for each of the next 10 years.

Insurance company: Annual payments of $2,654.77 for each of the next 10 years plus an additional (balloon) payment of $9,317.61 at the end of the tenth year.

Which of the three alternatives should H & M select?

Solution:

H & M should select among the available alternatives based on the annual effective cost of each.

Bank 1: The annual interest here is $2,160/$18,000 = 12\%$, with "add-on" interest such that the effective cost of this alternative is 12%:

$$\$18,000 = 2,160 \sum_{t=1}^{10} \frac{1}{(1+0.12)^t} + 1,800 \frac{1}{(1+0.12)^{10}}$$

Bank 2: The arrangement here is of the annual-installment variety, where the effective cost, k, is found by solving:

$$\$18,000 = \$3,185.72 \sum_{t=1}^{10} \frac{1}{(1+k)^t}$$

$$\sum_{t=1}^{10} \frac{1}{(1+k)^t} = \frac{\$18,000}{\$3,185.72} = 5.6502$$

5.6502 corresponds to a discount factor for a 10-year annuity at 12%. Thus, the effective cost of this alternative is 12%.

Insurance company: The answer here is not so easy. Actually, the loan repayment schedule reflects a set of annual installment payments based on 12% interest to repay a principal of $15,000 plus a lump-sum payment of $9,317.61 to repay an outstanding principal amount of $3,000 for 10 years:

$$\$18{,}000 = \$2{,}654.77 \sum_{t=1}^{10} \frac{1}{(1 + 0.12)^t} + \$9{,}317.61 \frac{1}{(1 + 0.12)^{10}}$$

Thus, this alternative, although disguised, represents a combination of an installment loan and an add-on loan carrying an effective rate of interest of 12% per annum.

2. Compute the annual installment payment, principal, and interest on a $100,000 5-year loan for each year of its existence carrying a 10% rate of interest.

Solution:

Compute the installment payments:

$$\text{payment} \times \sum_{t=1}^{5} \frac{1}{(1 + 0.10)^t} = \$100{,}000$$

$$\text{payment} \times 3.7908 = 100{,}000$$

$$\text{payment} = \$26{,}380$$

Principal and Interest Computation

Year	Payment	Interest	Principal	Remaining Balance
1	$26,380	$10,000*	$16,380†	$83,620‡
2	26,380	8,362§	18,018	65,601
3	26,380	6,560	19,820	45,782
4	26,380	4,578	21,801	23,980
5	26,380	2,398	23,982	0

*$100,000 × 0.10 = $10,000.
†$26,380 − 10,000 = $16,380.
‡$100,000 − 16,380 = $83,620.
§$83,620 × 0.10 = $8,362.

3. The Acme Real Estate Company is considering renting or leasing the company car as opposed to buying as it has done in prior years. The ABC Leasing Company has offered to lease Acme a car and to provide it with regular maintenance for $2,400 a year over a 3-year lease.

Information pertinent to the purchase of the car is found as follows:

Purchase price	$5,000
Salvage value at the end of 3 years	$2,000
Depreciation method	Straight line
Annual maintenance	$200
Interest rate on bank not for purchase of car (assume that the full $5,000 is borrowed)	8%
Tax rate	50%
Term of loan	3 years
Marginal cost of capital	0.10

Given the above information, analyze the lease or buy decision for Acme.

Solution:

Exhibit 1

Computing the Cost of Leasing

End of Year	Lease Payment	Tax Shield	Cash Flow after Taxes	Discount Fact or after Tax at Cost of New Devaluation (4%)	Present Value
0	$(2,400)	$ 0	$(2,400)	1.0	$(2,400)
1	(2,400)	1,200	(1,200)	0.9615	(1,154)
2	(2,400)	1,200	(1,200)	0.9246	(1,110)
3	–	1,200	1,200	0.8890	1,067
					$(3,597)

Exhibit 2

Computing the Cost of Borrowing

End of Year	Loan Payment*	Interest†	Principal†	Maintenance	Depreciation	Total Tax Expenditures	Tax Shield	Cash Expenditures	Annual Cash Expenditure	Discount Factors	Present Value
0	$1,940	$400	$1,540	$200	$1,000	$1,600	$800	$2,140	$(1,340)	0.9615	$(1,288)
1	1,940	277	1,663	200	1,000	1,477	738	2,140	(1,402)	0.9246	(1,296)
2	1,940	144	1,796	200	1,000	1,344	672	2,140	(1,468)	0.8890	(1,305)
									2,000	0.7513‡	1,503
											$(2,386)

*5,000 = x•2.5771
x = 1,940

†Year	Payment	Interest	Principal	Remaining Balance
1	1,940	400	1,540	3,460
2	1,940	277	1,663	1,796
3	1,940	144	1,796	—

‡Since the salvage value is not as certain a cash flow as the other cash flows being considered, we discount it at a higher rate. For want of a better rate we use the firm's cost of capital, 10%.

SELF-TESTS

True-False

___F___   1. One of the principal economic reasons for borrowing is the inability of a firm to utilize all of the tax benefits associated with the leasing of an asset.

___T___   2. A lease payment is deductible as an expense for federal income tax purposes.

___T___   3. If leases are capitalized on the balance sheet, it will permit easier analysis of the contractual obligations of the firm and investors.

___T___   4. The accounting treatment of leases has changed over the years— toward greater disclosure.

___F___   5. Omitting consideration of lease obligations will affect the company that leases by showing a slower turnover of its assets and a lower earning-power ratio than an identical company that engaged in debt financing.

___F___   6. Under a sale-and-lease-back arrangement, a company acquires the use of an asset that it did not own previously.

___T___   7. The distinguishing feature between a financial and an operating lease is cancellability.

___F___   8. A chattel mortgage is a lien on real property.

___F___   9. Insurance company term loans are highly competitive with bank term loans.

___T___   10. The working-capital requirement is probably the most commonly used and most comprehensive provision in a loan agreement.

___F___   11. The principal advantage of revolving credit is flexibility.

___F___   12. The interest rate on a term loan is higher than the rate on a short-term loan to the same borrower.

Multiple Choice

1. Features of a bank term loan that distinguish it from other types of business loans include:
   a. A final maturity of more than 1 year.
   b. Credit extended under an informal loan agreement.

c. Credit extended under a formal loan agreement.
d. a and b only.
e. a and c only.

2. Rarely will a bank make a term loan with a final maturity of more than:
   a. 5 years.
   b. 10 years.
   c. 20 years.
   d. 25 years.
   e. None of the above.

3. The interest rate on a term loan is *not* set by:
   a. Periodic negotiations between the borrower and the lender.
   b. A fixed rate effective over the life of the loan.
   c. A variable rate that is adjusted in keeping with changes in the prime rate.
   d. None of the above.

4. The important protective covenants of a loan agreement may be classified as follows:
   a. General provisions.
   b. Routine provisions.
   c. Specific provisions.
   d. All of the above.
   e. a and c only.

5. The definition of a small business depends:
   a. Upon its sales in relation to those of the industry.
   b Upon the number of employers.
   c. Upon its profits.
   d. Upon all of the above.
   e. a and b only.
   f. a and c only.

6. Participation by the SBA may be up to what percent of the loan?
   a. 20%.
   b. 48%.
   c. 50%.
   d. 80%.
   e. None of the above.

7. Which of the following is *not* a source of equipment financing?
   a. Commercial bank.
   b. Finance company.
   c. Seller of the equipment.
   d. None of the above.

Mathematics of Finance 12

Orientation: The purpose of this chapter is to provide a framework for the understanding the mathematics of finance. The mathematical formulas and calculations presented in this chapter provide a basis for the concepts of capital budgeting, valuation, and cost of capital (which are developed later in the book).

I. Compound interest refers to the rate of interest when interest in future periods is earned *both* on the initial principal and on the accumulated interest from prior periods.

    A. The terminal value of an amount compounded for n years at a rate of r is

$$TV_n = X_0(1 + r)^n$$

        1. TV_n is the terminal value at the end of n years.

        2. X_0 is the beginning or present value of the amount being compounded.

        3. r equals the compounding interest rate.

    B. For example, if you had $100 and put it in the bank at a compound interest rate of 5% for 10 years, it would compound as follows:

Time	Value at Time n	Generalized Form
Now	$100.00	X_0
1 yr	105.00	$X_0(1 + r)$
2 yr	110.25	$X_0(1 + r)(1 + r)$
3 yr	115.76	$X_0(1 + r)(1 + r)(1 + r)$
4 yr	121.55	$X_0(1 + r)^4$
5 yr	127.63	$X_0(1 + r)^5$
.		
.		
.		
10 yr	162.89	$X_0(1 + r)^{10}$

C. In the preceding example, returns were compounded once a year, or annually. However, there are other methods of compounding: semi-annually, quarterly, and other periods.

1. These more frequent compounding periods result in larger terminal values when the time horizon and interest rate are kept constant because interest is earned on interest more frequently.

2. If someone is earning 8% on his savings of $100 for 5 years and it is compounded semiannually, that is the same as saying that he earns 4% every 6 months for 10 6-month periods, or

$$TV_{\text{10 6-month periods}} = \$100(1 + 0.04)^{10}$$

3. If it is compounded quarterly, he is earning 2% every 3 months for 20 3-month periods, or

$$TV_{\text{20 3-month periods}} = \$100(1 + 0.02)^{20}$$

4. The generalized form of this equation is

$$TV_n = X_0(1 + \frac{r}{m})^{mn}$$

where TV_n = terminal value after n years
   m = number of times interest is compounded per year
   r = interest rate
   X_0 = beginning or present value of the amount being compounded

5. In the case of continuous compounding, this equation becomes

$$TV_n = X_0 e^{rn}$$

where $e = \lim_{m \to \infty} (1 + \frac{1}{m})^m$, or about 2.71828.

II. Present value is the value today of a payment to be received in the future.

    A.   The general formula for calculating the present value of a future cash flow is

$$PV = \frac{X_n}{(1 + k)^n}$$

        where X_n = cash flow in year n
                k = discount rate or required rate of return, an interest rate
                n = number of years until the cash flow is received
               PV = present value of the cash flow

    B.   If you look closely at this formula, you can see that it is merely the inverse of the compound-interest equation, where

           X_n corresponds to TV_n
           k corresponds to r
           PV corresponds to X_0

    C.   Actually, we only have one equation; however, in the first case we are moving money forward in time, that is, seeing how much we will have after n years if we compound at r; and in the second case we are moving money back in time, seeing what the present value of a future amount is.

    D.   In a manner similar to compounding, we have to modify our present-value formula somewhat to determine the present value of an amount when interest is compounded more than once a year:

$$PV = \frac{X_n}{\left(1 + \frac{k}{m}\right)^{mn}}$$

        where m is the number of times per year that interest is compounded:

III. Present-value tables: If one had to make all these calculations by hand, it would become quite time consuming; for that reason, present value and annuity tables are supplied.

    A.   The present-value table (Table A-1 of the text) gives you the value for $1/(1 + r)^n$ for all combinations of r and n.

    B.   Thus, to find the present value of $100 to be received in 5 years discounted back to the present at 15%, one need only look in Table A-1 in the 15% column and 5-year row and plug the value found into the following formula:

$$PV = X_n \frac{1}{(1+r)^n} = X_n \begin{bmatrix} \text{Table A-1} \\ n = 5 \text{ yr} \\ r = 15\% \end{bmatrix} = \$100(0.49718) = \$49.718$$

C.   As shown in Part IIB, the compound-interest formula is merely the inverse of the present-value formula. Thus, we can also use this table to find the terminal value of a present amount compounded at r for n years.

D.   Thus, to find the terminal value of \$49.718 compounded for 5 years at 15%, we merely look in Table A-1 in the 15% column and 5-year row and plug the value found into the following formula:

$$TV = X_0(1+r)^n = X_0 \begin{bmatrix} \dfrac{1}{\text{Table A-1}} \\ n = 5 \text{ yr} \\ r = 15\% \end{bmatrix} = \$49.718 \times \frac{1}{0.49718} = \$100$$

IV.   Annuity tables. An annuity is a series of equal payments for a specified number of years. As annuities occur frequently in finance (interest payments on bonds), you are also supplied with an annuity table (Table A-2).

A.   The annuity table gives you the value for $\sum\limits_{t=1}^{n} 1/(1+r)^t$ for all combinations of r and n.

B.   Thus, to find the present value of \$100 received at the end of each year for five years discounted to the present at 15%, one need only look in Table A-2 in the 15% column and 5-year row and plug the value found into the following formula:

$$PV_{\text{annuity}} = \sum_{t=1}^{n} \frac{X_t}{(1+r)^t} = X_t \begin{bmatrix} \text{Table A-2} \\ n = 5 \text{ yr} \\ r = 15\% \end{bmatrix} = \$100(3.3522) = \$335.22$$

V.   The final formula provided in this chapter is used to find the compound value when the uniform payments or receipts:

$$TV_n = \left(X_0 + \frac{x}{r}\right)(1+r)^n - \frac{x}{r}$$

where X_0 = initial deposit at time 0
      r = appropriate compound rate
      x = annual uniform payment or receipt
      n = number of years that X is deposited or withdrawn

A. Thus, if you deposited $1,000 initially in the bank to be compounded at 10% annually and withdrew $50 per year for 10 years, the terminal value of your account can be determined as follows:

$$TV_n = \left(X_0 + \frac{x}{r}\right)(1 + r)^n - \frac{x}{r}$$

$$= \left(\$1,000 + \frac{-50}{0.10}\right)(1 + 0.10)^{10} - \frac{-50}{0.10}$$

$$= (\$1,000 - 500)(2.5934) + 500$$

$$= \$1,296.70 + 500$$

$$= \$1,796.70$$

STUDY PROBLEMS

1. Suppose that you inherit $100,000 and are able to invest it in a bank at 8% annual compound interest. What would be the maximum uniform withdrawal that you could make at the end of the next 10 years?

Solution:

$$TV_n = 0 = \left(X_0 - \frac{x}{r}\right)(1 + r)^n + \frac{x}{r}$$

$$0 = \left(\$100,000 - \frac{x}{0.08}\right)(1.08)^{10} + \frac{x}{0.08}$$

$$= (\$100,000 - 12.5x)(2.15892) + 12.5x$$

$$= \$215,892 - 26.986x + 12.5x$$

$$14.4865x = \$215,892$$

$$= \$14,902.98$$

2. Suppose that you deposit $100,000 in a bank at 8% quarterly compound interest. What would be the terminal value at the end of 10 years?

Solution:

$$TV_n = X_0\left(1 + \frac{r}{m}\right)^{mn}$$

$$TV_{10} = \$100,000\left(1 + \frac{0.08}{4}\right)^{4 \cdot 10}$$

$$= \$100,000(1.02)^{40}$$

$$= \$220,804$$

3. Without using the present-value tables, what would be the present value of receiving $100, $200, and $300 at the end of years 1, 2, and 3, respectively, at an 8% annual compound interest?

Solution:

$$PV_n = \frac{X_n}{(1+k)^n}$$

$$PV_1 = \frac{1}{1.08} = 0.9259$$

$$PV_2 = \frac{1}{(1.08)^2} = 0.8573$$

$$PV_3 = \frac{1}{(1.08)_3} = 0.7938$$

$$PV_n = \$100(0.9259) + \$200(0.8573) + \$300(0.7938)$$

$$PV = \$92.59 + \$171.46 + \$238.14 = \underline{\$502.19}$$

or

$$PV = \frac{\$100}{1.08} + \frac{\$200}{(1.08)^2} + \frac{\$300}{(1.08)^3} = \$92.59 + \$171.46 + \$238.14 = \underline{\$502.19}$$

4. Without using the tables, solve for the present value of receiving $200 at the end of years 1, 2, and 3, using the appropriate annuity discount factor for an 8% annual compound interest opportunity cost.

Solution:

$$PV_1 = \frac{1}{1.08} = 0.9259$$

$$PV_2 = \frac{1}{1.08^2} = 0.8573$$

$$PV_3 = \frac{1}{1.08^3} = \frac{0.7938}{2.5770} \quad \text{(annuity factor)}$$

$$PV = \$200(2.577) = \$515.40$$

5. Suppose that for $2,000 you could receive $500 at the end of each year for an uncertain amount of time. With an opportunity cost of 8%, what would be the required length of time necessary for the cash inflows to make this investment worthwhile?

Solution:

$$\frac{\$2,000}{\$500} = 4$$

The closest discount factor under 8% in the annuity table is 3.993. The corresponding number of years for 8% and 3.993 is *5 years.*

SELF-TESTS

True-False

 1. If $100 was deposited in a bank at 5% compound annual interest, it would equal $115 at the end of 3 years.

___E___ 2. As the number of times per year that interest is compounded approaches infinity, the terminal value approaches infinity.

___T___ 3. A life insurance annuity pays a uniform series of receipts for a specified number of years, which is the result of an initial deposit.

___T___ 4. The only difference between computing compound values with uniform payments and compound values with uniform receipts is that payments are added into the formula and receipts are subtracted.

___T___ 5. Money has a time value.

___T___ 6. The present value of money bears a reciprocal relationship to the compound value.

___E___ 7. The present value of money increases as the discount rates increase.

___T___ 8. The expression $1/(1 + 0.10)^4$ should equal the present value of $1 received in 4 years with a discount rate of 10%.

___F___ 9. The present value of a series of cash flows decreases as the number of times per year interest is compounded.

___F___ 10. For an outlay of $1,000, two future series of $500 receipts would be necessary to make the investment worthwhile.

Multiple Choice

1. Terminal value increases as:
   a. The initial deposit increases.
   b. The interest rate increases.
   c. The number of years increases.
   d. All of the above.
   e. None of the above.

2. The terminal value of an initial deposit compounded continously would be calculated using the following equation:
   a. $TV_n = X_0(1 + r)^n$.
   b. $TV_n = X_0(1 + \frac{r}{\infty})^{\infty \cdot n}$.

c. $TV_n = X_0\left(1 + \dfrac{r}{365}\right)^{365 \cdot n}$.

d. $TV_n = X_0 e^{rn}$.

3. Present value of one cash flow increases as:
   a. The future cash flow decreases.
   b. The discount rate increases.
   c. The number of years decreases.
   d. All of the above.
   e. None of the above.

4. The discount factors in present-value tables increase as:
   a. The discount rate decreases (for a given number of years).
   b. The number of years increases (for a given interest rate).
   c. Both of the above.
   d. None of the above.

5. If earnings are expected to grow at 10% annual compound rate for 5 years, what is the total percentage that earnings would have grown at the end of 5 years?
   a. Need more information.
   b. 50%.
   c. $(1.10)^5 - 1.00$.
   d. $(1.10)^5$.

6. If you wish to double your money in 6 years, what yield should you seek?
   a. 6%.
   b. 8%.
   c. 10%.
   d. 12%.
   e. 14%.

Capital ${\large\mathbf{13}}$
Budgeting

Orientation: Capital-budgeting decisions involve capital allocations on investment proposals with expected returns extending beyond one year in the future. This chapter focuses on the estimation of cash flows from investment proposals and the evaluation of those cash flows based upon various decision criteria.

I. What criteria should we use in the evaluation of alternative investment proposals?

    A. Use cash flows rather than accounting profits, as this allows us to correctly analyze the time element of the flows.

    B. Examine cash flows on an after-tax basis as those are the flows available to shareholders.

    C. Only include the incremental cash flows resulting from the investment decision. Ignore all other flows.

II. Measuring cash flows: We are interested in measuring the incremental after-tax cash flows resulting from the investment proposal. In general, there will be three major sources of cash flows: initial outlays, differential cash flows over the project's life, and terminal cash flows.

    A. Initial outlays include whatever cash flows are necessary to get the project in running order; for example:

        1. The installed cost of the asset.

2. In the case of a replacement proposal, the selling price of the old machine plus (or minus) any tax gain (or loss) offsetting the initial outlay.

3. Any expense items (for example, training) necessary for the operation of the proposal.

4. Any other nonexpense cash outlays required, even if not expenses such as increased working-capital needs.

B. Differential cash flows over the project's life include the incremental after-tax flows over the life of the project, for example:

1. Added revenue (less added selling expenses) for the proposal.

2. Any labor and/or material savings incurred.

3. These values are measured on an after-tax basis, thus allowing for the tax savings (or loss) from incremental increase (or decrease) in depreciation to be included.

4. A word of warning not to include financing charges (such as interest or preferred stock dividends), as they are implicitly taken care of in the discounting process.

C. Terminal cash flows include any incremental cash flows that result at the termination of the project; for example:

1. The projects salvage value plus (or minus) any taxable gains or losses associated with the project.

2. Any terminal cash flow needed, perhaps disposal of obsolete equipment.

3. Recovery of any nonexpense cash outlays associated with the project, such as recovery of increased working-capital needs associated with the proposal.

III. Methods for evaluating projects

A. Average rate of return is

$$\text{average rate of return} = \frac{\text{average annual profits after tax}}{\dfrac{\text{investment + salvage value}}{2}}$$

1. This formula assumes straight-line depreciation; thus, the average investment in the project is equal to the sum of the investment plus the salvage value divided by 2.

2. While this measure has the advantages of being easy to calculate and having familiar terms, it uses profits rather than cash flows

in its calculations and does not consider the time value of money.

B. The payback method

1. The payback period of an investment tells the number of years required to recover the initial investment. If the annual cash flows are constant over the life of the project, it is

$$\text{payback period} = \frac{\text{initial fixed investment}}{\text{annual cash inflows}}$$

If the annual cash flows are not constant, the payback period must be calculated, adding the cash flows up until they are equal to the initial fixed investment.

2. While this measure does, in fact, deal with cash flows and is easy to calculate and understand, it ignores any cash flows that occur after the payback period and does not consider the time value of money within the payback period.

C. Internal rate of return is the rate of return that equates the present value of the expected cash outflows with the present value of the expected inflows. Thus, if the initial cash outlay occurs at time 0, the internal rate of return is represented by r:

$$A_0 = \frac{A_1}{1 + r} + \frac{A_2}{(1 + r)^2} + \cdots + \frac{A_n}{(1 + r)^r}$$

where A_t is the cash flow in time t.

1. The acceptance-rejection criteria are:

accept if IRR $>$ cutoff or hurdle rate
reject if IRR $<$ cutoff or hurdle rate

This cutoff or hurdle rate is often taken to be the firm's cost of capital, which will be discussed in Chapter 15.

2. The advantages of this method are that it deals with cash flows and recognizes the time value of money; however, the procedure is rather complicated and time consuming.

D. Present-value methods

1. The net present value of an investment project is the present value of the cash inflows less the present value of the cash outflows. Assigning negative values to cash outflows, it becomes

$$NPV = A_0 + \frac{A_1}{1+k} + \frac{A_2}{(1+k)^2} + \cdots + \frac{A_n}{(1+k)^n}$$

where k is the required rate of return.

   a. The acceptance criteria are:

accept if $NPV > 0$
reject if $NPV < 0$

   b. The advantage of this approach is that it takes the time value of money into consideration in addition to dealing with cash flows.

  2. The profitability index is the ratio of the present value of the expected future net cash flows to the initial cash outlay, or

$$\text{profitability index} = \frac{\displaystyle\sum_{t=1}^{n} \frac{A_t}{(1+k)^t}}{A_0}$$

   a. The acceptance criteria are:

accept if $PI > 1.0$
reject if $PI < 1.0$

   b. The advantages of this method are the same as those for the net present value.

   c. Either of these present-value methods will give the same accept-reject decisions to a project.

IV. Mutually exclusive projects: While the IRR and the present-value methods will, in general, give consistent accept-reject decisions they may not rank projects identically. This becomes important in the case of mutually exclusive projects.

   A. A project is mutually exclusive if acceptance of it precludes the acceptance of one or more projects. In this case, the project's relative ranking becomes important.

   B. Ranking conflicts come as a result of the different assumptions as to the reinvestment rate on funds released from the proposals.

   C. Thus, when conflicting ranking of mutually exclusive projects results from the different reinvestment assumptions, the decision boils down to which assumption is best.

   D. In general, we consider the present-value method to be theoretically superior.

V.   Capital rationing is the situation in which a budget ceiling or constraint is placed upon the amount of funds that can be invested during a time period.

   A.   Theoretically, a firm should never reject a project yielding more than the required rate of return. Although there are circumstances that may create complicated situations in general, an investment policy limited by capital rationing is less than optimal.

STUDY PROBLEMS

1. The cost of new machinery for a given investment project will be $100,000. Incremental cash flows after taxes will be $40,000 in years 1 and 2, and $60,000 in year 3. What is the payback period for this project and if acceptable projects must recover the initial investment in 2.5 years, should this project be accpeted or rejected?

   Solution:

   After 2 years they will have recovered $80,000 of the $100,000 outlay and expect to recover an additional $60,000 in the third year. Thus, the payback period becomes

$$2 \text{ years} + \frac{\$20,000}{\$60,000} = 2.33 \text{ years}$$

$$2.33 \text{ years} < 2.5 \text{ years}$$

   Therefore, accept the project.

2. A given investment project will cost $50,000. Incremental cash flows after taxes are expected to be $10,000 per year for the life of the investment, which is 7 years. There will be no salvage value at the end of the 7 years. The required rate of return is 14%. On the basis of the profitability index method, should the investment be accepted?

   Solution:

$$\text{PV of cash flow} = \$10,000(4.2883) = \$42,883$$

$$\text{PV of cash outlay} = \$50,000$$

$$\text{PI} = \frac{\$42,883}{\$50,000} = 0.8576 < 1$$

   Therefore, the project should be rejected.

3. Miller Electric Company is considering the replacement of an existing tool which has a current book value $10,000 and can currently be sold for $4,000.

The salvage value of the old machine in 5 years is zero, and it is being depreciated on a straight-line basis. The new machine would perform the same function as the old machine and would yield annual savings before depreciation and taxes of $10,000 per year. The new machine has a 5-year life, costs $34,000, and can be sold for an expected $4,000 at the end of the fifth year. Assuming straight-line depreciation, a 40% tax rate, and cost of capital of 12%, find the payback period and net present value.

Solution:

Initial outlay:

Purchase price	$34,000
Salvage value	−4,000
Tax savings on loss	−2,400
	$27,600

Annual Net Cash Flow (Years 1-5)

	Cash Method	*Book Method*
Savings	$10,000	$10,000
Incremental depreciation		−(6,000 − 2,000)
Taxable income		6,000
Taxes	−2,400	−2,400
Annual net cash flow	$ 7,600	

Terminal cash flow
Salvage value = $4,000

Cash-flow diagram:

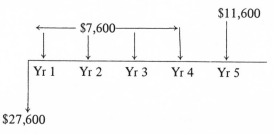

(a) Payback period: after 3 years they will have recovered $22,800 and during the fourth year expect to recover $7,600. Thus, the payback period becomes

$$3 \text{ years} + \frac{\$4,800}{\$7,600} = 3.63 \text{ years}$$

(b) Net present value = $7,600(3.0373) + $11,600(0.56743) − $27,600
$$= \$23,083 + \$6,582 - \$27,600$$
$$= \$2,065$$

4. What is the project's internal rate of return?

Solution:

Try 14%:
$$\$27,600 = \$7,600(2.9137) + \$11,600(0.51937)$$
$$= \$22,144.12 + \$6,024.69$$
$$= \$28,168.81$$

Try 15%:
$$\$27,600 = \$7,600(2.8550) + \$11,600(0.49718)$$
$$= \$21,698 + \$5,767.29$$
$$= \$27,465.29$$

Thus, the IRR is just a bit below 15%.

SELF-TESTS

True-False

_T_ 1. Cash flow, not income, is what is important in capital budgeting.

_T_ 2. The net present value of a project decreases as the required rate of return increases.

_T_ 3. The higher the discount rate, the more valued is the proposal with the early cash flows.

_T_ 4. The net-present-value approach is preferred over the profitability index for mutually exclusive projects because it measures worth in absolute terms and profitability index measures worth in relative terms.

_T_ 5. Capital rationing occurs when profitable projects must be rejected because of shortage of capital.

_F_ 6. The net present value of a project will equal zero whenever the average rate of return equals the required rate of return.

_F_ 7. The net present value of a project will equal zero whenever the payback period of a project equals the required payback period.

_F_ 8. The average rate of return will always equal the internal rate of return.

___)___   9. The only difference in the net-present-value approach and the
              internal-rate-of-return method is the reinvestment-rate
              assumption.

___/___   10. Capital rationing is not an optimal capital budgeting strategy.

Multiple Choice

1. Which of the following considers the time value of money?
   a. Payback method.
   b. Average rate of return.
   c. Profitability index.
   d. None of the above.

2. Which of the following is important to capital-budgeting decisions?
   a. Depreciation method.
   b. Salvage value.
   c. Timing of cash flows.
   d. Taxes.
   e. All of the above.

3. Which of the following is an estimate approach?
   a. Average rate of return.
   b. Profitability index.
   c. Internal rate of return.
   d. Net present value.

4. The net-present-value approach and the internal-rate-of-return method may
   lead to discrepancies when:
   a. Projects are dependent.
   b. The discount rate equals zero.
   c. Projects are mutually exclusive.
   d. All of the above.

5. The average-rate-of-return method will always lead to the same accept
   or reject decision as the:
   a. Profitability index.
   b. Net-present-value method.
   c. Payback method.
   d. Internal rate of return.
   e. None of the above.

Risk and Capital Budgeting 14

Orientation: The focus of this chapter will be on how to measure and adjust for the riskiness of a given project or combination of projects, in addition to understanding how risk affects the value of a firm.

I. The riskiness of an investment project is defined as the variability of its cash flows from the expected cash flow.

A. Standard deviation is a mathematical measure of cash-flow dispersion.

$$\sigma = \sqrt{\sum_{X=1}^{n} (A_X - \bar{A})^2 P_X}$$

where σ = standard deviation
A_X = cash flow for the Xth possibility
$\bar{A}$ = expected value of the cash flow
P_X = probability of occurrence of that cash flow

Example I

State	Probability	Proposal A	Weighted Average	Proposal B	Weighted Average
Deep recession	0.2	$20,000	$ 4,000	$10,000	$ 2,000
Normal	0.6	25,000	15,000	25,000	15,000
Major boom	0.2	30,000	6,000	40,000	8,000
		Expected value =	$25,000		$25,000

$$\sigma_A = \sqrt{(\$20{,}000 - \$25{,}000)^2\,(0.2) + (\$25{,}000 - \$25{,}000)^2\,(0.6) +}$$
$$\overline{(\$30{,}000 - \$25{,}000)^2\,(0.2)}$$

$$= \sqrt{\$5{,}000{,}000 + \$5{,}000{,}000} = \underline{\underline{\$3{,}162.28}}$$

$$\sigma_B = \sqrt{(\$10{,}000 - \$25{,}000)^2\,(0.2) + (\$25{,}000 - \$25{,}000)^2\,(0.6) +}$$
$$\overline{(\$40{,}000 - \$25{,}000)^2\,(0.2)}$$

$$= \sqrt{\$45{,}000{,}000 + \$45{,}000{,}000} = \underline{\underline{\$9{,}486.833}}$$

1. The standard deviation simply measures the tightness of a probability distribution.

2. The lower the standard deviation of the cash flow, the lower the perceived risk.

3. Sixty-eight percent of all cash flows in a normal distribution lie within 1 standard deviation of the mean.

4. Ninety-five percent of all cash flows in a normal distribution lie within 2 standard deviations of the mean.

B. The coefficient of variation is the measure of relative dispersion or risk in a project.

$$CV = \frac{\sigma}{\overline{A}}$$

1. Business risk is defined as the relative dispersion of net cash flows as measured by the coefficient of variation for the firm as a whole.

2. Whereas the standard deviation gives us a measure of absolute risk, the coefficient of variation gives us a measure of relative risk (i.e., risk per unit of return).

II. Methods for treating risky investments begin with the assumption of the independence of cash flows over time.

A. The expected value of the net present value of a proposal from its probability distribution is

$$NPV = \sum_{T=0}^{\infty} \frac{\overline{A}_T}{(1 + i)^T}$$

where i is the risk-free rate.

B. The variation of expected net-present value from its probability
distribution is

$$\sigma = \sqrt{\sum_{T=0}^{\infty} \frac{\sigma_T^2}{(1+i)^{2T}}}$$

In order to calculate the probability of a proposal's net present
value being less or more than a specified a unit (call it X), we first
standardize the difference between this specified amount (X) and
the expected net present value. We use the following formula to
do this:

$$S = \frac{X - \overline{NPV}}{\sigma}$$

where   X = outcome in which we are interested in knowing the
probability of the net present value of the project
being more or less than $\overline{NPV}$
$\overline{NPV}$ = expected value of the NPV
σ = standard deviation of the NPV

1. To determine the probability that the present value will be more
or less than X, we must consult a normal probability distribution
table, such as the one found in Appendix B to Chapter 14 of the
text.

2. To do this we look up the value of S in the "Number of Standard
Deviations from the Mean (X)" column and find the probability
of the net present value being more or less than the specified
outcome in the column labeled "Area to the Left or Right (One
Tail)."

Example II

Assume that the risk-free rate is 5% and a given investment outlay will cost
$15,000. The probability distribution of the cash flows for the life of the project
is given in the table. What is the expected value of the net present value?
What is the standard deviation about the expected value? What is the probability
of the NPV being less than $6,000?(Assume a normal distribution.)

Period 1		Period 2		Period 3	
Probability	*Net Cash Flow*	*Probability*	*Net Cash Flow*	*Probability*	*Net Cash Flow*
0.20	$ 8,000	0.20	$ 5,000	0.20	$ 4,000
0.60	12,000	0.60	9,000	0.60	10,000
0.20	16,000	0.20	13,000	0.20	16,000

$\overline{A}_1 = 0.2(\$8,000) + 0.6(\$12,000) + 0.2(\$16,000) = \$12,000$

$\overline{A}_2 = 0.2(\$5,000) + 0.6(\$9,000) + 0.2(\$13,000) = \$9,000$

$\overline{A}_3 = 0.2(\$4,000) + 0.6(\$10,000) + 0.2(\$16,000) = \$10,000$

$\sigma_1 = (\$8,000 - \$12,000)^2 (0.2) + (\$12,000 - \$12,000)^2 (0.6) + (\$16,000 - \$12,000)^2 (0.2) = \$2,529.82$

$\sigma_2 = (\$5,000 - \$9,000)^2 (0.2) + (\$9,000 - \$9,000)^2 (0.6) + (\$13,000 - \$9,000)^2 (0.2) = \$2,529.82$

$\sigma_3 = (\$4,000 - \$10,000)^2 (0.2) + (\$10,000 - \$10,000)^2 (0.6) + (\$16,000 - \$10,000)^2 (0.2) = \$3,794.73$

$$\text{NPV} = \$-15,000 + \frac{\$12,000}{1.05} + \frac{\$9,000}{(1.05)^2} + \frac{\$10,000}{(1.05)^3} = \$-15,000 + \$11,428.56 +$$
$$\$8,163.27 + \$8,638.40 = \$13,230.23$$

Under the assumption of mutual independence of cash flows over time, the standard deviation about the expected value is

$$\sigma = \sqrt{\sum_{t=0}^{\infty} \frac{\sigma_t^{\,2}}{(1+i)^{2t}}} = \sqrt{\frac{(\$2,529.82)^2}{(1.05)^2} + \frac{(\$2,529.82)^2}{(1.05)^4} + \frac{(\$3,794.73)^2}{(1.05)^6}} = \$4670.73$$

$$S = \frac{\$6,000 - \$13,230.23}{\$4670.73} = -1.54799$$

$$P = (X \leq \$6,000) = 6\%$$

III. For many investment proposals the cash flow in a future period is in part dependent upon the cash flow in previous years.

    A. Project correlation means that if the current cash flow deviates from the expected flow, all succeeding flows will deviate in exactly the same manner. In effect, all future cash flows depend upon what has happened in the past.

        1. The formula for the standard deviation of a perfectly correlated stream of cash flows is

$$\sigma = \sum_{T=0}^{\infty} \frac{\sigma_T}{(1+i)^T}$$

        2. Standard deviation in this case is significantly higher than it would be under the alternative assumption of independence of cash flows.

    B. When a project's cash flows are moderately correlated, probability trees provide a useful analytical tool.

$$\overline{NPV} = \sum_{X=1}^{Z} NPV_X(P_X)$$

where $\overline{NPV}$ = the expected value

NPV_X = NPV for series X of cash flow

P_X = probability of series X

Z = total number of cash-flow series

$$\sigma = \sqrt{\sum_{X=1}^{Z} (NPV_X - \overline{NPV})^2 P_X}$$

= standard deviation of net present value

Example III

What is the NPV? What is the standard deviation of the expected NPV? Initial cost is $200 and the risk-free rate is 5%. Cash flows and probability distribution are as follows:

Period 1			*Period 2*	
Probability	*Net Cash Flow*	*Conditional Probability (2/1)*	*Cash Flow*	*Joint Probability*
		0.25	$-1,500	0.05
0.20	$-200	0.25	-1,100	0.05
		0.50	-700	0.10
		0.10	-300	0.06
0.60	+200	0.80	+100	0.48
		0.10	+500	0.06
		0.50	+900	0.10
0.20	+600	0.25	+1,300	0.05
		0.25	+1,700	0.05

$$NPV = \sum_{X=1}^{Z} NPV_X P_X$$

$$NPV_1 = \$-200 - \frac{\$200}{1.05} - \frac{\$1,500}{(1.05)^2} = \$-1,751$$

$$NPV_2 = \$-200 - \frac{\$200}{1.05} - \frac{\$1,100}{(1.05)^2} = \$-1,388$$

$$NPV_3 = \$-200 - \frac{\$200}{1.05} - \frac{\$700}{(1.05)^2} = \$-1,025$$

$$NPV_4 = \$-200 + \frac{\$200}{1.05} - \frac{\$300}{(1.05)^2} = \$-282$$

$$NPV_5 = \$-200 + \frac{\$200}{1.05} + \frac{\$100}{(1.05)^2} = \$+81$$

$$NPV_6 = \$-200 + \frac{\$200}{1.05} + \frac{\$500}{(1.05)^2} = \$+444$$

$$NPV_7 = \$-200 + \frac{\$600}{1.05} + \frac{\$900}{(1.05)^2} = \$+1187.76$$

$$NPV_8 = \$-200 + \frac{\$600}{1.05} + \frac{\$1,300}{(1.05)^2} = \$+1550.56$$

$$NPV_9 = \$-200 + \frac{\$600}{1.05} + \frac{\$1,700}{(1.05)^2} = + \$1913.38$$

Cash-Flow Series	NPV	Probability of Occurrence	Weighted	$NPV - \overline{NPV}$	$(NPV - \overline{NPV})^2\, P_X$
1	$-1,751	0.05	$ -88	$-1833	$167,994
2	-1,388	0.05	-69	-1470	108,045
3	-1,025	0.10	-103	-1107	122,545
4	-282	0.06	-17	- 364	7,950
5	+81	0.48	+39	- 1	0
6	+444	0.06	+27	362	7,863
7	+1188	0.10	+119	1106	122,324
8	+1551	0.05	+78	1469	107,898
9	+1913	0.05	+96	1831	167,628

$$\overline{NPV} = +82$$

$$\sigma = \sqrt{\sum_{X=1}^{Z} (NPV_X - \overline{NPV})^2 P_X}$$

$$= \sqrt{\$167,994 + \$108,045 + \$122,545 + \$7,950 + 0 + \$7,863 +}$$
$$\sqrt{\$122,324 + \$107,898 + \$167,628}$$
$$= \sqrt{\$812,247} = \$901.25$$

IV. The measurement of risk for a portfolio differs from the procedure for measuring risk for a single project.

$$\sigma = \sqrt{\sum_{j=1}^{m} \sum_{k=1}^{m} \sigma_{jk}}$$

where   j = refers to project J
         k = refers to project K
         m = total number of projects in the portfolio
         σ_{jk} = variance of NPV when j = k
         $\sigma_{jk} = r_{jk}\sigma_j\sigma_k$ when j ≠ k
         r_{jk} = correlation between project J and K
         σ_j = standard deviation of project J
         σ_k = standard deviation of project K

Example IV

Compute the standard deviation of the following portfolio:

Projects	Standard Deviation	Correlation Coefficient
1	$100	1
2	300	1
3	400	1
1 and 2		0.5
1 and 3		0.25
2 and 3		0.25

$$\sigma = \sqrt{r_{11}\sigma_1^2 + r_{22}\sigma_2^2 + r_{33}\sigma_3^2 + 2r_{12}\sigma_1\sigma_2 + 2r_{13}\sigma_1\sigma_3 + 2r_{23}\sigma_2\sigma_3}$$

$$= \sqrt{(1)(\$100)^2 + (1)(\$300)^2 + (1)(\$400)^2 + 2(0.5)(\$100)(\$300) + }$$

$$\overline{2(0.25)(\$100)(\$400) + 2(0.25)(\$300)(\$400)}$$

$$= \sqrt{\$370,000} = \$608.28$$

V.   The set efficient portfolios can be chose by comparing all possible combinations of projects on two dimensions (i.e., the standard deviation of a portfolio and its expected net-present value). The efficient set or frontier are those portfolios that give the maximum return for any given level of risk or the minimum risk for any given level of return.

STUDY PROBLEMS

1. Project A is expected to net a present value of $24,000 for each of the next 3 years. Project A's standard deviation is expected to be $12,000 for each of the next 3 years. Project B is expected to net a present value of $60,000 with a standard deviation of $20,000 for each of the next 3 years. Which of the two projects has the least business risk?

Solution:

$$CV_a = \frac{\$12,000}{\$24,000} = 0.5$$

$$CV_b = \frac{\$20,000}{\$60,000} = 0.33$$

Project B has the least business risk.

2. Project C has standard deviations over the next 3 years calculated to be $100, $300, and $800, respectively. Assume that the cash flows are independent over time. The risk-free rate is 5%. What is the standard deviation of project C?

Solution:

$$\sigma = \sqrt{\sum_{T=0}^{3} \frac{\sigma_T^2}{(1+i)^{2T}}}$$

$$= \sqrt{\frac{(\$100)^2}{(1.05)^2} + \frac{(\$300)^2}{(1.05)^4} + \frac{(\$800)^2}{(1.05)^6}}$$

$$= \sqrt{\$9,070.30 + \$74,043.23 + \$477,577.90}$$

$$= \sqrt{\$560,691.43} = \$748.79$$

3. If the cash flows from project C (in problem 2) are considered to be perfectly correlated, what is the standard deviation of the project?

Solution:

$$\sigma = \sum_{T=0}^{\infty} \frac{\sigma_T}{(1+i)^T}$$

$$= \frac{\$100}{1.05} + \frac{\$300}{(1.05)^2} + \frac{\$800}{(1.05)^3}$$

$$= \$95.24 + \$272.11 + \$691.07 = \$1,058.42$$

4. Suppose that a company has only one current investment project, project 1. If it accepts project 2, how will it affect the business risk of the firm?

Projects	Expected NPV	σ	Correlation Coefficient
1	$1,000	$1,500	1
2	700	500	1
1 and 2	$1,700		0.20

Solution:

$$\sigma = \sqrt{r_{11}\sigma_1^2 + 2r_{12}\sigma_1\sigma_2 + r_{22}\sigma_2^2}$$

$$= \sqrt{1(\$1,500)^2 + 2(0.2)(\$1,500)(\$500) + 1(\$500)^2}$$

$$= \sqrt{\$2,250,000 + \$300,000 + \$250,000} = \sqrt{\$2,800,000}$$

$$= \$1,673.32$$

$$CV_1 = \frac{\$1,500}{\$1,000} = 1.5$$

$$CV_{1 \text{ and } 2} = \frac{\$1,673.32}{\$1,700} = 0.98$$

Therefore, project 2 would reduce the business risk of the firm.

SELF-TESTS

True-False

1. Business risk is synonymous with financial risk.
2. Independent cash flows means that the outcome in period T is not dependent upon the outcome of the T − 1 cash flow.
3. If two projects are mutually exclusive, the one with the highest expected value should always be chosen, even if it is riskier.
4. The independence of cash flows is a realistic assumption.
5. The coefficient of variation serves as a relative measure of risk.

F **6.** The standard deviation of NPV for a portfolio is always the sum of the standard deviation of the individual projects.

T **7.** The opportunity set is all possible combinations of projects available.

T **8.** Business risk is the risk associated with the operations of the firm and as such is many times measured through the use of the coefficient of variation.

T **9.** The correlation among projects is an essential element in measuring the risk of a portfolio.

T **10.** Standard deviation is a measure of dispersion from an expected value.

Multiple Choice

1. If two projects are completely independent, the measure of correlation between them is:
   a. +1.
   b. 0.
   c. −1.

2. To reduce risk most effectively, projects would ideally be chosen with the following coefficient correlation:
   a. +1.
   b. 0.
   c. −1.

3. Which of the following formulas assumes that the cash flows in different periods are independt of one another?

   a. $$\sigma = \sqrt{\sum_{T=0}^{\infty} \frac{\sigma_T^2}{(1+i)^{2T}}}.$$

   b. $$\sigma = \sqrt{\sum_{T=0}^{\infty} \frac{\sigma_T}{(1+i)^T}}.$$

   c. $$\sigma = \sqrt{\sum_{j=1}^{m} \sum_{k=1}^{m} \sigma_{jk}}.$$

4. The proposal with the greatest relative risk would have:
   a. The greatest standard deviation.
   b. The greatest coefficient of variation.
   c. The highest expected NPV.

5. On a normal curve, all values within 2 standard deviations of the mean represent:
   a. 68% of the possible outcomes.
   b. 95% of the possible outcomes.
   c. It varies with each project.

15 *The Valuation Process*

Orientation: This chapter introduces the concepts that underlie the valuation of securities. Specifically, we are concerned with the valuation of bonds, preferred stock, and common stock, although the principles discussed also apply to other financial instruments.

I. Risk and required return—the security market line

    A. The foundations of security valuation are based upon perceived risk and required return, with increased returns necessary to entice investors to assume higher risks.

    B. Risk can be partitioned into two subcomponents: avoidable and unavoidable.

        1. Avoidable risk is that risk which can be eliminated through diversification in the investor's portfolio of investments.

        2. Unavoidable risk is unaffected by diversification; thus, higher returns are required to induce investors to undertake investments with higher levels of unavoidable risk.

        3. The relationship between unavoidable risk and expected return in an *efficient market* can be described using the security market line (SML). The SML is a straight line having two parameters:

       a.   The intercept of the line with the vertical return axis represents the risk-free rate of interest, which carries zero unavoidable risk.

       b.   The slope of the SML depicts the trade-off between risk and return.

   4. The SML is not a static concept and changes over time and with changes in interest rates, investor psychology, and expected return.

II.   Valuation of fixed income securities

   A.   The general equation for valuation of a bond is

$$P_B = \frac{I}{(1+k)^1} + \frac{I}{(1+k)^2} + \cdots + \frac{I+F}{(1+k)^n}$$

where I is the annual interest paid on the bond, k is the rate at which both principle and interest are discounted (capitalized), and F is the face value of the bond that must be repaid at maturity.

   B.   For payments on other than an annual basis, the valuation equation becomes

$$P_B = \frac{I/m}{(1+k/m)^1} + \frac{I/m}{(1+k/m)^2} + \cdots + \frac{I/m+F}{(1+k)^n}$$

where m equals the number of payments per annum.

   C.   For perpetuities the valuation equation simplifes to

$$P_B = \frac{I}{k}$$

   D.   The longer the term to maturity for a fixed income security, the greater will be the change in yield associated with a change in market price. Likewise, the longer the maturity of the bond, other things being equal, the greater will be the corresponding change in market price that is associated with a given change in yield.

III.   Preferred stock valuation

   A.   In most general cases, where the preferred stock issue carries no maturity, its value is determined as a perpetuity (i.e.,

$$P_p = \frac{D_p}{k_p}$$

where D_p is the annual dividend per preferred share and k_p is the rate of discount).

B.   The discount rate, or required rate of return, can be viewed as the sum of the risk-free rate of interest, i, and some risk premium, θ, such that $k_p = i + \theta$.

C.   The SML can be used as the basic for estimating k_p.

IV. Valuation of common stock

A.   A common stock's value lies in its risk-return characteristics as assessed in relation to the investor's entire portfolio of assets.

B.   The return from owning common stock is equal to the sum of dividends received plus any capital appreciation or loss during the relevant holding period minus the price paid for the stock, all divided by the original purchase price of the stock.

C.   The foundation for a stock's value lies in dividends which represent the cash flow associated with owning a share of stock. Even firms that presently pay no dividends are expected to eventually pay them, with the result that their value, too, is based on dividend expectations.

D.   Growth models of stock valuation can be devised to deal with either constant or sporatic growth expectations.

1.   When dividends are expected to grow at a constant rate, we can define the value of a common stock as the present value of a growing stream of dividends as follows:

$$P_c = \frac{D_0(1+g)}{1+k_c} + \frac{D_0(1+g)^2}{(1+k_c)^2} + \cdots + \frac{D_0(1+g)^\infty}{(1+k_c)^\infty}$$

where D_0 is the most recent dividend payment, g is the anticipated rate of growth individends, and the remaining terms retain their previous meanings.

a.   If k is greater than g and g is constant, the valuation model above can be shown to be equal to

$$P_c = \frac{D_0(1+g)}{k_c - g}$$

b.   If dividends are not assumed to grow at a constant rate g forever, then the simple valuation model in part (a) is no longer appropriate.

E.   The dividend-valuation model encompasses both dividends and market-price changes, where the current market-price change is simply a function of changes in anticipated future dividends.

V. The required rate of return on a stock is that rate which
equates the present values of the stream of expected future
dividends with the current market price of the share of stock.

VI. The capital-asset pricing model

A. Under conditions of market equilibrium, the value of a security
depends on its risk in relation to risks in alternative investments.

B. To derive the equilibrium risk-return relationships as prescribed in
the capital-asset pricing model, the following assumptions were
made:

1. Capital markets are efficient.

2. Investors are well informed.

3. Transaction costs are very low or zero.

4. There are only negligible restrictions on the investments that
can be made.

5. No investor is large enough to affect the market price of any
stock.

6. General agreement exists among investors with regard to the
likely performance of the various securities available for
purchase.

7. Investors all base their expectations regarding future returns
on the same holding period (e.g., 1 year).

C. The market portfolio becomes the attainable set of investment
opportunities within which diversification can take place.

D. The characteristic line measures the expected relationship between
excess returns for a share of stock and excess returns for the
market portfolio. Generally, greater expected excess returns for
the market mean greater excess returns for the stock.

E. Three measures are of importance in interpreting the characteristic
line.

1. Alpha (α) is the intercept of the characteristic line on the vertical
(return) axis and has an expected value of zero.

2. Beta (β) measures the slope of the characteristic line and represents
the relationship between market returns and those of an
individual security. The larger a security's beta, the greater is the
market related or systematic risk for that security.

3. The unsystematic line represents the dispersion in excess returns about the stock's characteristic line. This dispersion represents unsystematic risk, which can be eliminated through diversification in the investor's portfolio.

VII.   Measuring the required rate of return

A.   The risk most important to a stock is its unavoidable or systematic risk, which is measured using the beta coefficient from the characteristic line. A higher beta indicates higher systematic risk and vice versa.

B.   The required return for a stock J, $\overline{R}_J$, where systematic risk, B_J, comprises the total risk of the investor's portfolio (as a result of effective diversification) can be defined in terms of the capital-asset pricing model:

$$\overline{R}_J = i + B_J(\overline{R}_m - i)$$

where $\overline{R}_m$ is the expected return on the market portfolio and all other terms retain their prior definitions.

C.   Given that investors are risk-averse, expected returns for individual securities should bear a positive relationship to their marginal contributions to the risk of the market portfolio. It is this relation that is depicted in the capital-asset pricing model.

VIII.   When in an efficient market stocks become over (under)-priced with regard to their systematic risk, investors will sell (buy) those securities as long as the unwarranted price differential continues to exist.

STUDY PROBLEMS

1. Seeking to gain more liquidity in its assets, United Mutual Life Insurance has decided to convert part of its bond holdings to cash and commercial paper. It currently holds $500,000 in 6% bonds of $1,000 face value due in 9 years. Rising interest rates, which prompted the move to the more liquid portfolio, currently stand at 10%. For the risk class associated with United's bond holdings, what price per bond should United realize on their sale? (Ignore transaction costs.)

Solution:

$$I = 6\% (\$1,000) = \$60$$

$$k = 10\%$$

$$P = \sum_{t=1}^{9} \frac{\$60}{(1 + 0.1)^t} + \frac{\$1,000}{(1 + 0.1)^9} \times 500$$

$$\$60(5.759) + \$1,000(0.424) = \$345.54 + \$424.00 =$$
$$\$769.54 \times 500 = \$384,770$$

2. Ellis Transport has paid an annual dividend of $1 per share over the last 5 years. Recently, the firm's management changed and dividends are expected to grow by 7% per year. Indications are that the market anticipates that dividends will continue to grow at this pace for the indefinite future. If the appropriate discount rate (capitalization rate) for Ellis is 9%, what should be the market price for its stock?

Solution:

$$9\% = \frac{\$1}{P_0} + 7\%$$
$$9\%P = \$1 + 7\%P$$
$$0.02P = \$1$$
$$P = \$50$$

3. As a newly appointed portfolio manager with a large insurance company, your employer has just called you in on a special project. The firm has been experiencing returns on its portfolio that are not as good as the market as a whole. Since management feels the market is on a general and sustained upswing, they are worried about the long-run effect this could have on their earnings when compared with other insurance companies. Your task is to place the firm's portfolio in a more aggressive position, so as to take advantage of the expected upturn in the market. What steps would you take in remedying the situation? Defend your solution to the problem.

Solution:

Given the firm's expectations of a market upsurge, they could increase the anticipated returns of the portfolio by altering the portfolio's composition so as to increase its average beta coefficient. This would involve selling those issues that have low beta coefficients and acquiring securities with high betas. Note, however, that this strategy increases the unavoidable risk of the portfolio, which in turn means that portfolio returns will outpace changes in the market price level in both a downward and an upward direction.

4. Based upon a risk-free rate of 0.06 and an expected rate of return for the market portfolio of 0.12, compute the required rate of return for each of the stocks below, using the capital-asset pricing mode.

Stock	Beta
A	2.1
B	0.4
C	1.8
D	−0.1
E	1.0

What is the underlying rationale for the capital-asset pricing model (CAPM)?

Solution:

$$\bar{R}_A = 0.06 + (0.12 - 0.06)(2.1) = 0.186$$
$$\bar{R}_B = 0.06 + (0.12 - 0.06)(0.4) = 0.084$$
$$\bar{R}_C = 0.06 + (0.12 - 0.06)(1.8) = 0.168$$
$$\bar{R}_D = 0.06 + (0.12 - 0.06)(-0.1) = 0.054$$
$$\bar{R}_E = 0.06 + (0.12 - 0.06)(1.0) = 0.120$$

The rationale underlying the CAPM is that only unavoidable (systematic) risk should be rewarded with higher returns in an efficient market. Thus, the required return on a stock is the sum of the risk-free rate plus a risk premium related to its systematic risk, B.

SELF-TESTS

True-False

_____ 1. Since the level of systematic risk is the same to all investors for any given security, portfolio returns should be commensurate with the level of avoidable risk of the portfolio.

_____ 2. For the valuation of a stock to be consistent with market equilibrium the required return must be a positively related to risk.

_____ 3. For firms that do not pay a dividend (e.g., Litton Industries), earnings per share are an acceptable surrogate for dividends in evaluating the stock.

_____ 4. The true return on investment is that rate of discount that equates the present value of expected dividends with the current market price of the stock.

_____ 5. Diversification can effectively reduce the level of unavoidable or systematic risk.

_____ 6. The terms "risk premium" and "excess return" are interchangeable when dealing with the capital-asset pricing model.

_____ 7. An investor seeking an aggressive portfolio should seek stocks with betas greater than 1.

_____ 8. The capital-asset pricing model, while establishing the relationship between excess security returns and excess market returns, has nothing to say about security valuation.

Multiple Choice

1. For a $1,000-par-value bond carrying a 6% coupon (interest paid quarterly) and whose current yield to maturity is 8%, periodic interest payments would be:
   a. $20.
   b. $60.
   c. $15.
   d. $40.
   e. $30.

2. Dividends are currently paid out at $1.25 annually. According to the stock's risk class, the appropriate required rate of return is 6%. Growth is anticipated to be 5% annually for an indefinite period of time. The market price of the stock should be:
   a. $125.00.
   b. $12.50.
   c. $60.00.
   d. $25.83.
   e. $31.00.

3. If growth were expected to be 5% for 2 years and then drop to 3% for an indefinite period, what would be the price of the stock described in question 2?
   a. $154.33.
   b. $92.93.
   c. $69.79.
   d. $82.70.
   e. $42.22.

4. Which of the following is not an assumption underlying the security market line?
   a. Minimal transaction costs.
   b. Perfect markets (i.e., no investor is large enough to affect market prices).
   c. A stable, risk-free rate of interest.
   d. A common time horizon for all investors.
   e. None of the above.

5. A beta coefficient for a common stock which is greater than 1 denotes:
   a. The stock shares the same systematic risk as the market portfolio.
   b. Excess returns for the stock are proportionately greater than excess returns on other stocks of the same risk class.
   c. Unsystematic risk for the stock is greater than that of the market portfolio.
   d. Excess returns for the stock vary more widely than market excess returns.
   e. Avoidable risk for the stock is greater than that of the market as a whole.

6. As additional stocks are added to a portfolio:
   a. Systematic risk is necessarily lowered.
   b. Dispersion in excess returns about the characteristic line for the portfolio is diminished.
   c. Unsystematic risk is descreased.
   d. The investor's anticipated returns increase.
   e. Alpha approaches 1.

Required Returns on Capital Investments 16

Orientation: In Chapter 15 we considered the valuation of debt and equity instruments. The concepts advanced there serve as a foundation for determining the required rate of return for the firm and for specific investment projects. The objective in this chapter is to determine the required rate of return to be used in evaluating investment projects. This minimum required rate of return should result in acceptance of only those projects that will at worst leave the market value of the firm's stock unchanged and hopefully increase it.

I. Overall cost of capital for the firm

    A. The overall cost of capital reflects the business risk of the firm's entire asset portfolio and as a result is useful as a cutoff rate for new investment only under very restricted circumstances.

        1. The assets of the firm must be homogeneous with respect to risk.

        2. Investment proposals under consideration must have the same risk characteristics as the firm's existing assets.

    B. The overall cost of capital of a firm is comprised of the costs of the various components of financing, which must each be estimated.

        1. The explicit cost of debt can be derived by solving for that discount rate, k, which equates the net proceeds of the debt issue with the present value of interest plus principal payments, and then adjusting the explicit cost obtained for the tax effect.

The after-tax cost of new debt, k_i, is found by multiplying the before-tax cost, k, by 1 minus the firm's marginal tax rate, t [i.e., $k_i = k(1 - t)$].

2. As preferred stock has no maturity date, its cost may be represented by

$$k_p = \frac{D}{I_0}$$

where D is the stated annual dividend and I_0 represents the net proceeds per share from the preferred stock issue.

3. The cost of equity capital is by far the most difficult to measure.

   a. One method for estimating the cost of equity capital, k_e, relies on the dividend-valuation model presented in Chapter 15,

$$k_e = \frac{D_1}{k_e - g}$$

   b. Rather than estimating the future dividend stream of the firm and then solving for the cost of equity capital, one may approach the problem directly using the capital-asset pricing model,

$$R_j = i + (\overline{R}_m - i)B_j$$

   where i is the risk-free rate, $\overline{R}_m$ is the expected return for the market portfolio, and B_j is the beta coefficient for stock j.

C. Once the costs of the individual components of the capital structure have been computed, a weighted-average cost of capital can be calculated.

   1. The critical assumption in any weighting system is that the firm will, in fact, raise capital in the proportions specified.

   2. Because the firm raises capital to make incremental investments, it is the marginal cost of capital to the firm which we desire to estimate.

   3. The rationale for use of the weighted-average cost of new capital in making investment decisions lies in the fact that this average reflects both the explicit and implicit costs of capital funds.

II. Acceptance criterion for individual projects

   A. When the existing investment projects of the firm and investment proposals under consideration are not homogeneous with respect to risk, the use of the firm's cost of capital as an acceptance criterion is inappropriate.

B. One method for determining individual project required rates of return involves use of the capital-asset pricing model,

$$R_k = i + (\overline{R}_m - i)B_k$$

where R_k is the required return on the kth investment project, B_k is the beta coefficient for the proposal, and each of the remaining terms retain their previous definitions.

C. When for either theoretical or practical reasons it is inappropriate to compute a required rate of return for a project using the capital-asset pricing model, we must turn to more subjective means for evaluating risky investments.

   1. One such approach involves the use of project profiles based on expected values and standard deviations in NPV, PI, or IRR.

   2. The serious shortcoming of any subjective technique lies in the fact that there is no direct link between the technique used and the share value.

D. Considerations of firm solvency and bankruptcy suggest that the firm should evaluate asset acquisitions in light of their impact on expected returns and "total" variability in those returns. This approach involves considering the impact of proposed investments on the risk-return characteristics of the firm's portfolio of assets.

STUDY PROBLEMS

1. As a consultant to a firm of moderate size, you have been called in to discuss the potential effects of the firm's diversifying its asset holdings. One proposed investment is into the trucking industry; the firm has no knowledge of what return it should expect from such an investment. Using McLean Trucking as a surrogate with beta equal to 1.3 and assuming a risk-free rate of 5% coupled with a market portfolio return of 12%, explain to the firm's management what return level they should require.

   Solution:
   $$R_k = i + (\overline{R}_m - i)B_k$$
   Therefore,
   $$R_k = 0.05 + (0.12 - 0.05)(1.3)$$
   $$= 0.05 + (0.07)(1.3)$$
   $$= 0.05 + 0.091$$
   $$= 14.10\%$$

The McLean Trucking Company would act as a surrogate for the new investment and therefore free the firm from having to develop the characteristic line required in estimating the systematic risk of the trucking investment.

2. Harper Drug Co. has recently engaged in a complete review of its capital-budgeting procedures. One of the first tasks suggested to the review committee involved estimating the cost of capital for a major expansion. Harper plans to finance the expansion as follows:

10% Debentures due 2001	$3,000,000
9% Preferred stock (par value $100)	1,000,000
Common stock (200,000 shares)	6,000,000

The firm's common stock can be sold to net the company $30 per share and the current dividend on common is $1.50, which is expected to grow at a rate of 0.08 per year into the indefinite future. New preferred stock and debentures can be sold to net their par value carrying the yields stated above. Compute Harper's cost of new capital for the expansion. (Assume a 50% marginal tax rate.)

Solution:

$$\text{Cost of common equity} = k_e = \frac{D_0(1+g)}{I_0} + g = \frac{1.50(1+0.08)}{30} + 0.08$$

$$= 0.054 + 0.08$$
$$= \underline{0.134}$$

$$\text{Cost of preferred stock} = k_p = \frac{D_p}{I_0} = \frac{9}{100} = \underline{0.09}$$

$$\text{Cost of debentures} = k_D$$

where k_D is found by solving for itself in the following valuation model:

$$I_0 = \sum_{t=1}^{25} \frac{100}{(1+k_D)^t} + \frac{1,000}{(1+k_D)^{25}}$$

However, where $I_0 = \$1,000$, or the face value of the bond, we know that $k_D = 0.10$, or the coupon rate on the bond.

The after-tax cost of the debentures, k_D', is found as follows:

$$k_D' = k_D(1 - \text{tax rate})$$
$$= 0.10(1 - 0.5) = \underline{0.05}$$

The weighted-average cost of capital is found as follows:

Source	Proportion		×	After-Tax Cost	=	Product
Debentures	(3/10)	0.3	×	0.05	=	0.015
Preferred stock	(1/10)	0.1	×	0.09	=	0.009
Common stock	(6/10)	0.6	×	0.134	=	0.080
			Weighted-average cost of capital =			0.104

3. Assume a marginal tax rate of 48% and compute the after-tax cost of each of the following:

(a) An 8½% bond selling for $900 (face value is $1,000) with a 20-year maturity and flotation costs of $50 per bond.

(b) A preferred stock issue with a 7% dividend, $100 par value, which nets $90 to the issuer.

(c) A common stock issue with a current market price of $60 per share, recent dividend of $2.50, flotation and underpricing of $10 per share, and an anticipated growth rate in future dividends of 5% per annum forever.

Solution:

(a) k_p is found by solving the following equation via trial and error:

$$\$900 - 50 = \sum_{t=1}^{20} \frac{\$85}{(1+k_B)^t} + \frac{\$1,000}{(1+k_B)^{20}}$$

Trying k_B = 8.5%, we obtain a present value of interest and principal of $1,000. Trying k_B = 12%:

$$PV = \$85 \times 7.469 + \$1,000 \times 0.104$$
$$= \$738.87$$

Interpolation:

	Rate	Present Value		
	0.12	$ 738.87		
0.035 (×	k_B	850.00	$111.13)	$261.13
	0.085	1,000.00		

$$\frac{x}{0.035} = \frac{\$111.13}{\$261.13}$$

$$x = 0.035 \times 0.42557 = 0.0149$$

Thus, k_B = 0.12 − 0.0149 = 0.105, or 10.5%.

Eliminating the influence of taxes:

$$k_B = 0.105(1 - 0.48) = \underline{0.0546}$$

(b) $k_p = \dfrac{D_p}{I_0} = \dfrac{\$7}{90} = \underline{0.078}$

(c) $k_e = \dfrac{D_0(1 + g)}{I_0} + g$

$$= \frac{2.50(1 + 0.05)}{50} + 0.05$$

$$= \frac{2.625}{50} + 0.05 = 0.0525 + 0.05$$

$$= \underline{0.1025}$$

SELF-TESTS

True-False

_____ 1. When the security market line is applied to risky investments, the investment opportunities lying above the SML are to be avoided, owing to the fact that they are overpriced and because of the anticipated drop in price that will occur once arbitrage in the marketplace adjusts for the temporary imbalance.

_____ 2. As a result of the heterogeneity of risk in the usual corporate capital structure, the concept of weighted-average cost of capital is not always applicable.

_____ 3. Stock rights are treated much the same as common equity in computing flotation costs because it is assumed that the rights will eventually be exercised.

_____ 4. The implicit assumption behind the use of NPV and standard deviation is the belief that systematic risk, not total risk, is the major concern for the firm; therefore, investments are evaluated according to their marginal addition to systematic, not total, risk.

_____ 5. The cost of preferred stock is not adjusted for taxes because payment of preferred dividends occurs after taxes.

_____ 6. By application of the capital-asset pricing model, the need to compute future changes in market price due to unsystematic risk is circumvented.

_____ 7. Efforts by the firm to reduce total risk through diversification are of no value in enhancing its market value since the investor can eliminate systematic risk through diversification.

_____ 8. The profitability index provides a relative as opposed to an absolute measure of risk.

_____ 9. Because of its numerous theoretical shortcomings (i.e., no concern for investors or existing investment projects), the NPV/standard deviation approach is not popular among corporate decision makers, whereas the capital-asset pricing model is.

_____ 10. Regardless of the risk aversion of a firm's management, they should always choose a combination of investment projects lying on the efficient frontier of the firm's opportunity set of projects.

Mutliple Choice

1. The general subject area of the cost of capital is most concerned with the:
   a. Diversification of risk.
   b. Marginal addition to risk.
   c. Maximization of expected return and minimization of risk.
   d. Marginal cost of financing sources.
   e. Net effect of dividends on the capital structure.

2. A bond of $1,000 par at 6% is currently selling for $1,050. The appropriate federal tax rate is 48%. What is the cost of debit to the issuing firm?
   a. 3.12%.
   b. 6.00%.
   c. 6.35%.
   d. 5.45%.
   e. 3.75%.

3. On a sale of preferred stock the firm realized $95 on $100 par. If the dividend was $8 per annum, what is the cost of preferred stock financing for the company?
   a. 8.00%.
   b. 8.42%.
   c. 7.50%.
   d. 9.00%.
   e. 8.35%.

4. To compute the required rate of return for equity in a company using the capital asset pricing model, it is necessary to know all the following except:
   a. The risk-free rate.
   b. The beta for the firm.

c. The earnings for the next quarter or year.

d. The market return expected for the time period.

e. The slope of the characteristic line.

5. The more inefficient the capital markets are:
   a. The larger beta is for the firm.
   b. The higher are the flotation costs.
   c. The greater importance total risk plays in allowance for risk.
   d. The smaller your residual risk becomes.
   e. The lower the rate of return required by investors.

6. The major problem (aside from the lumpiness of raising capital) in maintaining the capital structure is:
   a. The changing costs of equity and debt in the marketplace.
   b. The short-term nature of most financing episodes.
   c. The constraining effect of retained earnings.
   d. The sale of common stock in the secondary markets.

7. The most important factor in the evaluation of investment decisions by subjective methods (i.e., not the capital-asset pricing model) is:
   a. The accurate determination of earnings.
   b. The degree of systematic risk involved.
   c. The associating risk/profitability with share price.
   d. The determination of the true standard deviation.

8. Given the following diagram of investment combinations and expected returns:

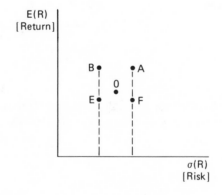

which of the following relationships is not true?

a. B dominates A.

b. E dominates F.

c. A dominates F.

d. For a strongly risk-adverse investor, E dominates D.

e. None of the above.

The Concept of Leverage

17

Orientation: The attention of this chapter is upon the analysis of operating and financial leverage. Ordinary cost-volume-profit analysis is employed to present the concept of operating leverage. A form of indifference analysis is applied to the study of alternative financing choices. The joint relationship between operating and financial leverage is then presented.

I. Operating leverage

    A. When the firm incurs fixed costs, *operating leverage* results. *Fixed costs* represent those cash outflows that must be met by the company regardless of the volume of product that it is producing and selling. The analysis of operating leverage deals with the time period that economists would call the "short run." Upon the use of assets that result in fixed costs, the firm will find that percentage changes in output (sales) will translate into even greater percentage changes in profits. The tool of break-even analysis or cost-volume-profit analysis facilitates the study of the concept of operating leverage.

    B. The technique of *break-even analysis* is a simple one but useful in many situations. To apply it, the array of costs that confront the firm must be separated into two categories: fixed and variable. Fixed costs do not vary in total with the firm's volume of output; notice, however, that as more units of a product are produced and sold, the fixed costs per unit of output will decline. Variable costs are constant per unit of output; consequently, as output rises, so do variable costs (in total). A typical fixed cost is administrative salaries. Raw materials used in the product are a typical variable cost.

1. By definition, at the break-even point, variable costs plus fixed costs will be equal to total sales revenue:

$$F + V(X) = P(X)$$

where F = fixed costs
          V = variable costs per unit
          X = volume of output (in units)
          P = selling price per unit

2. Solving the above equation for X, the break-even level of output, results in the following relationship:

$$X = \frac{F}{P - V}$$

3. Suppose that your company produces a single product which sells in the marketplace for $6 per unit. Your controller has determined that every unit produced results in $4.80 in variable expenses. He also forecasts that annual fixed costs will be $12,000. With this information you can determine the break-even volume of output. This break-even volume of output will leave operating profits before taxes equal to $0. Substituting into the basic break-even formula, we find that

$$X = \frac{\$12,000}{\$6.00 - 4.80} = \frac{\$12,000}{\$1.20} = 10,000 \text{ units}$$

At the output level of 10,000 units, total fixed costs of $12,000 plus total variable costs of $48,000 will equal exactly the total sales revenue of $60,000.

4. It is now possible to define explicitly the concept of operating leverage. At a given level of output, the degree of operating leverage can be measured by dividing a percentage change in profits (net operating income) by the percentage change in output (sales) that caused the profit change. This can be expressed as follows:

$$\frac{\text{degree of operating leverage}}{\text{(DOL) at X units of output (sales)}} = \frac{\text{percentage change in profits}}{\text{percentage change in output}}$$

An alternative way of stating this relationship, and one that is computationally easier to deal with, is

$$\text{DOL at X units} = \frac{X(P - V)}{X(P - V) - F}$$

Observe that this method of expressing the operating leverage concept emphasizes that it is nothing more than "sales revenue before the deduction of fixed costs" (the numerator of the above equation) divided by "sales revenue after the deduction of fixed costs." The only factor providing the operating leverage is the level of operating fixed costs.

a. To illustrate this measurement of the degree of operating leverage, assume the same cost structure for the firm described in the break-even example. Let us suppose that the firm plans to produce and sell 12,000 units of the product. The degree of operating leverage at this volume of output would be determined as follows:

$$\text{DOL at 12,000 units} = \frac{12,000(\$6.00 - \$4.80)}{12,000(\$6.00 - \$4.80) - \$12,000}$$

$$= 6.00 \text{ times}$$

b. It is reasonable to ask about the significance of this derived figure of 6.00 times. It means that from the output level of 12,000 units for every 1% percent increase in output (sales), a 6.00% increase in operating profits will result (if the tenets of break-even analysis hold).

5. Cost-volume-profit analysis can be a very useful financial management planning tool. Knowledge of the approximate break-even point allows forecasted fluctuations in sales volume to be analyzed with regard to the effect upon profits. This is especially important in planning the debt-carrying capacity of the firm. Further, knowledge of the firm's cost structure is helpful in ascertaining whether a price cut might be used to increase profits through hoped-for sales increases.

6. No model of the profit-generating capability of the company should be followed blindly. Cost-volume-profit analysis is no exception. Confident usage of the approach is dependent upon a thorough understanding of its prime assumptions.

a. It is assumed that price and variable cost per unit are unaffected by volume changes.

b. All costs are forced into two mutually exclusive categories: (1) fixed or (2) variable.

c. A constant product mix is implied.

Other limitations concerning this procedure are the tendency to derive the crucial variables from historical patterns that may not be stable, and the fact that method is not particularly useful in a long-range setting.

II. Financial leverage

A. Financial leverage is used by the firm when it finances a portion of its assets with funds bearing a fixed (limited) cost in the hope of increasing the ultimate return to the common stockholders. The terms "financial leverage" and "trading on the equity" will be used interchangeably. The analysis that follows deals only with explicit (contractual) costs, not with opportunity costs.

B. The study of whether financial leverage has been used to the benefit of the shareholders will focus upon the relationship between earnings per share (EPS) and earnings before interest and taxes (EBIT). While we will concentrate primarily upon this relationship, please note that not all analysts follow it exclusively. Some center their analysis of the favorableness of the leverage on the relationship between the rate of return on the common equity investment and EBIT.

C. Within the context of financial leverage study, the term "break-even analysis" (or "indifference analysis") has a different meaning than in our previous examination of operating leverage. Break-even or indifference point now refers to a level of EBIT that will equate EPS between two financing choices. This indifference point can be found, often with good success, through the careful use of graph paper. It can be exactly and directly located, however, through the application of a little algebra. The following equation will be applied to an example contained in Chapter 17 of the text:

$$\frac{[(EBIT - C)(1 - t)] - P}{S_1} = \frac{[(EBIT - C)(1 - t)] - P}{S_2}$$

where EBIT = indifference level of earnings before interest and taxes
    C = interest expense associated with a given financing choice
    t = the firm's marginal tax rate
    P = preferred dividend payments associated with a given financing choice
    S_1 = number of common shares outstanding under financing arrangement 1

S_2 = number of common shares outstanding under financing arrangement 2

D. Now, suppose the firm is currently financed with $10 million of common equity, represented by 200,000 common shares. The company wishes to raise an additional $5 million. Plan 1 calls for selling 100,000 new common shares at $50 per share. Plan 2 calls for selling $5 million of bonds that carry a 9% interest rate. The federal income tax rate is 50%. We wish to ascertain at what level of EBIT the firm's EPS will be the same regardless of which financing plan is selected. The solution is as follows:

$$\frac{[(\text{EBIT} - 0)(1 - 0.5)] - 0}{300,000} = \frac{[(\text{EBIT} - 450,000)(1 - 0.5)] - 0}{200,000}$$

$$\frac{0.5 \text{ EBIT}}{3} = \frac{0.5 \text{ EBIT} - 225,000}{2}$$

$$1.5 \text{ EBIT} - 675,000 = 1.0 \text{ EBIT}$$

$$0.5 \text{ EBIT} = 675,000$$

$$\text{EBIT} = \underline{\$1,350,000} \text{ indifference level}$$

The break-even point with respect to EPS turns out to be $1,350,000 between the common stock and debt-financing alternatives. This is a most useful number to have when financing strategy is being decided. In the present case, if EBIT should consistently be greater than $1,350,000, debt financing would provide for a higher EPS. If EBIT should fall below $1,350,000, the common stock financing choice would offer the shareholders a higher EPS.

E. One method of measuring the firm's degree of financial leverage from a given level of EBIT is to divide a percentage change in EPS by the percentage change in EBIT that occasioned it. Thus, we have

$$\frac{\text{degree of financial leverage}}{\text{(DFL) at EBIT of } y} = \frac{\text{percentage change in EPS}}{\text{percentage change in EBIT}}$$

An equivalent expression is

$$\text{DFL at EBIT of } y = \frac{\text{EBIT}}{\text{EBIT} - \text{C}}$$

where C is annual interest expense, or the before-tax equivalent of the preferred stock dividend.

F. It will be helpful to apply the expression just offered as a measure of financial leverage from a given level of EBIT. Suppose that the current level of EBIT for the firm is $2,400. The company must meet annual interest payments of $1,000. It faces a federal income tax rate of 50% and has 70 shares of common stock outstanding. The degree of financial leverage for this firm is found to be

$$\text{DFL at } \$2,400 = \frac{2,400}{2,400 - 1,000} = \frac{2,400}{1,400} = 1.714 \text{ times}$$

In this case a 100% increase in EBIT would result in a 171.4% increase in earnings per share.

III. Combined effect of two types of levarage

A. An extremely large effect upon earnings per share (EPS) can result when financial leverage and operating leverage are combined. That is, a relatively small fluctuation in sales can be translated into a large change in EPS through the combined leverage effect. This combined leverage effect can in general be measured as the *product* of the individual financial leverage and operating leverage measures that have previously been advanced in this chapter.

B. It can also be measured directly through use of an equation:

$$\frac{\text{Degree of operating and financial}}{\text{leverage at X units}} = \frac{X(P - V)}{X(P - V) - F - C}$$

C. The application of this formula will be illustrated in the Study Problems.

D. Combining the two types of leverage can be an important policy decision confronting the financial manager. It is possible, for example, to dampen a high level of operating leverage with a financial structure that contains little or no financial leverage.

STUDY PROBLEMS

1. The Redstone Corporation projects that next year its fixed costs will total $80,000. Its only product sells for $10 per unit, of which $5 is a variable cost. The management of Redstone is considering the purchase of a new machine that will lower the variable cost per unit to $4. The new machine, however, will add to fixed costs through an increase in depreciation expense.

a. How large can the *addition* to fixed costs be in order to keep the firm's break-even point in units produced and sold unchanged?

Solution:

Compute the present level of break-even output:

$$X = \frac{F}{P - V}$$
$$= \frac{\$80,000}{10 - 5} = \frac{\$80,000}{5} = 16,000 \text{ units}$$

Compute the new level of fixed costs at the break-even output:

$$F + (4)(16,000) = (10)(16,000)$$
$$F + 64,000 = 160,000$$
$$F = \$96,000$$

Compute the addition to fixed costs:

$$\$96,000 - \$80,000 = \underline{\underline{\$16,000 \text{ addition}}}$$

2. The management of Redstone Corporation decided not to purchase the new piece of equipment. Using the existing cost structure, calculate the degree of operating leverage at 20,000 units of output.

Solution:

$$\text{DOL at 20,000 units} = \frac{20,000(\$10 - \$5)}{20,000(\$10 - \$5) - \$80,000}$$
$$= \frac{\$100,000}{\$20,000} = 5 \text{ times}$$

This indicates, for example, that a 10% increase in sales for the Redstone Corporation will result in a 50% increase in EBIT, provided the assumptions of cost-volume-profit analysis hold.

3. Construct a break-even chart for the Redstone Corporation under its present cost structure.

Solution (see chart on following page):

4. An analytical income statement for the Redstone Corporation is shown. It is based upon an output level of 32,000 units.

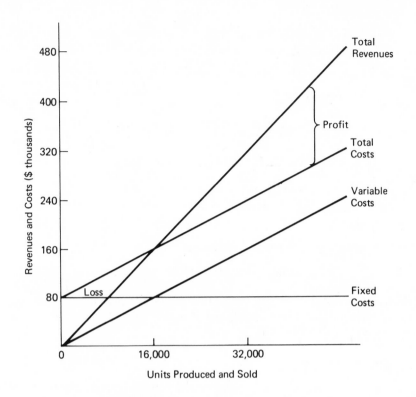

Redstone Corporation Break-Even Chart

Sales	$320,000
Variable costs	160,000
Revenue before fixed costs	$160,000
Fixed costs	80,000
EBIT	$ 80,000
Interest expense	20,000
Earnings before taxes	$ 60,000
Taxes	30,000
Net income	$ 30,000

(a) Calculate the degree of operating leverage at this output level.

(b) Calculate the degree of financial leverage at this level of EBIT.

(c) Determine the combined leverage effect at this output level.

Solution:

(a) DOL at 32,000 units $= \dfrac{32,000(\$10 - \$5)}{32,000(\$10 - \$5) - \$80,000} = 2$ times

(b) DFL at EBIT of \$80,000 = $\dfrac{\$80,000}{\$80,000 - \$20,000}$ = 1.333 times

(c) Combined leverage effect = $\dfrac{32,000(\$10 - \$5)}{32,000(\$10 - \$5) - \$80,000 - \$20,000}$

$$= 2.667 \text{ times}$$

Notice that the combined leverage effect is the product of the degrees of operating and financial leverage. A 1% increase in sales for Redstone would be magnified into a 2.667% increase in net income, owing to the combined leverage effect.

SELF-TESTS

True-False

_____ 1. The concept of cost-volume-profit analysis dwells upon the "long run."

_____ 2. Break-even analysis is better suited for multiple-product firms than for single-product firms.

_____ 3. Your firm adds to its facilities a completely automated production line. This will cause the break-even point (in units of output) to rise.

_____ 4. All other things being the same, if the firm raises its next increment of funds by selling common stock, it will increase its degree of financial leverage.

_____ 5. The firm is utilizing financial leverage when it raises funds by selling preferred stock and pays the contractual preferred stock dividend.

_____ 6. Financial leverage and operating leverage exactly offset each other.

_____ 7. Actually, in practice some costs are best termed "semivariable," as they are partly fixed and partly variable.

_____ 8. Operating leverage and trading on the equity are interchangeable terms.

_____ 9. If the actual level of EBIT exceeds the indifference level of EBIT, the use of financial leverage can be called favorable.

_____ 10. If EBIT were to remain constant while the firm incurred additional interest expense, the degree of financial leverage would increase.

Multiple Choice

1. Which of the following is *not* a limitation of break-even analysis?
   a. The price of the product is assumed to be constant.
   b. Variable cost per unit is assumed to be constant.
   c. In multiple-product firms, the product mix is assumed to be fixed.
   d. It provides a method for analyzing operating leverage.

2. In the context of cost-volume-profit analysis, if selling price rises per unit, and all other variables remain constant, the break-even point in units will:
   a. Fall.
   b. Rise.
   c. Stay the same.
   d. None of the above.

3. The combined effect of financial and operating leverage is:
   a. The sum of the degree of operating leverage and the degree of financial leverage.
   b. The degree of financial leverage minus the degree of operating leverage.
   c. The product of the two separate measures of leverage.
   d. None of the above.

4. An operating leverage factor of 5.00 indicates:
   a. If sales rise by 5%, EBIT will rise by 5%.
   b. If sales rise by 1%, EBIT will rise by 1%.
   c. If sales rise by 5%, EBIT will fall by 25%.
   d. If sales rise by 1%, EBIT will rise by 5%.

5. The degree of financial leverage will be increased with all of the following financing methods except:
   a. Retained earnings.
   b. Common stock.
   c. First mortgage bonds.
   d. Debentures.
   e. Preferred stock.
   f. Second mortgage bonds.

Capital Structure of the Firm 18

Orientation: This chapter concentrates on the way the firm arranges its sources of funds. The theory of an optimal capital structure is presented, along with various arguments related to that concept. The discussion is concluded with a description of techniques useful to the practitioner faced with the problem of determining an appropriate financing mix.

I. Theory of capital structure

    A. In the broadest sense, *financial risk* is made up of two components: the risk of possible insolvency, and variability in the earnings available to common stockholders. Both of these aspects of financial risk increase as the firm employs greater degrees of financial leverage. The increased risk is borne by the common stock investor. In light of this increased risk, can the firm affect its cost of capital and the worth of its outstanding debt and equity securities by altering its financing mix?

    B. In a well-known article, David Durand suggested alternative methods for valuing the earnings of a firm with regard to the degree to which it utilizes financial leverage.[1] These valuation methods have become so familiar in the literature of finance that they are recognized by their initials—NI, for net-income approach, and NOI, for net-operating-income approach.

---

[1] David Durand, "The Cost of Debt and Equity Funds for Business," in *The Management of Corporate Capital,* Ezra Solomon, ed. (New York: The Free Press, 1959).

1. The NI approach will be illustrated first. Assume that a firm has $5,000 in debt outstanding, and that it carries a 6% interest rate. In addition, annual net operating earnings are expected to be $2,000. Finally, the appropriate equity-capitalization rate for the firm is 10%. The equity-capitalization rate is defined as the earnings available to common shareholders divided by the market value of common stock outstanding. This is designated as $K_e = E/S$. According to the assumptions of the NI valuation method and the assumptions stated in Chapter 18 of the text, it is possible to compute the market value of the firm's outstanding securities.

O	Net operating earnings	$ 2,000
F	Interest expense	300
E	Earnings available to common	1,700
k_e	Equity-capitalization rate	0.10
S	Market value of common stock	$17,000
B	Market value of debt	5,000
V	Total value of the firm	$22,000

This methodology for arriving at the market value of the firm's securities (assuming that debt is selling in the marketplace at face value) produces an implied overall capitalization rate (from the above example) of 9.1%.

$$K_0 = \frac{O}{V} = \frac{\$2,000}{\$22,000} = 9.1\%$$

This overall capitalization rate, when there are no income taxes, is also defined as the weighted-average cost of capital.

Continuing with our analysis of the NI method, suppose that a capital-stucture change is effected by having the firm sell $5,000 worth of additional bonds, the proceeds of which are used to repurchase its common stock. Further, assume that the interest rate on all outstanding debt remains at 6%. Note what will happen to the total value of the firm's securities.

O	Net operating earnings	$ 2,000
F	Interest	600
E	Earnings available to common	$ 1,400
k_e	Equity capitalization rate	0.10
S	Market value of common stock	$14,000
B	Market value of debt	10,000
V	Total value of the firm	$24,000

This action by the company results in a reduction of the implied overall capitalization rate to a level of 8.3%.

$$K_0 = \frac{O}{V} = \frac{\$2,000}{\$24,000} = 8.3\%$$

The upshot of this valuation approach is that increases in the degree of financial leverage utilized by the company will increase its total market value and lower its overall cost of capital, K_0. It can also be shown that this type of action (i.e., assumption of greater degrees of financial risk) will raise the market price per share of the common stock. Figure 1(b), which depicts the NI valuation model, reflects the implication of the model that investors and lenders do not believe that the firm's expected returns are more risky as the leverage use increases. Maximum leverage use would provide the lowest cost of capital and highest stock price.

2. Durand's second method for appraising the market value of the firm's securities, the NOI method, will now be described. This approach operates upon the key assumption that the overall capitalization rate, k_0, of the firm's operating income is unchanged for all degrees of financial leverage. We will use the same initial example as before, where $5,000 of debt is outstanding, but now let k_0 be equal to 10%. This model capitalizes (discounts) net operating income at k_0 to arrive at the total market value of outstanding debt and common equity. From the total market value of these securities is subtracted the market value of the debt, leaving the market value of the common stock.

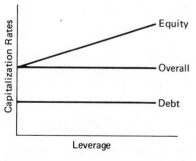

(a) The Net Operating Income Approach

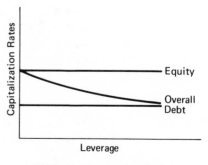

(b) The Net Income Approach

FIGURE 1. Leverage and Capitalization Rates

O	Net operating earnings	$ 2,000
k_0	Overall capitalization rate	0.10
V	Total value of the firm	$20,000
B	Market value of debt	5,000
S	Market value of stock	$15,000

This methodology produces an implied equity-capitalization rate, k_e, of 11.3%.

$$k_e = \frac{E}{S} = \frac{\$1,700}{\$15,000} = 11.3\%$$

Again, suppose that the firm markets new debt totaling an additional $5,000; this brings the total debt level to $10,000. Also assume that the debt proceeds are used to retire outstanding common shares. Using the format for the NOI model just outlined, you should be able to show that the total value of the firm will remain at $20,000. Note, however, from your own calculations that k_e will rise to 14%. The implication of this valuation model is that the value of the firm, including the per share price of the common stock, will not be changed by capital-structure alterations. This is depicted in Figure 1(a), where the overall capitalization rate is left unchanged as the firm incurs more financial risk. This happens because an increase in the use of supposedly cheaper debt is offset by a rise in the required return on common equity, leaving the overall capitalization rate unchanged. As the overall cost of capital to the firm, k_0, and the value of its common shares are not affected by capital-structure alterations, no one capital structure can be deemed "optimal."

3. Lying between the NI and NOI valuation methods is an approach generally referred to as the *traditional* approach. The thrust of this traditional position is that the judicious use of financial leverage can (for a while) lower the firm's overall cost of capital and raise the total market value of its outstanding securities. The traditional position, however, recognizes that the benefits of substituting debt for common equity cannot go on forever. Eventually the increased financial leverage will result in rising debt costs (say k_i for the interest rate on the debt) and increased equity-capitalization rates. Thus, k_0, the overall cost of capital, must start to rise. According to this position, then, the firm's cost of capital and its financial (or capital) structure are not independent. The traditional view on capital structure and valuation holds that either (a) an optimal degree of financial leverage use exists for the firm, or that (b) an optimal *range* of

financial leverage use can be found for the firm where its cost of capital will be minimized. The optimum range variant of the traditional view is illustrated in Figure 2. It shows that k_0, the overall capitalization rate, would be minimized between degrees of financial leverage use X_1 and X_2.

4. A famous attack upon the traditional position regarding capital-structure importance was launched by Modigliani and Miller (MM).[1] They took the purely definitional NOI model and offered a theory of investor behavior to account for the posited independence between total firm value and capital structure. By assuming perfect capital markets where all information is available to all investors, MM argue that perfect substitutes cannot sell at different prices. In the present context, this means that firms which differ only with regard to their capital structures cannot sell at differing total market values. Thus, MM contend that the total risk of the firm is not affected by a change in its capital structure. Arbitragers (profit seekers) will see to it that a more heavily levered firm does not sell at a higher total market

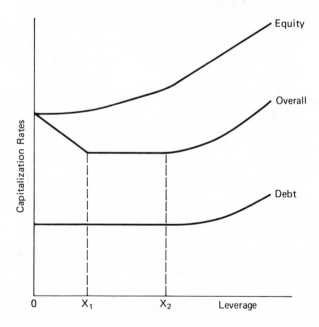

FIGURE 2. The Traditional View—Optimum Range Variant

[1] Franco Modigliani and Merton H. Miller, "The Cost of Capital, Corporation Finance and the Theory of Investment," *American Economic Review, 48* (June 1958), 261-297.

value than one which uses a lesser degree of fixed-charge financing. An equilibrium will be reached when firms competing in the same homogeneous risk class sell at the same total market values. This will equate their overall costs of capital. The major implication of this MM position is that in a world without corporate income taxes, one capital structure is as good as the next.

5. Many arguments against the MM arbitrage process have been advanced.

    a. Where the possibility of corporate bankruptcy exists, carrying with it significant costs, a levered company could be less preferable to investors than an unlevered firm.

    b. The MM arbitrage process rests upon the assumption that personal financial leverage and corporate financial leverage are perfect substitutes. With corporate borrowings, however, the individual investor has limited liability.

    c. The individual investor probably can borrow only at a higher interest cost than the corporation.

    d. A multitude of restrictions upon institutional investor behavior will preclude the arbitrage mechanism from working perfectly enough to uphold the MM position.

6. The MM argument is changed drastically when corporate income taxes are admitted into the argument. The final result is that the cost of capital, k_0, can be lowered as more financial leverage is employed by the firm. With corporate taxes, the value of the firm, according to the MM position, is given by the following relationship:

$$V = \frac{O(1 - t)}{p_k} + tB$$

where t = corporate tax rate
     p_k = after-tax capitalization rate for a firm with no debt in a given risk class
     O = expected net operating income
     B = market value of debt

The expression above shows that as more corporate debt is used in the capital structure, the value of the firm, V, will rise. The overall cost of capital, on a tax-adjusted basis, now becomes

$$k_0 = p_k \frac{(1-t)B}{B+S}$$

where all the variables are as previously defined. If you will take any set of variables and substitute them into the expression above, you will find that as B rises, the cost of capital, k_0, will fall. With taxes, then, the MM position implies an optimal capital structure made up almost (one share of common stock would be needed to be a legal corporation) entirely of debt. This is far from the traditional view, where increased financial-risk exposure would cause the cost of capital curve to bend upward as more fixed-charge financing is used.

II. The appropriate capital structure in practice

    A. In the world where financial policy is determined, attempts *are* made to approximate an optimal capital structure. One way to view this problem is to consider it to be that of ascertaining where the k_0 curve would start to rise as financial leverage use is increased. Some basic and practical approaches will be described.

    B. One popular technique used in making financing decisions can be referred to as *EBIT-EPS* analysis.

        1. In Chapter 17 we discussed the concept of indifference analysis as applied to mutually exclusive financing arrangements. We noted that an indifference (break-even) level of EBIT could be found, either by algebra or graphic analysis, that would equate EPS between two financing plans. It would be helpful at this point for you to review that example.

        2. Although EBIT-EPS analysis focuses upon the explicit costs of fixed-charge financing, it is a useful tool for the financial manager concerned with selection of a financing arrangement.

        3. An EBIT-EPS table, constructed according to the given financing choices under various economic conditions (recession, normal, boom) can provide added insight into the effect of EBIT changes on EPS.

        4. A study problem in this chapter will again illustrate this simple, but useful, technique.

    C. The search for an appropriate capital structure and a *cash-flow analysis* of the firm's ability to service fixed financing charges go hand in hand. The financing charges must be thought of in the broadest sense, encompassing (1) interest payments on debt,

(2) lease payments, (3) principal payments on debt, and (4) preferred stock dividends.

1. Large and stable cash flows permit the firm to carry and service more debt and other financing arrangements that result in fixed charges.

2. Cash budget preparation, discussed earlier in the text, should be extended to include the fixed charges associated with possible financing contracts.

3. The best way for the firm to analyze financial risk and the market's way of assessing the financial-risk exposure of a given firm probably are different.

  a. Large lenders and institutional investors clearly relate the firm's ability to service fixed charges with the level of those charges.

  b. Many individual investors, however, probably rely more on book-value relationships (say, the ratio of debt to equity) in assessing financial risk.

D. Another approach, often used in practice, to arrive at desired capital-structure relationships is to compare the financing mix of the given firm with other firms competing in similar lines of business activity. Advice can also be obtained from investment analysts, institutional investors, and investment banking houses.

STUDY PROBLEMS

1. The Oklahoma Fertilizer Company has $8,000,000 of net operating earnings. In its capital structure, $12,500,000 worth of debt is outstanding, with an interest rate of 8%. The debt is selling in the marketplace at its book value. Parts (a) and (b) assume that there is no tax upon corporate income.

(a) According to the NOI valuation method, compute the total value of the firm and the implied equity-capitalization rate. Assume an implied overall capitalization rate, k_0, of 16%.

(b) Compute the total value of the firm and the implied overall capitalization rate, k_0, according to the NI capitalization model. Assume an equity-capitalization rate, k_e, of 20%.

(c) Now, allow for the existence of a federal tax on corporate income at a 50% rate. Calculate the value of Oklahoma Fertilizer according to the Modigliani-Miller position (with taxes considered). Assume an after-tax capitalization rate,

p_k, of 16% for a firm with no debt and in the same risk class as Oklahoma Fertilizer.

Solution:

(a)

O	Net operating earnings	$ 8,000,000
k_o	Overall capitalization rate	0.16
V	Total value of the firm	$50,000,000
B	Market value of debt	−12,500,000
S	Market value of stock	$37,500,000

$$k_e = \frac{O - F}{S} = \frac{\$7,000,000}{\$37,500,000} = \underline{\underline{18.67\%}}$$

(b)

$$
\begin{array}{l}
O = \$\ 8,000,000 \\
F = \underline{\ \ 1,000,000} \\
E = \$\ 7,000,000 \\
k_e = \underline{\ \ \ \ \ \ 0.20} \\
S = \$35,000,000 \\
B = \underline{\ 12,500,000} \\
V = \underline{\$47,500,000}
\end{array}
$$

$$k_o = \frac{O}{V} = \frac{\$8,000,000}{\$47,500,000} = 16.84\%$$

(c)
$$V = \frac{O(1 - t)}{p_k} + tB$$

$$= \frac{\$8,000,000(0.5)}{0.16} + \$(0.5)(\$12,500,000)$$

$$= \underline{\underline{\$31,250,000}}$$

2. Louisiana Leather Outlets, Inc., ended this past year of operations with the capital structure shown below:

First mortgage bonds at 8%	$ 2,000,000
Debentures at 9%	1,000,000
Common stock (1,000,000 shares)	6,000,000
Retained earnings	1,000,000
Total	$10,000,000

The federal income tax rate is 50%. The firm wants to raise an additional $1,000,000 to open new facilities in Alabama and Tennessee. Two approaches are open to the firm. It can sell a new issue of 20-year debentures with a 10% interest rate. Alternatively, 20,000 new shares of common stock can be sold to the public to net the company $50 per share. A recent study performed by an outside consulting organization projected Louisiana Leather's long-term EBIT level at approximately $4,750,000.

(a) Find the indifference level of EBIT (with regard to earnings per share) between the suggested financing plans.

(b) Which alternative do you recommend that Louisiana Leather pursue?

> **Solution:**
>
> (a) In the following equations, E = EBIT.
>
> $$\frac{(E - \$250,000)(0.5)}{1,020,000} = \frac{(E - \$350,000)(0.5)}{1,000,000}$$
>
> $$\frac{0.5E - \$125,000}{102} = \frac{0.5E - \$175,000}{100}$$
>
> $$50E - \$12,500,000 = 51E - \$17,850,000$$
>
> $$E = \underline{\$5,350,000}\ \text{indifference level of EBIT}$$
>
> (b) The consulting firm projected Louisiana Leather's long-term EBIT at $4,750,000. Since this projected level of EBIT is *less* than the indifference level of $5,350,000, the earnings per share of the firm will be greater if the common stock is issued.

SELF-TESTS

True-False

_____   1. Business risk and financial risk are just different ways of expressing the same concept.

_____   2. Two approaches to the valuation of the earnings of a company, the net income approach and the net operating income approach, were first suggested by Modigliani and Miller.

_____   3. EBIT-EPS analysis does not consider directly the implicit costs associated with debt financing.

_____   4. Consider EBIT-EPS analysis. The indifference point between a common stock and debt financing alternative has been calculated. If the projected level of EBIT is well below the indifference point, debt financing is favored.

_____   5. The debt capacity of the firm is directly related to its cash-flow-generating ability.

_____   6. In selection of the appropriate financing mix for a given company, comparison of the capital structures of other

companies having similar business risk may be used as
one benchmark.

_____   7. When corporate income taxes are admitted into the analysis,
the MM position fails to recognize that the cost of capital can
be lowered with financial leverage.

_____   8. In a world of both taxes and bankruptcy costs, there likely
will be an optimal capital structure even if all the other
behavioral assumptions of the MM argument hold.

_____   9. If you did not have to pay your broker to sell your stock, the
MM position on capital structure would be strengthened.

_____   10. Knowledge of balance-sheet relationships only is adequate for
the making of optimal capital-structure decisions.

Multiple Choice

1. The dispersion of operating income is most often known as:
   a. Financial risk.
   b. Trading on the equity.
   c. Financial leverage.
   d. Business risk.
   e. The correlation coefficient.

2. Possible methods to use in the approximation of an optimal capital
   structure include:
   a. Cash-flow analysis.
   b. EBIT-EPS analysis.
   c. Comparison of selected financial ratios with those of similar firms.
   d. All of the above.

3. Which of the following is *not* a major argument against the MM arbitrage
   process?
   a. In the business world, bankruptcy costs can be significant.
   b. The cost of borrowing for individuals is usually higher than for
      corporations.
   c. Personal leverage and corporate leverage are not equally risky to an
      individual.
   d. Earnings per share can be increased with the careful use of financial
      leverage.

4. Analysis of a firm's cash flows under "adverse circumstances" would most
   likely be associated with:
   a. Modigliani and Miller.
   b. Gordon Donaldson.
   c. Ezra Solomon.
   d. David Durand.

19

Dividend Policy and Retained Earnings

Orientation: The corporate dividend policy is considered to be primarily a function of the firm's investment opportunities and the required rate of returns associated with such investments. In addition, a number of other factors may contribute to making the dividend policy a relevant decision variable for the financial manager. Stated differently, the dividend decision may not simply be a passive residual of the firm's investment decision. Also, stock splits, stock dividends, as well as the repurchase of stock, represent means by which the outstanding stock of a company is altered to achieve the firm's goals.

   I. Dividend-payout ratio: If the payment of cash dividends can affect the shareholders' wealth, the optimal dividend-payout ratio (dividend/ earnings) is that ratio which maximizes shareholder wealth.

      A. Assume:

          1. Business risk to be constant.

          2. Financial risk to be constant.

      B. Dividends as a financing decision: If dividend policy is treated *strictly* as a financing decision (whether or not to retain earnings), the payment of cash dividends is a passive residual.

          1. Given that the firm has investment opportunities with expected returns exceeding the cost of capital, retained earnings available for reinvestment will be employed in financing the equity portion of these projects.

2. If the company has internally generated funds remaining after financing all acceptable investment opportunities, these funds would be distributed as dividends.

3. Conclusion: The amount of dividend payout will change from period to period in keeping with fluctuations in the amount of acceptable investment opportunities available to the firm.

4. Walter's formula illustrates the impact of dividends upon the market price when the dividend policy is purely a financing decision.

C. Irrelevance of dividends

1. Contention:

   a. Dividends are irrelevant, in that the investor is indifferent between (1) receiving dividends and (2) the retention of earnings resulting in capital gains.

   b. With irrelevance, the required rate of return of the investor does not change in response to changes in dividend payout.

2. The Modigliani and Miller argument

   a. Given the investment decision of the firm, the dividend-payout ratio is a mere detail, having no effect upon the wealth of shareholders.

   b. The value of the firm is determined solely by the earning power of the firm's assets and not by the division of earnings between dividends and retained earnings.

   c. Bases of the argument

      (1) The value of a stock today (P_0) is the present value of dividends to be received in the forthcoming period (D_1) plus the present value of the price to be received at year end (P_1), with both being discounted at the investors' required rate of return (ρ). This relationship may be represented as follows:

$$P_0 = \frac{D_1 + P_1}{1 + \rho} \tag{1}$$

Accordingly, solving for the price at the end of the forthcoming period (P_1) from equation (1) yields

$$P_1 = (1 + \rho)P_0 - D_1 \tag{2}$$

As may be noted in equation (2), the price after the

dividend (P_1) is exactly reduced by the amount of the dividend, which provides no incremental benefit to investors.

(2) Since dividends have no way of affecting the value of the stockholder (i.e., $P_0 = P_1 + D_1$), investment opportunities may be financed by either:

(a) Retention of earnings.

(b) Paying dividends and in turn issuing stock.

(3) If a new stock issue is required, the size of the issue would equal the common portion of the investment not financed by internally generated funds. This amount would be equal to the number of new shares to be issued (m) times the price per share after the dividend (P_1), determined as follows:

$$mP_1 \quad = \quad I \quad - \quad (X - nD_1)$$

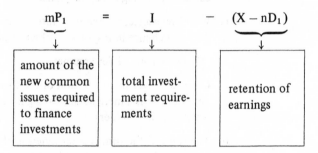

| amount of the new common issues required to finance investments | total invest- ment require- ments | retention of earnings |

where   m = number of new shares to be issued
$\quad\quad P_1$ = price after dividend
$\quad\quad$ I = corporate investment requirements
$\quad\quad$ X = total net profits of the company
$\quad\quad$ n = number of shares outstanding prior to the new issue
$\quad\quad D_1$ = dividend per share

d. The underlying Modigliani and Miller assumptions are

(1) Perfect capital market, which requires rational investors, costless information, infinitely devisible securities, no transaction cost, and small investors.

(2) No flotation cost.

(3) No tax.

(4) No change in investment policy.

        (5) Perfect certainty by the investor as to future investment opportunities and profits of the firm; however, this assumption is later removed.

    e. In summary, the crux of the Modigliani and Miller argument is that the effect of dividend payments on shareholders' wealth is exactly offset by other means of financing.

D. Argument for relevance

    1. The payment of current dividends resolves uncertainty in the minds of investors; therefore, an investor may not be indifferent between dividends and capital gains.

    2. Dividends may have an impact on share price as a result of the favorable connotations associated with the payment of dividends.

    3. To issue a block of stock sufficiently large to finance investments, the shares may have to be sold at a discount, which is not recognized by Modigliani and Miller.

E. Removal of other assumptions

    1. Tax effect: An important tax effect is the beneficial capital-gains tax rate; thus, a preference for capital gains through the retention of earnings may develop.

    2. Flotation costs: The recognition of flotation costs incurred in the issuance of securities by a firm favors financing investments by the retention of earnings.

    3. Transaction costs and divisibility of securities

        a. If the dividend payment is not sufficient to satisfy the shareholder's current desire for income, a sale of stock may be required, resulting in transaction costs to the investor.

        b. The smallest integer in the sale of stock for current income, that being one share, may result in "lumpiness," possibly acting as a deterrent to the sale of stock in lieu of dividends.

    4. Certain institutional investors are restricted in their investment policies to firms having a history of continuous dividends.

F. Investment opportunities and dividend policy: In theory, the optimal dividend policy of the firm should be determined in light of the firm's investment opportunities and any preference the investors have for dividends as opposed to capital gains.

II. Dividend stability: Investors may assign a premium in value to firms maintaining a stable dividend policy over a period of time.

A. Reasons for the valuation of stability:

   1. Stable dividends may provide informational content to the investors.

   2. Investors who desire a specific periodic income will prefer a company with stable dividends.

   3. Many institutional investors are only allowed to invest in stocks that have an uninterrupted pattern of dividends.

B. Target-payout ratios: A number of companies may follow the policy of a target dividend-payout ratio.

   1. Lintner contends that dividends are adjusted to changes in earnings, but only with a lag.

   2. Companies tend to be strongly averse to reducing the absolute amount of the cash dividend.

C. Regular and extra dividends: By declaring a year-end extra dividend, the company attempts to prevent investors from considering the year-end extra as representing an increase in the established dividend rate.

III. Additional factors: A number of other practical considerations influence a company in its dividend policy.

A. Liquidity: The greater the cash position and overall liquidity of a company, the greater its ability to pay a dividend.

B. Ability to borrow: The greater the ability of a firm to borrow, the greater its flexibility and the greater its ability to pay a cash dividend.

C. Control: The controlling shareholders may prefer to retain earnings rather than issue stock, which might pose a threat to control; however, companies in danger of being acquired may establish a a high dividend payout in order to please stockholders.

D. Nature of stockholders: If stockholders are in high tax brackets and prefer capital gains to current income, the firm may establish a low dividend payout.

E. Timing of investment opportunities: A company having sporadic investment opportunities may be justified in retaining earnings to meet these needs.

F. Restrictions in bond indenture of loan agreement: The protective covenants in a bond indenture or loan agreement often include a restriction on the payment of dividends.

IV. Procedural aspects of dividend payments

    A. A shareholder, as of the *date of record* which is specified by the board of directors, is entitled to the dividend being declared.

    B. After the date of record, the stock is said to trade *ex-dividend,* that is, being without the right to receive the declared dividend.

    C. For listed stocks, the ex-dividend date is 4 business days before the date of record.

    D. Theoretically, the market price of a stock should decline by the amount of the dividend when the stock goes ex-dividend; however, other influences in the market may alter this principle.

    E. Once a dividend is declared, stockholders become creditors of the corporation.

V. Stock dividends and stock splits

    A. The only significant difference between a stock dividend and a stock split comes from the accounting treatment and is not a function of any economic differences.

    B. Stock dividends

        1. A stock dividend is the payment of additional shares to stockholders.

        2. The additional shares represent no more than a recapitalization of the company.

        3. A stockholder's proportional ownership remains unchanged.

        4. The accounting treatment results in a reduction in retained earnings, countered by increases in the capital stock and capital surplus accounts.

        5. Earnings per share are proportionably reduced.

        6. Value to the investor

            a. Conceptually, the stockholder receives nothing, since the proportioned ownership in the company and the total value of holdings would remain unchanged.

            b. In practice, the stock dividend may be of merit as a result of the following:

                (1) The cash dividend per share may not be reduced proportionally.

                (2) The stock dividend may have a favorably psychological effect on the stockholders.

          (3) The stock dividend conveys favorable informational content, such as management expecting earnings to grow at a rate sufficient to offset the immediate dilution in earnings per share.

    7. Advantages to the company:

       a. Conserves cash for investment needs.

       b. Alleviates cash-flow problems for a company experiencing financial difficulties.

       c. Contributes to maintaining the market price of the stock within a desired trading range.

    8. Disadvantages to the company:

       a. More costly to administer than cash dividends.

       b. Potentially distorts the firm's earnings per share.

  C. Stock splits

    1. The number of shares are increased, with a proportional reduction in the par value of the stock.

    2. The common stock, capital surplus, and retained earnings remain unchanged.

    3. The stock split may provide informational content but does not increase a shareholder's proportionate interest.

  D. A reverse split occurs when a company reduces the number of shares outstanding.

VI. Repurchase of stock

  A. Reasons for repurchasing:

    1. Have shares available for stock options.

    2. Have shares available for the acquisition of other companies.

    3. The retirement of stock.

  B. Repurchasing as a dividend decision

    1. Excess cash resulting from insufficient profitable investment opportunities may be distributed either by repurchasing stock or by paying the funds out in increased dividends.

    2. In the absence of personal income taxes and transaction costs, the two distribution alternatives should be equally appealing to stockholders.

      a. If a dividend is paid, the stockholder is benefited by the amount of the dividend.

      b. If a repurchase plan is instigated, the price per share should increase by the same amount as would be paid in dividends.

    3. As a result of the differential tax rate on dividends and capital gains, the repurchase of stock may offer a significant tax advantage over the payment of dividends.

    4. The Internal Revenue Service may impose a penalty if it deems a steady program of repurchases as being performed in lieu of paying dividends.

  C. Investment or financing decision?

    1. The repurchase of stock should not be considered to be an investment decision.

    2. By issuing debt and in turn repurchasing stock, a firm may immediately change its debt/equity ratio, thereby altering the firm's financial mix, which represents a financing decision.

  D. Method of repurchase

    1. Two common methods of repurchase include the following:

      a. Tender offer: The company makes a formal offer to the existing shareholders to purchase a certain number of shares, typically at a set price above the current market price.

      b. Purchase of stock in the market place: The company makes open-market purchases through a brokerage house in the same manner as does any other investor.

    2. The corporate management should take considerable care in providing stockholders with full disclosure during a repurchase.

STUDY PROBLEMS

1. (a) Using Walter's model, if the return on investment is 8%, the market capitalization rate is 7%, and earnings per share equals $2.00, what amount of dividends per share would maximize the price of the stock? What will be the maximum price?

(b) How would your answer change if the return on investment is 6%, the market capitalization rate is 8% and the earnings per share is $3?

Solution:

(a) If dividends per share is $0, price would be $32.65.

(b) If dividends per share is $3, price is maximized at $37.50.

2. The Griggs Corporation has the following capital structure:

Common stock ($10 par, 100,000 shares)	$ 1,000,000
Capital surplus	4,000,000
Retained earnings	5,000,000
	$10,000,000

(a) Provide the journal entries to record a 10% stock dividend if the current market price is $20 per share.

(b) Indicate how the capital accounts would appear subsequent to a 4-for-1 split.

Solution:

(a) Retained earnings ($20 × 10,000) $200,000
        Common stock ($10 × 10,000) $100,000
        Capital surplus   100,000

(b) Common Stock ($2.50 par, 400,000 shares) $1,000,000
        Capital surplus   4,000,000
        Retained earnings   5,000,000

3. The Smith Company operates within an industry that has been relatively stable for some time. The market value of its stock has not appreciated significantly for a number of years. At the present time, management is planning an expansion program and has decided to issue common stock to meet its financing needs. The table below lists relevant earnings, dividends, and market price data. What dividend-policy recommendations would you recommend to the company? Why?

	1974	*1975*	*1976*	*1977 (Projected)*
Dividends per share	$2.00	$2.10	$2.20	?
Earnings per share	$4.00	$4.25	$4.42	$4.60
Payout ratio	50%	49%	50%	?
Price/earnings ratio	18	19	18	18
Average market price	$72.00	$80.75	$79.56	$82.80

Solution:

Financing the expansion program via common stock seems to be a likely move. The firm should continue to maintain approximately the same retention rate, in that a discontinuous or irregular dividend pattern (should the firm decide to retain the dividends in order to finance the expansion) could adversely affect the market price of the stock. This implication might prove particularly true if the stockholders of Smith are more dividend- than growth-oriented, which seems to be the case from the facts of the problem. The firm should maintain about a 50% payout, which would result in dividends per share of $2.30 being paid.

4. Johnson Motors has decided to pay a $2 dividend to its stockholders at the end of the current year. It has 500,000 shares outstanding selling at $50 per share. The company is in a risk class such that a 15% capitalization rate is applicable. Based upon Modigliani and Miller's model, and assuming no taxes:

(a) What would be the value of its stock at the end of the year if a dividend is paid? What if a dividend is not paid?

(b) Assuming that the firm pays the dividend, with a net income of $5,000,000, and makes investments of $8,000,000 during the year, how many new shares must be issued?

Solution:

(a) According to Modigliani and Miller:

$$P_0 = \frac{1}{1+p}(D_1 + P_1)$$

where P_0 = market price of the stock at the beginning of the year
P_1 = market price of the stock at the end of the year
p = capitalization rate
D_1 = dividend per share

Rearranging the equation,

$$P_1 = P_0(1+p) - D_1$$

Thus, if a dividend is not paid ($D_1 = 0$), we have

$$P_1 = \$50(1.15) - 0$$
$$= \$57.50$$

However, if the dividend is paid ($D_1 = \$2$), we have

$$P_1 = \$50(1.15) - \$2$$
$$= \$55.50$$

(b) According to Modigliani and Miller,

$$mP_1 = I - (X - nD_1)$$

where m = number of new shares of stock sold at time 1 at a price of P_1

n = number of shares of record at time 0

I = total new investments during the period

X = total net profit of the firm for the period

Thus, we have

$$\$55.50(m) = \$8,000,000 - [\$5,000,000 - (500,000)(\$2)]$$
$$\$55.50(m) = \$8,000,000 - \$4,000,000$$
$$m = \frac{4,000,000}{\$55.50}$$
$$= 72,072.07 \text{ shares}$$

5. Peoria Limited has a policy of treating dividends as a passive residual. Management has forecasted that net income for the upcoming year will be $500,000. The firm has only equity in its capital structure and its cost-of-equity capital is 12%. However, if new common stock were issued, flotation costs will raise this cost to 14%. If the firm treats the 12% cost as the opportunity cost of retained earnings:

(a) (1) How much in dividends should be paid if the company has $400,000 in projects whose expected returns exceed 12%? (2) How much should be paid out if it has investment projects of $500,000 which yield greater than 12%?

(b) How much in dividends should be paid if it has $1,000,000 in projects whose expected return exceeds 14%?

Solution:

(a) (1) According to Modigliani and Miller, the firm should pay dividends only when it has exhausted its investments whose returns exceed the firm's cost of capital. Thus, the firm should pay $100,000 in dividends. (2) Using the same rationale as in (1), the firm should use all of the $500,000 for investing in the projects and not pay any dividends.

(b) Modigliani and Miller would contend that under these circumstances, the firm should raise an additional $500,000 in common stock and invest the entire $1,000,000 in the investment projects.

6. The *San Angelo Chronicle,* a successful newspaper, earned $1,000,000 after taxes this year. The 500,000 shares outstanding recently traded for $28 per share. One dollar of this value is thought to be the result of investor anticipation of a cash dividend. As chairman of the board of directors, you are considering a recommendation to repurchase the company's stock by means of a tender offer at $28 per share, in lieu of the cash dividend.

(a) How many shares could the firm repurchase?

(b) Without considering the tax consequences, which alternative should be selected?

(c) Considering taxes, which alternative should be selected?

> **Solution:**
>
> **(a)** The number of shares that could be repurchased can be found by (1) multiplying the expected dividend times the number of shares outstanding; and (2) dividing this amount by the market price of the stock. In other words,
>
> $$\text{number of shares that could be repurchased} = \frac{(\$1)(500,000)}{\$28}$$
> $$= 17.857 \text{ shares}$$
>
> **(b)** If taxes are ignored, the correct decision would be a function of (1) the informational content of the dividends; and (2) the ability and ease of the investor in substituting a sale of stock in place of the anticipated dividends.
>
> **(c)** The presence of taxes favors a repurchase decision; however, the tax benefit may or may not offset any preference investors have for current dividends.

7. The two firms Richardson Chemicals and Sandstone Products are identical in terms of (1) being in the same industry, (2) producing the same products, (3) being subject to the same risks, and (4) even having equivalent earnings per share. Only one difference exists. Richardson Chemicals has paid a constant cash dividend, whereas Sandstone Products has followed a constant percentage payout ratio of 40%. The financial vice-president of Sandstone Products is concerned by the generally lower price for Sandstone's stock. This lower price has resulted in spite of Sandstone's dividend being substantially larger than Richardson's in certain years. Given the data below:

	Richardson Chemicals				Sandstone Products		
Year	EPS	Dividend	Market Price		EPS	Dividend	Market Price
1973	$2.50	$0.75	$8½		$2.50	$1.00	$5¾
1974	−0.25	0.75	8¼		−0.25	0	5½
1975	3.00	0.75	8¾		3.00	1.20	10
1976	2.00	0.75	8½		2.00	0.80	9½

(a) What might account for the differences in the market prices of the two companies?

(b) What might be done by both companies to enhance the market prices of their respective shares?

174

Solution:

(a) The dissimilarity between market prices might be a function of the different dividend policies, with a lower capitalization rate, and, accordingly, a higher price being assigned to Richardson as a result of the stable dividend stream.

(b) From the data presented, it appears that neither company would appear to be growth-oriented. If both of the firms are valued in terms of their dividend yield, which seems to be the case, higher dividend payouts might produce higher prices.

8. The Monsanto Corporation's capital structure on June 30, 1976, is as follows:

Common stock ($2 par, 5,000,000 shares outstanding)	$10,000,000
Capital surplus	700,000
Retained earnings	5,300,000
Net worth	$16,000,000

The firm's 1976 earnings after taxes was $1,000,000, of which the company paid out 25% in cash dividends. Furthermore, the price of the firm's common stock, as of the date of the capital structure, was $6.

(a) If the firm declared a 10% stock dividend on June 30, 1976, how would the capital structure appear?

(b) If the firm declared a 30% stock dividend as opposed to the 10% dividend, what would be the end result upon the capital structure? (*Hint:* Stock dividends in excess of 25% should be calculated on the basis of book value less retained earnings, instead of market value.)

(c) What would be the price of the stock after each of the foregoing stock dividends?

(d) Assuming the 10% stock dividend, what would be the earnings per share and the dividends per share in 1976? What would be the earnings per share and the dividends per share for 1976 if a 30% stock dividend is issued?

Solution:

(a)   10% X 5,000,000 shares = 500,000 shares

Increase in the common stock account:

$2 X 500,000 shares = $1,000,000

Increase in the capital-surplus account:

$4 X 500,000 shares = $2,000,000

Result:

Common stock (5,500,000 shares)	$11,000,000
Capital surplus	2,700,000
Retained earnings	2,300,000
Net worth	$16,000,000

(b) Calculating the 30% stock dividend on the basis of book value:

$$30\% \times 5,000,000 \text{ shares} = 1,500,000 \text{ shares}$$

Amount transferred to common stock:

$10,000,000 × 30%	$ 3,000,000

Amount transferred to capital surplus:

$700,000 × 30%	210,000

Amount transferred from retained earnings:	$ 3,210,000

Common stock (6,500,000 shares)	$13,000,000
Excess over par	910,000
Retained earnings	2,090,000
Net worth	$16,000,000

(c) In theory, the *total* market value of the stock should remain the same after the payment of the stock dividend. The market value per share will go down; however, more shares are outstanding.

Price after 10% stock dividend:

$$\$6 \left(1 - \frac{1.00}{1.10} \right) = \$0.55$$

Price = $6.00 − $0.55 = $ 5.45 per share

Price after 30% stock dividend:

$$\$6 \left(1 - \frac{1.00}{1.30} \right) = \$1.38$$

Price = $6.00 − $1.38 = $4.62 per share

(d) Earnings per share after a 10% stock dividend:

$$\frac{\$1,000,000}{5,500,000} = \$0.18$$

Dividends per share after a 10% stock dividend:

$$\frac{\$250,000}{5,500,000} = \$0.045$$

Earnings per share after a 30% stock dividend:

$$\frac{\$1,000,000}{6,500,000} = \$0.15$$

Dividends per share after a 30% stock dividend:

$$\frac{\$250,000}{6,500,000} = \$0.0385$$

SELF-TESTS

True-False

_____ 1. If dividend policy is treated as a passive residual, dividends are paid once a firm has exhausted its investment opportunities.

_____ 2. The firm should invest retained earnings as long as the required rate of return exceeds the expected rate of return from the investment.

_____ 3. The greater the ability of a firm to borrow, the less its ability to pay a cash dividend.

_____ 4. If a firm has sporadic investment opportunities, it might be expected to pay out more dividends.

_____ 5. A stock dividend results in a recapitalization of retained earnings.

_____ 6. In a stock split, the only accounting change is the shifting of amounts from retained earnings to the common stock account.

_____ 7. In theory, the decision to repurchase or pay dividends should leave the shareholder's net worth unchanged.

_____ 8. Since a repurchase decision involves the firm investing in its own stock, it is often considered to be an investment decision.

_____ 9. The crux of Modigliani and Miller's position concerning the relevance of dividends is that the effect of dividend payments on shareholder wealth is offset exactly by other means of financing.

_____ 10. The introduction of flotation costs to Modigliani and Miller's argument favors the *retention* of earnings in the firm.

Multiple Choice

1. Which of the following is *not* an assumption of Modigliani and Miller in their argument for dividend irrelevancy?
   a. No taxes.
   b. Efficient capital markets.
   c. No flotation costs.
   d. Costless information.

2. Which of the following is an argument for the relevance of dividends?
   a. Informational content.
   b. Resolution of uncertainty.
   c. Preference for current income.
   d. Both of the above.
   e. Neither of the above.

3. Which of the following is *not* an advantage of stock dividends?
   a. Helps to conserve cash.
   b. Tends to increase the market price.
   c. Keeps the price of the stock within a desired trading range.

4. When we remove the assumption of no taxes from Modigliani and Miller's argument:
   a. There is a preference for retention of earnings.
   b. There is a preference for paying out dividends.
   c. The preference depends upon the individual investor's investment needs.

5. Which of the following does not represent a "market imperfection"?
   a. Taxes.
   b. Flotation costs.
   c. Legal restrictions.
   d. All of the above are "market imperfections."

6. Which of the following is not a possible reason for an investor valuing the stability of dividend payments?
   a. Legal considerations.
   b. Informational content of dividends.
   c. Certainty of taxes.
   d. Desire for current income.

7. Which of the following are factors which influence the dividend policy a company undertakes?
   a. The liquidity of the firm.
   b. Capital structure.
   c. The ability to borrow.
   d. a and c.
   e. a and b.

8. Certain legal restrictions prohibit a firm from paying dividends. These restrictions would include:
   a. Capital restriction.
   b. Insolvency.
   c. Excess accumulation of cash.
   d. None of the above.
   e. All of the above.

Money and Capital Markets

20

Orientation: This chapter centers upon the money and capital markets from which a company raises external funds. The underlying purpose of financial markets is discussed, and the flow of funds through various sectors of the economy is clarified. Several factors that affect security yields are also examined.

I. Classification of different financial markets

    A. A popular criteria used by businessmen, the financial press, and academicians to distinguish financial markets does so on the basis of the final maturity of the different securities traded in those markets.

    B. The *money markets* deal in securities that are (1) short-term, (2) highly marketable, and (3) very safe from the investor's viewpoint. These are invariably debt instruments. Prominent examples include (1) treasury bills, (2) commercial paper, (3) bankers' acceptances and negotiable certificates of deposit.

    C. *Capital markets* involve trading in securities with longer maturity periods than those exchanged in the money markets. Conventionally, capital market instruments have maturities greater than one year and also include equity-type financial assets.

II. The purpose of financial markets

    A. From a fundamental standpoint, financial assets exist in a given economy because for some chosen period of time, economic units save and invest in *real* assets at different rates.

B.   When an economic unit, such as a corporation, desires to invest in real assets (e.g., in plant and equipment) to a greater degree than it has saved (through retentions), it might try to issue (market) a financial asset and finance the excess by borrowing or issuing equity securities. Such behavior would create a financial asset.

C.   The purpose of having a system of financial markets in an economy is to allocate savings *efficiently* to the ultimate users of the savings.

   1.   If capital formation was accomplished by the very economic units that saved, financial markets would be unnecessary.

   2.   In developed economies, however, nonfinancial corporations typically are most responsible for capital formation and are savings-deficit units. Households are savings-surplus units (in the aggregate). Thus, financial markets channel the savings from the surplus units to the deficit units, and the wealth of the economy increases as a result of this process.

D.   The channeling of savings from surplus to deficit units can be done at a lower cost to the economy and with greater convenience if *financial intermediaries* are present.

   1.   Financial intermediaries are institutions such as (a) commercial banks, (b) savings banks, (c) savings and loan associations, (d) life insurance companies, (e) pension funds, and (f) profit-sharing funds.

   2.   Intermediaries step between the ultimate borrower and lender by issuing their own indirect securities, which, in effect, transform the direct claims issued by deficit economic units into funds more attractive to the bulk of savings-surplus units.

      a.   As an example, consider a savings and loan association. For the most part, savings and loan associations purchase the mortgages issued by deficit units wanting to finance homes, buildings, or real estate. These mortgages are the primary (or direct) security issued by the deficit unit. The savings and loan association then issues savings accounts or certificates of deposit. These are known as indirect securities.

   3.   The attractiveness of funds to ultimate savers is increased by the wide variety of services and economies provided by financial intermediaries. These include:

      a.   Economies of scale that can be passed on to both borrower and lender in the form of lower operations costs. Brokerage costs provide one example.

b. The financial capacity to pool savings to purchase primary (direct) securities of varying sizes.

c. The ability and capacity to diversify risk for the individual saver.

d. The ability to transform the maturity of a direct security into indirect securities of different maturities.

e. The provision of investment expertise.

E. In general, our economy can be thought of as being comprised of *four main sectors:* (1) households, (2) nonfinancial business firms, (3) governments, and (4) financial institutions.

1. The flow of savings between these sectors can be studied through flow of funds data presented in matrix form in the *Federal Reserve Bulletin.*

2. The tabulation that follows is a hypothetical matrix for a closed economy comprising four key sectors. In effect, it consists of a source and use of funds statement for each sector. These funds-flow statements are then combined to monitor the flow of funds throughout the entire economy.

3. In this example notice that the household sector is the major savings-surplus sector. Its savings (change in net worth during the given time period) of $116 exceeded its real asset investment of $94 by $22. This excess was accumulated by the household sector investing in financial assets (including money) to an extent equal to $46, whereas financial liabilities were only increased by $24.

4. The business sector was the major savings-deficit sector to an extent of $21 ($110 − $89). This deficit was financed by a net increase in financial liabilities outstanding of the same amount [i.e., $21 ($45 − $24)].

5. The interaction determining funds transfer can be traced in a similar manner by study of all the sectors whose data are contained in the matrix.

6. By looking at the last column ("All Sectors") it can be seen that for the entire economy there is no such thing as saving through financial asset accumulation. One unit's financial asset must be offset by another unit's financial liability.

Matrix of Flow of Funds of Entire Economy 197X   (billions of dollars)

	Households		Business Firms		Financial Institutions		Governments		All Sectors	
	U	S	U	S	U	S	U	S	U	S
Net worth (savings)		116		89		5		−4		206
Real assets (investment)	94		110		2		—		206	
Money	3		3			7	1		7	7
Other financial assets	43		21		69	59	19		152	
Financial liabilities		24		45				24		152
	140	140	134	134	71	71	20	20	365	365

For the economy, then, saving amounts to the net addition to the stock of real assets.

III. Channels of funds flows to and from business firms

    A.   Business firms in the aggregate comprise a savings-deficit sector.

        1. Financing the excess of business firms' investment in real assets over savings are households (a direct flow) and financial institutions (an indirect flow).

        2. Consistently, over time, the major use of funds by business firms is for purchases of plant and equipment.

        3. Internal funds sources (retained earnings and depreciation allowances) account for about three-fifths of the total sources of funds.

        4. Of the external funds sources, net new bond and stock issues were the most important categories over the 1969-1974 period. Mortgage debt and bank loans were next in importance.

    B.   Financial intermediaries are crucial to the channeling of funds to business firms. They invest in corporate stocks and bonds, of course, but are also major participants in mortgage financing and the granting of bank credit.

        1. We recall that the indirect claims issued by intermediaries are mostly held by individuals. Thus, individuals are the ultimate source of net financing for business firms.

IV. Allocation of funds through yields

    A.   In a free economy the allocation of savings occurs primarily on the basis of *price*. The price of savings is affected by both *expected return* and *risk*.

    B.   Characteristics possessed by financing instruments differ. As a result, the risk to the investor and his required return will vary across the spectrum of securities. Some of these differing characteristics will now be identified.

        1. *Default risk* refers to violation of principal and/or interest payments, as previously agreed to in the loan contract (say, the bond indenture), on the part of the borrowing economic unit. A higher default risk results in a higher return premium demanded by potential investors. Investors can judge default risk on bonds and commercial paper indirectly by inspection of published bond and paper ratings.

2. *Marketability* refers to the conversion of a security into cash. The price actually realized and the time necessary to liquidate the security are the two facets of marketability.

3. The relationship between yield and *maturity* of securities, which differ only with respect to their maturity periods, is known as the term structure of interest rates. Over time there is an observed tendency for longer-term securities to offer greater yields than shorter-term instruments. For any given time period, however, this tendency can be violated.

4. Different securities are affected differently by *tax regulations.* Of the various *taxability* features, the income tax is the most important. Only the interest income from state and local government securities is tax exempt at the federal level. Yields also differ on securities because of another type of tax consideration. Interest income is taxed as ordinary income, whereas securities held for over 6 months that result in a capital gain are taxed at a more favorable capital gains tax rate.

5. These differences in default risk, marketability, maturity, and taxability cause the cost of funds to corporations to vary. Typically short-term yields (say, on commercial paper) fluctuate more than do long-term yields (say, on bonds) of similar default risk. Short-run demand and supply situations affect short-term rates more so than long-term rates; the latter are more susceptible to alterations in long-run expectations.

6. The most important factors affecting interest-rate expectations are economic conditions, monetary policy, and fiscal policy.

7. *Bond yields versus stock yields* are not directly comparable. The actual return on holding a share of common stock is comprised of two components: the dividend yield, and the capital gain or loss that occurs at the end of the holding period. As only the dividend yield is directly observable, bond and stock yields cannot be compared.

SELF-TESTS

True-False

_____ 1. Between 1900 and 1950 bond yields were consistently greater than stock yields.

_____ 2. The return on a negotiable certificate of deposit is tax-exempt at the federal level of government.

_____ 3. Generally, the yield-maturity relationship is upward-sloping when interest rates are expected to rise.

_____ 4. Bond ratings are regularly published by the SEC.

_____ 5. The marketability of a financial asset has one key dimension: the length of time necessary to convert it into cash.

_____ 6. Savings are allocated not only on the basis of expected return but on the basis of risk as well.

_____ 7. The practice of capital rationing by firms does not affect the actual allocation of any savings.

_____ 8. The principal means of financing asset growth by business firms is through their internal generation of funds.

_____ 9. In recent years (1969-1974) individuals have been net purchasers of corporate stocks.

_____ 10. Corporate equities are actively traded in the U.S. money markets.

Multiple Choice

1. The purpose of financial markets is to:
   a. Raise stock prices.
   b. Lower bond yields.
   c. Allocate savings efficiently.
   d. All of the above.

2. The maturity boundary dividing the U.S. money and capital markets is:
   a. Set by the Federal Reserve Board.
   b. Periodically reviewed and altered by the SEC.
   c. Determined by the U.S. Treasury.
   d. An arbitrary classification system.

3. Which of the following is *not* an example of a financial intermediary?
   a. A commercial bank.
   b. A mutual fund.
   c. A savings and loan association.
   d. A manufacturer of computers.

4. Which of the following holds (owns) the greatest amount (dollars) of corporate bonds?
   a. Commercial banks.
   b. Fire and casualty insurance companies.
   c. Open-end mutual funds.
   d. Life insurance companies.

5. Which of the following financial institutions holds the greatest amount of corporate stocks?

    a. Fire and casualty insurance companies.
    b. Open-end mutual funds.
    c. Private noninsured pension funds.
    d. Life insurance companies.

External Financing of Long-Term Needs

Orientation: This chapter examines many of the critical aspects concerned with the raising of long-term funds in the capital markets. The various services provided by investment bankers are explored, public offerings of security issues are distinguished from private placements, and the regulation of the new-issues market is discussed.

I. Offerings through investment bankers

    A. Investment bankers perform many functions for corporations that utilize their services. The most important function of the investment banker is to purchase an issue of securities from the company and then resell this issue to ultimate investors.

        1. This function is often referred to as the *underwriting function.*

        2. For performing this underwriting function, the investment banker receives the difference between the price paid for a specific security and the resale price to the investing public. This difference in prices is called the *spread.*

    B. The investment banker is also a specialist in the distribution or marketing of securities.

        1. As corporations typically raise funds in the capital markets on an occasional basis, it would be inefficient for them to attempt to distribute their new issues themselves.

2. The investment banker, however, will have the sales organization necessary for effective distribution of these securities.

C. It is necessary to distinguish competitive bidding from negotiated offerings.

    1. When securities are marketed by way of the *competitive bid method,* the issuing company solicits bids from several investment bankers.

    2. The bids usually do not come from a single investment banker but from a *syndicate* comprised of several houses.

        a. A syndicate is formed so that one investment banker does not have to assume all of the underwriting risk. Also, a syndicate provides for a much larger sales organization.

        b. Underwriting syndicates may be either *divided* or *undivided.* When the syndicate provides for divided accounts, the member is liable only for selling those securities allotted to the particular house. With undivided accounts, the syndicate member is liable for his percentage participation in any unsold securities.

    3. The right to distribute the new offering will be awarded to the syndicate that bids the highest price per security.

    4. In the *negotiated offering* the firm raising funds in the capital markets selects its investment banker in advance of the price being set. The term *negotiated,* then, refers to the process that determines the amount the investment banking house and its syndicate will pay the issuing firm for the securities.

        a. The negotiated offering permits the firm to discuss with the investment banking house the critical features of the issue.

        b. Advocates of this procedure also feel that it permits the investment banker more time to locate investors for the issue.

    5. In most instances public utilities and railroads are mandated by legal regulations to issue securities on a competitive bid basis.

D. It is possible for an investment banker to participate in the distribution of securities and assume no underwriting risk. That is, he may sell the issue on a *best-efforts* basis.

    1. In this situation the investment banker sells what securities he can at an agreed-upon price.

    2. Unsold securities are returned to the issuing firm and are not the responsibility of the investment banker.

3. For small companies, because of their inherent riskiness, this may be the only method available to place securities in the hands of the investing public.

E. In some instances the investment banker will *make a market* in a security after it has been issued and sold to the public.

   1. This procedure dictates that the investment banking house maintain an investment position in the given security, say, a new common stock issue.

   2. The investment banker then buys and sells the stock at bid and ask prices that he quotes.

   3. This secondary market provides greater liquidity to investors and, thereby, increases the chances that the primary offering will be successful.

F. In addition to the underwriting and distribution (or selling) functions, the investment banker can perform the valuable service of providing sound advice to his client.

   1. The firm that makes infrequent trips to the capital market must lean heavily upon the expertise of its chosen investment banker.

   2. The elements of a successful security distribution include (a) timing of the issue, (b) its pricing, and (c) contract features. Few nonfinancial firms have the insights into these elements that the investment banker possesses. One problem with the competitive-bid type of offering is that the advising function to the client (issuing company) is for practical purposes eliminated.

G. Setting the price for a new security issue is a difficult task.

   1. Recall that in a negotiated offering the issuing firm and the investment banker jointly determine the price of the security.

      a. From the investment banker's viewpoint, a low price will increase the likelihood of a successful sale.

      b. The issuing firm, though, will desire a high price for obvious reasons, including the avoidance of earnings dilution in the case of new equity issues.

   2. Bond ratings provide one guide in the case of new debt issues.

   3. Recent and expected interest-rate movements must be assessed.

   4. Other factors that must be considered include (a) the prospective supply of new security issues, (b) expectations as to the direction the economy will take, and (c) forecasts of monetary and fiscal actions.

      5. In the case of new common stock issues, the principal pricing factor is the market price of the existing stock, provided that some is already outstanding.

  H. Often the investment banker or syndicate manager will try to stablize the price of the security being distributed.

      1. This is done by placing buy orders at a pegged price.

      2. Stabilization is attempted because it is thought that a volatile price behavior would lessen investor interest in the issue.

  I. Even though flotation costs are very important to firms selling securities, recent empirical evidence on this topic is lacking.

      1. A study covering the time period of 1963-1965 demonstrated that the larger the issue, the lower the cost of flotation as a percentage of gross proceeds. This occurs because certain costs of flotation are essentially "fixed" regardless of size.

      2. Flotation costs for common stock are greater than those for debt issues.

II. The rights offering

  A. An offering of securities to existing shareholders prior to selling all or part of the issue to the general public is called a *rights offering.*

  B. The firm's corporate charter may grant the *preemptive right* to the owners of its common stock.

      1. The preemptive right protects the existing shareholders' proportionate ownership in the firm.

      2. The details of the preemptive right differ across the 50 states. Most state statutes do offer that the preemptive right is granted unless the corporate charger specifically denies it.

  C. When a firm elects to sell new common stock by means of the privileged subscription method, each stockholder will receive in the mail one *right* for each share of stock owned.

      1. The specific terms of the offering will spell out the number of rights needed to buy one new share of stock, the subscription price of the stock, and the expiration date of the offering.

      2. The existing stockholder may exercise his rights and buy additional shares, sell his rights for cash, or simply do nothing.

  D. The market value of a right is determined by three major factors. These are (1) the current market price of the stock, (2) the subscription price of the new shares, and (3) the number of rights needed to buy one new share.

1. The theoretical market value of one right can be determined through use of the following relationship:

$$R_0 = \frac{P_0 - S}{N + 1}$$

where R_0 = market value of one right when the stock is selling rights-on

P_0 = market value of a share of stock selling rights-on

S = subscription price per share of stock

N = number of rights needed to buy one share of stock

2. When the stock is selling ex-rights, this relationship will provide the theoretical value of one right:

$$R_x = \frac{P_x - S}{N}$$

where R_x = market value of one right when the stock is selling ex-rights

P_x = market price of the stock when it sells ex-rights

3. These relationships will be illustrated through the use of problems at the end of the chapter.

4. Factors such as (a) transactions costs, (b) speculation, and (c) the irregular exercise and sale of rights over the subscription period will cause the actual value of a right to differ from its theoretical value as determined by the formulas above.

E. Note that the subscription price of the new shares of stock must be set below the current market price of the stock in order for the offering to be successful. No one would buy the new shares if the market price fell below the subscription price.

F. It is possible to ensure the success of the rights offering by having an investment banker or investment banking syndicate "stand by" to underwrite any unsold portion of the issue.

G. In a rights offering: (1) investors familiar with the firm are tapped for additional investment, which usually increases the chances of a successful sale; (2) the flotation costs are lower than with a public offering, because the effort is not underwritten; and (3) many stockholders are kept happy, as they feel they deserve the first opportunity to purchase new common shares. On the other side of the coin, however, a rights offering relative to a public offering

(1) results in a greater dilution in earnings per share, and (2) a narrowing of the distribution of share ownership.

III. Government regulation of security offerings

    A. Two major federal securities laws affect both firms and investment bankers concerned with issuing and trading securities.

        1. The Securities Act of 1933 focuses upon the sale of new securities and requires full disclosure of information to investors.

            a. It requires that most corporations selling securities to the public must register the issue with the SEC.

            b. Exemptions from registration do pertain in certain situations. For example, if the size of the offering is small enough to warrant the attention and time of the SEC (less than $500,000), it does not have to be registered. Also, if the issuing firm is already regulated by some other authority (as is the case with railroads), registration with the SEC is not required.

            c. If not exempted from registration, a detailed registration statement must be filed with the SEC and examined by that same agency.

            d. In addition to the registration statement, a copy of the prospectus must also be filed. The prospectus is simply a summary of the registration statement. This prospectus, which does not yet have the selling price of the security printed on it, is referred to as a "red herring." It is a "red herring" until approved by the SEC.

            e. If the information in the registration statement and the prospectus is satisfactory to the SEC, the firm can proceed to sell the new issue. If the information is not satisfactory, a *stop order* will be issued which prevents the immediate sale of the issue. Deficiencies will have to be corrected by the firm before it can sell the securities.

            f. The SEC does not pass on the investment quality or value of the issue being examined. It is concerned only with the presentation of complete and accurate information.

        2. The Securities Exchange Act of 1934, which established the SEC, centers upon trading in already existing securities. Thus, the secondary financial markets are also highly regulated.

    B. State laws also seek to prevent fraudulent sale of securities.

1. These regulations, known as "blue-sky" laws, are particularly critical when the issue is too small to be examined by the SEC.

2. A real difficulty here is the wide variation in effectiveness of these laws across the states. Many states are quite permissive, which allows shoddy promotion of some new issues to exist.

IV. Private placements

A. It is possible for a firm desiring to raise funds to bypass both the public and its existing shareholders and sell an issue to a small number of institutional investors. Such sales are referred to as *private placements* or *direct placements.*

B. The bulk of private placements involve debt issues. Occasionally a common stock issue will be privately placed.

C. In recent years about one-fourth of the external funds raised by corporations have been garnered through the private-placement method. This percentage, however, is volatile over time.

D. The private-placement method offers a great deal of *flexibility* to the firm raising cash.

1. A private placement usually does not have to be registered with the SEC. Obviously, this saves time and money, as a large number of documents do not have to be prepared.

2. Because the number of investors is small, the terms of the issue can be altered.

3. All of the borrowing does not have to take place at the same time. It can be spread over a period of time, unlike the raising of funds through a public issue.

E. Small and medium-sized firms that would be unable to float debt issues publicly can often place them privately.

F. While a private placement involves no underwriting expenses, an investment banking firm may still be involved as an agent or finder in locating the institutional investors who will purchase all or part of the issue.

G. Studies have shown that the *initial* costs of private placements are less than those of public offerings. *Interest* costs, though, generally are higher on the privately placed issue.

STUDY PROBLEMS

1. Ballinger Construction, Inc., a regional contracting firm, currently has 600,000 shares of common stock outstanding. The company will issue another 100,000 shares through a rights offering. The market price of the firm's common stock is $80 per share. The subscription price to the new issue has been set at $73 per share.

(a) Compute the number of rights necessary to buy one new share at the subscription price of $73.

(b) Compute the value of a right.

(c) What will be the theoretical value of one share of stock when it goes ex-rights?

(d) Prior to the rights being exercised but after the stock goes ex-rights, some adverse economic news startles the market and the price of Ballinger stock drops to $78 per share. Determine the price of one right under these conditions.

> **Solution:**
>
> **(a)** The ratio of old or existing common shares to the new shares that will be sold determines the number of rights needed to buy one new share: 600,000/100,000 = 6.
>
> **(b)** $R_0 = \dfrac{P_0 - S}{N + 1} = \dfrac{80 - 73}{6 + 1} = \dfrac{7}{7} = \$1$ (value of one right)
>
> **(c)** Theoretically, the value of the common stock will fall by the value of one right: $R_X = P_0 - R_0 = 80 - 1 = \$79$.
>
> **(d)** $R_X = \dfrac{P_X - S}{N} = \dfrac{78 - 73}{6} = \$0.833$

2. You own 6 shares of Ballinger Construction common stock (see Problem 1). Demonstrate that you will neither gain nor lose any monetary return if you exercise your rights and the stock sells at its theoretical value after the rights have been exercised.

> **Solution:**
>
> The value of 6 old shares at the current market price: 6(80) = $480
>
> The cost of exercising the rights is the subscription price   =   73
>
> The value of your 7 shares (what you could have received had you sold your old shares plus your out-of-pocket subscription price cost) $553

The average value of your 7 shares to you, then, is: $553/7 = $79 per share. Notice that this is the theoretical value of the stock when it goes ex-rights. This analysis, of course, ignores any transaction fees.

SELF-TESTS

True-False

_____ 1. Placing a security in the hands of the ultimate investor is known as the underwriting function of investment banking.

_____ 2. Automobile manufacturers are required by law to issue securities on a competitive bid basis.

_____ 3. Private placements typically do not have to be registered with the SEC.

_____ 4. The underwriting costs associated with private placements are higher than those associated with public offerings of new securities.

_____ 5. The term "red herring" refers to a security issue that was not completely sold by the investment banking syndicate.

_____ 6. With regard to underwriting commissions, the selling concession typically exceeds the gross underwriting profit.

_____ 7. Most investment banking syndicates involved in underwriting corporate securities provide for undivided accounts.

_____ 8. Flotation costs on common stock issues are relatively higher than those on bond issues.

_____ 9. The majority of the 50 states provide that a stockholder does have the preemptive right unless the corporate charter otherwise denies it.

_____ 10. Blue Sky Laws were designed by Congress at the urging of the SEC to regulate security issues of $350,000 or less.

Multiple Choice

1. What is it called when an investment banker agrees to sell only as many securities as he can at an established price?
   a. A bear market.
   b. A best efforts agreement.
   c. A demoralized market.
   d. A private placement.

2. Assume that a firm currently has common stock outstanding. The principal factor governing the negotiated price (with the firm's investment banker) of a new offering of shares is:
   a. The price of other common stock of similar companies.
   b. The firm's price/earnings ratio over the previous 12 months.
   c. The market price of the firm's existing common stock.
   d. The firm's debt/equity ratio.

3. In recent years, private placements have accounted for what proportion of total funds raised externally by corporations?
   a. 75%.
   b. 25%.
   c. 45%.
   d. 50%.

4. Which of the following is *not* an advantage of offering securities through the competitive-bid method (the offering firm's point of view):
   a. Increased competition through the bidding of several investment banking syndicates.
   b. The issue does not have to be registered with the SEC.
   c. A lessened advising function from the investment banking syndicate that ultimately wins the bid.
   d. None of the above.
   e. Both b and c.

5. The SEC was created by:
   a. The Securities Act of 1933.
   b. The Hunt Commission.
   c. The SEC special study.
   d. A concerned group of investment bankers and securities dealers.
   e. None of the above.

6. In a rights offering of common stock the subscription price is
   a. Set equal to the current market price of the stock.
   b. Set below the current market price of the stock.
   c. Set above the current market price of the stock.
   d. None of the above.

7. In calculating the value of one right when the stock is selling rights-on, the analyst needs to know the number of rights needed to buy one share of stock and:
   a. The length of the rights offering period.
   b. The transactions costs involved.
   c. The price/earnings ratio of the firm's stock.
   d. The subscription price per share to the stock issue.

Long-Term Debt

Orientation: In this chapter detailed variations of long-term debt financing are examined. Key terminology is introduced. Most of the major types of bond financing are described and their usefulness to the corporation discussed. An analysis dealing with the question of whether to refund an existing bond issue is presented.

I. Features of debt

    A. Certain terms are common to the practice of financing long-term needs through bond issues. Some of these key definitions are noted below.

        1. The *coupon rate* determines the fixed return on a long-term debt contract. A coupon rate of 9% on a $1,000-face-value bond indicates that the investor will receive $90 in interest receipts annually.

        2. Do not confuse the coupon rate with the *yield to maturity* on the bond. The yield to maturity is the discount rate that equates the present value of interest and principal payments with the current market price of the bond. From our discussions on capital-budgeting evaluation methods, it is clear that this discount rate is nothing more than the internal rate of return for this bond.

3. When a debt issue of over $1 million is offered to the public, a *trustee* must be designated by the issuing corporation to act on behalf of the bond investors. The formal agreement is actually between the issuing firm and the trustee who acts for the bondholders. The contract between the firm and the trustee is called the bond *indenture.*

   a. As the trustee is compensated by the corporation, a conflict of interest could easily result, so the obligations of the trustee are regulated by the *Trust Indenture Act of 1939.*

   b. This regulation is administered by the SEC.

   c. In brief, the trustee is to see that the terms of the indenture are actually carried out.

4. The indenture contains the terms of the bond issue and any restrictions placed upon the issuing firm. These restrictions are called *protective covenants.*

B. Two major methods of retiring bonds are accomplished through periodic repayment. These involve sinking-fund payments or serial bond issues.

   1. A bond which has a sinking-fund requirement detailed in its indenture provides for periodic payments to the trustee.

   2. The trustee will retire bonds (by using the sinking-fund payments) in two ways:

      a. The bonds can be purchased in the open market.

      b. Also, the bonds can be called for redemption at the *call price* denoted in the indenture.

      c. The trustee will use the method that will retire the greater volume (as measured by face value) of bonds.

   3. Sinking-fund payments can be either *fixed* or *variable.* Variable payments can be tied to some index of corporate performance (e.g., earnings). Then, if earnings are high in some years, the sinking-fund payment can be higher than if poor earnings are experienced.

   4. A *serial bond* issue actually consists of a number of different bond issues sold at the same time but with different maturity dates. In addition, the interest rates usually differ along with the maturity dates. Notice that this differs from a sinking-fund

issue. With a sinking-fund issue, all bonds within the issue mature on the same date.

II. Debt instruments

A. A *debenture* is an unsecured or general credit bond. Specific property is not pledged as collateral for these long-term promissory notes.

   1. The investor in a debenture obtains his protection from both the general credit-worthiness of the firm and the bond indenture.

   2. The indenture for this type of security will typically contain the *negative pledge clause.* This clause disallows the firm to pledge its assets to other creditors subsequent to the issuance of these particular securities.

B. *Subordinate debentures* have a lower claim on assets in the event of liquidation than do other senior debt holders.

   1. Because of the subordination to existing and future debt, senior bond holders can view these instruments as equity when evaluating the financial position of the firm.

   2. From the corporation's standpoint the use of subordinated debt provides for a tax-deductible expense (interest), whereas the issuance of preferred stock would not provide this benefit (preferred dividends being non-tax-deductible).

C. A mortgage bond is secured by a lien on specific assets of the firm.

   1. In the *mortgage,* preference in a specific asset is granted by the borrower to a class of creditors.

   2. In the event of default of a provision contained in the bond indenture, the trustee can seize the pledged property, sell it, and use the proceeds to settle the lender's claims.

   3. It is possible to sell more than one class of mortgage bonds using the same property as collateral. Thus, *first-mortgage* bonds and *second-mortgage* bonds could be sold pledging the same fixed asset. In the event of default, however, the holders of the first-mortgage bonds must be paid in full prior to any distribution of proceeds to the second-mortgage bondholders.

   4. A mortgage may be either *closed-end* or *open-end.*

      a. With a closed-end mortgage, additional bonds with equal rank against the same security may not be issued.

b. With an open-end mortgage, additional bonds under an existing lien may be issued.

5. Many mortgage issues have written into their indenture the *after-acquired property clause.* Under this clause all property subsequently acquired becomes subject to this given mortgage. This clause is often used to strengthen what would otherwise be a weak issue.

6. Investors still look to the basic earning power of the bond-issuing firm as the key test of credit-worthiness.

D. *Collateral trust bonds* are another form of secured, long-term financing.

1. This type of financing is secured by a pledge of stocks or bonds by the borrowing company to the trustee.

2. If default occurs, the securities are sold by the trustee and the proceeds used to pay the bondholders.

E. *Income bonds* represent a departure from the forms of debt financing previously discussed.

1. With these promissory notes, interest is paid to investors only when it is earned.

2. A cumulative feature may be written into the bond indenture but is usually limited to 3 years.

3. The income bonds are senior to any subordinate debt or equity claims. Unlike dividend payments, however, the interest paid on the income bond is tax-deductible.

4. Their main use is in corporate reorganizations.

F. *Equipment trust certificates,* which are actually a form of lease financing, are used extensively by both railroads and airlines to acquire needed equipment.

1. According to this method, a manufacturer builds the equipment to meet the firm's specifications. The equipment is then sold to a trustee.

2. The trustee sells equipment trust certificates to pay the manufacturer. The trustee then leases the equipment to the firm.

3. The lease payments are used by the trustee to pay a fixed return to investors in the certificates. The annual installments provide for retirement of the certificates well within the

economic life of the assets being leased. When the certificates are retired, title to the assets passes to the firm (railroad or airline).

G. *Project financing* refers to specific arrangements made to finance large, separate (i.e., individual) projects.

   1. Because the sums of money involved are so large, often a separate legal entity comprising several companies is created to finance the project.

   2. Energy-related projects provide recent examples of these arrangements. Their sheer size may necessitate financing schemes apart from the sponsoring firm's major line of business.

   3. When a consortium of firms is formed to spread the risk associated with a huge project, usually the sponsoring firms are liable for no more than their equity participations in the legal entity standing behind the proposal.

   4. Examples of these projects include (1) explorations for gas, oil, and coal supplies; (2) tankers; (3) port facilities; (4) refineries; (5) pipelines; (6) alumina plants; (7) fertilizer plants; and (8) nuclear plants.

   5. The actual arrangements may take many forms.

      a. Sometimes the sponsors will guarantee only that the project will be built; then after completion the lender or equipment lessor has no recourse against any sponsoring firm. This means that repayment to the lender must come from the earnings stream of the project.

      b. Another plan exists whereby a sponsor guarantees his share of the project's financing obligations. In this case the credit standing of the sponsoring firm, as well as the economic feasibility of the project, is important to a potential lender or lessor.

III. The call provision

   A. Most bond indentures allow the borrowing firm the right to buy back their bonds at a stated price prior to maturity. This is the *call provision.*

   B. Typically, the *call price* exceeds the par value of the bond, is begun at 1 year's interest rate above the par value, and decreases over time as the bond approaches maturity.

    C. Call provisions are of two types:

        1. Some bonds can be called immediately.

        2. Others cannot be called until a deferment period has expired. Conventionally, the deferment period is 5 years for utility bonds and 10 years for industrial bonds.

    D. The call provision offers the firm financing flexibility.

        1. Should interest rates decline, the outstanding bonds can be called and new bonds issued with the lower interest rate.

        2. If certain protective covenants prove burdensome to the company, the bonds can be called and (hopefully) new ones issued without the same covenants.

    E. From the issuing firm's viewpoint, the call privilege is not free.

        1. The yield on a callable bond will exceed that necessitated were the bond noncallable.

        2. When interest rates are high and expected to decline, the value of the call privilege can be considerable.

IV. Refunding a bond issue

    A. It is possible to analyze the profitability of *refunding a bond issue* prior to its maturity as a type of capital-budgeting decision.

    B. The decision carries with it an initial cash outlay, which is followed by interest savings in the future, if new bonds are marketed with a lower interest rate. A complete example will be given in the Study Problems.

    C. In the analysis of a refunding operation, most analysts favor discounting the projected savings *not* at the firm's cost of capital, but at the after-tax cost of borrowing on the new (refunding) bonds. This is because the cash benefits are known with certainty once the refunding bonds have been sold.

    D. Even if projected to be profitable, a refunding operation may be postponed if interest rates are expected to continue to decline.

STUDY PROBLEMS

1. This problem illustrates the major principles involved in the determination of whether an existing bond issue should be refunded. First the financial characteristics of the existing (old) bond issue are listed; then the financial data related to the proposed (new) issue are presented.

Bonds currently outstanding:

Principal amount outstanding: $20,000,000
Coupon rate: 7%
Years to maturity: 15
Unamortized bond discount: $300,000
Unamortized issue expense: $120,000
Call premium: 5%

Proposed issue of bonds:

Principal amount outstanding: $20,000,000
Coupon rate: 6%
Years to maturity: 15
Proceeds to the firm: $20,000,000
Issue expense: $100,000

The corporate income tax rate: 50%
Both issues will be outstanding simultaneously for a period of 30 days.

(a) Using the net-present-value method (on an after-tax basis), determine whether or not the firm should refund the old bond issue.

(b) What would be the internal rate of return on this proposed financing decision?

Solution:

(a) Calculation of net cash outflow

Cost of calling old bonds (1.05 × $20 million)		$21,000,000
Net proceeds of new bond issue		20,000,000
Difference		$ 1,000,000
Expenses:		
Issuing expense of new bonds	$ 100,000	
Interest expense overlap		
($1,400,000/12)	116,667	216,667
Gross cash outlay		$ 1,216,667
Less tax savings:		
Interest expense overlap	$ 116,667	
Call premium (0.05 × $20 million)	1,000,000	
Unamortized bond discount on old bond	300,000	
Unamortized issue expense on old bond	120,000	
Total	$1,536,667	
Tax savings (tax rate × above)		− 768,334
Net cash outflow		$ 448,333

Calculation of annual net cash outflow on old bonds:

Interest expense at 7%		$1,400,000
Less tax savings:		
Interest expense	$1,400,000	
Amortization of bond discount		
($300,000/15)	20,000	
Amortization of issuing costs		
($120,000/15)	8,000	
Total	$1,428,000	
Tax savings (tax rate × above)		− 714,000
Annual net cash outflow—old bonds		$ 686,000

Calculation of annual net cash outflow on new bonds:

Interest expense		$1,200,000
Less tax savings:		
Interest expense	$1,200,000	
Amortization of bond discount	0	
Amortization of issuing costs		
($100,000/15)	6,667	
Total	$1,206,667	
Tax savings (tax rate × above)		− 603,334
Annual net cash outflow—new bonds		$ 596,666

Difference between annual net cash outflows:

$$\$686,000 - \$596,666 = \underline{\$89,334}$$

Calculation of net present value of the refunding savings:

The proper discount rate to use in the refunding analysis is the after-tax cost of borrowing on the new bonds. In this example: $(6\%)(1 - 0.5) = 3\%$.

The present-value annuity factor for 3% and 15 years is 11.9379. This permits the present value of the cash savings to be computed as follows:

$89,334 (11.9379) =	$1,066,460
−net cash outflow	448,333
Net present value	$ 618,127

The positive net present value of $618,127 indicates that the refunding should be undertaken.

(b) Calculation of the internal rate of return:

$$\$448,333 = \$89,334 \times \text{(annuity factor)}$$

$$\frac{448,333}{89,334} = 5.019$$

The present-value annuity factor for 18% and 15 years is 5.0916. To the nearest whole percent, the internal rate of return of this refunding operation would be 18%.

SELF-TESTS

True-False

_____ 1. The call privilege on a bond issue will be mostly costly to the issuing firm when the general level of interest rates is low and is expected to rise.

_____ 2. The generally accepted discount rate to be used in the analysis of a bond-refunding operation is the after-tax cost of borrowing on the refunded bond.

_____ 3. The yield on a bond is calculated in the same manner as the average rate of return on an investment project.

_____ 4. The trustee, who represents the bondholders (investors), is compensated directly by the bondholders.

_____ 5. Mortgage bonds are typically regarded as common equity by security analysts, who evaluate the financial condition of a given corporation.

_____ 6. Variable sinking-fund payments are used to a much greater extent than fixed payments.

_____ 7. Collateral trust bonds are actually a form of lease financing used to a large degree by the railroad industry.

_____ 8. Most debentures have the "after-acquired property clause" written into their indentures.

_____ 9. The interest payments on income bonds are not tax-deductible to the borrowing corporation.

_____ 10. Some corporate bonds have no call deferment period.

Multiple Choice

1. What is the name for a bond secured by a lien on designated assets of the firm?
   a. Debenture.
   b. Serial bond.
   c. Bankers' acceptance.
   d. Mortgage bond.

2. The distinguishing feature(s) of project financing as opposed to other forms of financing is (are):
   a. Size and complexity of the project.
   b. Location of the project in a foreign country.

    c. Tax considerations to the investor.

    d. Environmental considerations.

    e. The Trust Indenture Act of 1939.

3. Bonds that mature periodically until the final maturity date are:
    a. Sinking fund bonds.
    b. Debentures.
    c. Commercial paper.
    d. Convertible bonds.
    e. Stock purchase warrants.
    f. Serial bonds.
    g. Money market mutual funds.

4. Which of the following bonds offers investors the most protection?
    a. Debentures.
    b. Subordinated debentures.
    c. Income bonds.
    d. First mortgage bonds.
    e. Second mortgage bonds.
    f. A second mortgage bond where the mortgage is open-ended.

5. A bond not secured by a mortgage will share equally in bankruptcy with:
    a. Common stock.
    b. Preferred stock.
    c. First mortgage bonds.
    d. Unsecured general creditors.

Preferred Stock and Common Stock 23

Orientation: In the present chapter we will consider two important sources of equity financing: preferred stock and common stock. The features and uses of common and preferred stock are examined, as are the rights of the preferred and common stockholders.

I. Preferred stock and its features

    A. Preferred stock is a hybrid form of financing, combining features of debt and common stock.

        1. Preferred stockholders' claims on assets come after those of creditors but before those of common stockholders. The claims are usually limited to the par value of the stock.

        2. Although preferred stock carries a stipulated dividend, the actual payment of a dividend is discretionary. The omission of a payment does not result in the default of the obligation.

        3. Preferred stockholders are usually limited to the specified dividend yield and do not ordinarily share in any residual earnings.

    B. Almost all preferred stocks have a cumulative feature, providing for unpaid dividends in any one year to be carried forward.

        1. The accrued preferred stock dividends must be paid before the company can meet the dividend obligation of the common stockholders.

2. There is no guarantee or obligation that the preferred stock dividends in arrears will be paid.

   a. If the preferred stock dividends are in arrears and the company wishes to pay a common stock dividend, it may choose not to clear up the arrearage, but to make an exchange offering to preferred stockholders.

   b. In order to eliminate the preferred stock, the company must obtain the approval of a required percentage of the (preferred) stock outstanding.

3. If a preferred stock issue is noncumulative, dividends not paid in one year are not carried forward.

   a. As a result, a company can pay a common stock dividend without regard to any dividends it did not pay in the past on its preferred stock.

   b. Noncumulative preferred stock is little more than an income bond and, therefore, is used primarily in reorganization plans.

C. A participating feature allows preferred stockholders to participate in the residual earnings of the corporation according to some specified formula.

   1. The essential feature is that preferred stockholders have a prior claim on income and an opportunity for additional return if the dividends to common stockholders exceed a certain amount.

   2. Practically all preferred stock issues are *nonparticipating.*

D. Preferred stockholders normally do not participate in the election of the corporate board of directors.

E. Preferred stock, like common stock, has no maturity.

   1. Still, most preferred stock issues are not regarded as a means of perpetual financing because provisions for retirement of the stock are made.

   2. Most preferred stock issues have a stated call price, which is above the original issuance price and may decrease over time.

   3. Without this feature, the corporation would be able to retire the issue only by the more expensive and less efficient methods of purchasing the stock in the open market.

F. Many preferred stock issues provide for a sinking fund which can be used to either buy the stock in the open market or call a portion of it.

    1. A sinking fund is advantageous to investors because the retirement process exerts upward pressure on the market price of the shares outstanding.

        a. Because the sinking fund is beneficial to preferred stockholders, the company should be able to sell the issue at a lower dividend yield.

        b. The sinking fund is a disadvantage to common stockholders because it represents another prior charge and, thus, contributes to the financial risk of the company.

    2. Over all, sinking funds are used much less with preferred stock than with bonds.

  G. Certain preferred stock issues are convertible into common stock at the option of the holder.

    1. Since practically all convertible securities have a call feature, the company can force conversion by calling the preferred stock if the market price of the preferred is significantly above the call price.

    2. Convertible preferred stock is often used in the acquisition of other companies.

II. Use in financing

  A. The main advantage of preferred stock financing lies in its inherent flexibility.

    1. The dividend is not a legal obligation and, therefore, can be omitted during adverse economic conditions.

    2. It has no final maturity, and also it adds to the equity base of the company's capital structure.

  B. The principal disadvantage of preferred stock financing is that its dividends are nondeductible for tax purposes.

III. Common stock and its features

  A. The common stockholders of a corporation are its residual owners. They assume the ultimate risk associated with ownership.

    1. In the event of liquidation, these stockholders have a residual claim on the assets of the company (i.e., after the claims of all creditors and preferred stockholders are settled in full).

    2. Common stock has no maturity date. It can be liquidated by the owner's selling the stock in the secondary market.

B. The corporate charter of a company specifies the number of authorized shares of common stock. This number can be increased by charter amendment.

   1. The number of outstanding shares represents those shares which have been issued and are held by the public.

   2. Treasury stock is issued stock that has been bought back by the corporation.

C. A share of common stock can be authorized either with or without par value.

   1. The par value of a stock has little economic significance; but common stock should not be issued at a price below its par value, as stockholders can be held liable to creditors for the difference between the price paid and the par value.

   2. The difference between the issuing price and the stated value is reflected as capital surplus.

D. The book value of a share of stock is the net worth of a corporation less the par value of preferred stock outstanding, divided by the number of shares outstanding.

   1. The liquidating value per share is usually less than book value per share because many of the assets can be liquidated only at distressed prices.

   2. To the extent that the liquidating value per share of a company exceeds its market value, the company may be subject to "raids."

E. The market value per share is the current price at which the stock is traded.

   1. The market value of a stock will usually differ from the book or liquidating value.

   2. The market value of stock is a function of the current and expected future dividends of the company discounted at a rate which incorporates the risk of the stock.

F. Unregistered stock is common stock that has been authorized and issued but has not been registered with the Securities and Exchange Commission.

   1. This type of stock is often used as promotional stock. It is given to the founders of the company apart from any cash investment they might make.

    2. Because of its illiquid nature, this stock must be sold at significant discounts from the market price of registered shares outstanding.

  G. If a company's stock is traded over one of the major stock exchanges, its stock is said to be listed.

    1. Reasons often cited for listing include greater marketability, wider disperson of stockholder ownership, and more prestige for the company.

    2. The larger the exchange, such as the New York Stock Exchange versus the American Stock Exchange, the more stringent the requirements for listing.

IV. Rights of stockholders

  A. Common stockholders are entitled to share in the earnings of the company only if cash dividends are paid.

    1. Stockholders prosper from the market-value appreciation of their stock and the dividends paid (if the stock pays dividends).

    2. Creditors can take legal actions if contractual interest and principal payments are not met, but stockholders have no legal recourse if the company defaults on dividend payments.

  B. The common stockholders of a company are the residual owners, and thus are entitled to elect the board of directors.

    1. In most large corporations, the average stockholder has very little power over who manages and how the company is managed.

      a. Each stockholder is entitled to one vote for each share of stock he owns.

      b. Most stockholders vote by proxy, which is a form by which the stockholder assigns his right to another person.

        (1) If minority stockholders can accumulate enough proxy votes, they can exercise limited control or influence over the board of directors of the company.

        (2) In most proxy contests, the existing management wins because they have both the organization and the use of the company's financial resources to fight the unhappy stockholders.

    2. Depending upon the corporate charter, the board of directors is elected either under a majority voting system or under a cumulative voting system.

a. Under the majority voting system, each stockholder has one vote for each share of stock he owns. He must vote for each director position that is open.

b. Under the cumulative voting system, a stockholder is able to accumulate his votes and cast them for less than the total number of directors being elected.

c. A cumulative voting system, in contrast to the majority system, permits minority interests a possible chance to elect a certain number of directors.

C. A preemptive right entitles a common stockholder to maintain his proportional ownership by offering him an opportunity to purchase, on a pro rata basis, any new stock being offered or any securities being converted into common stock.

V. Classified common stock

A. A company may have both class A and class B common stock.

1. Class A common stock may have no voting privilege but may be entitled to a prior claim to dividends. Class B common stock may have voting rights but a lower claim to dividends.

2. The promoters of a corporation and its management often hold class B common, while the general public holds class A common.

STUDY PROBLEMS

1. Five years ago the Brush Mountain Corporation marketed 5,000 shares of cumulative, preferred stock. This issue has a par value of $100 and is callable at $107. The dividend rate on the preferred stock is 8%. Because of depressed business conditions, the firm has not paid the preferred dividend for the past 3 years. The Brush Mountain Corporation, however, is certain that the recent economic recovery will permit net income to stabilize around a long-term norm of $300,000 per year. The firm's 60,000 common shares usually sell at a price/earnings ratio of 13 times. As the preferred dividend has not been paid for 3 years, the common stock is currently selling at $40 per share. The preferred is selling at $110. Brush Mountain's tax rate is 50%. The company faces these alternatives:

(a) Exchange common stock for the outstanding preferred stock, where the exchange ratio is based upon their current market values; or

(b) Call the preferred stock and finance the transaction by selling debentures that will carry a 10% interest rate. (At present, no debt is outstanding.)

Which alternative would the common shareholders prefer?

Solution:

(a) Find the projected price of the common stock, if an exchange is used:

$$\frac{\$110}{\$40} = \underline{2.75} \text{ common shares must be issued}$$
for every outstanding preferred share

(2.75)(5,000 preferred shares) = 13,750 new common shares

The number of common shares outstanding after the exchange is 73,750. Projected net income of $300,000 divided by 73,750 common shares gives a projected earnings per share level of $4.07. Therefore, ($4.07)(13) = $52.91 projected common stock price.

(b) Find the projected price of the common stock if debentures are issued:

Call price of each preferred share	$107
Arrearages per share	24
Value of debentures per preferred share	$131

($131)(5,000 preferred shares) = $655,000 debentures to be issued

($655,000)(0.10) = $65,500 annual interest expense on
the new debentures

Next, find earnings per share under this financing arrangement:

EBIT	$600,000
I	65,500
EBT	$534,500
T	267,250
NI	$267,250

Projected net income of $267,250 divided by 60,000 common shares gives a projected earnings-per-share level of $4.454. Therefore, ($4.454)(13) = $57.90 projected common stock price. All other things equal, financing the call of the preferred shares through the issue of debentures would be the choice of the common shareholders. It promises to increase the stock price more than if the exchange alternative is used. The crucial assumption here is that the price/earnings ratio would *not* be penalized by the marketplace for the simultaneous increase in financial risk that the debenture issue causes.

2. A group of environmentalists desire to have one director on the board of Pittsburgh Smelting, Inc. The firm's board consists of 12 members. The corporate

charter provides for cumulative voting. There are 7 million common shares outstanding. How many shares will the group have to own (control) to be assured they can elect one member to the board?

Solution:

The minimum number of shares necessary to elect a specific number of directors can be calculated by:

$$\frac{(\text{total shares outstanding}) \times (\text{number of directors desired})}{(\text{total numbers of directors to be elected}) + (1)} + 1$$

In the present situation this gives

$$\frac{7,000,000}{13} + 1 = 538,461 + 1 = \underline{\underline{538,462}} \text{ shares}$$

SELF-TESTS

True-False

_____ 1. Most preferred stock issues have a noncumulative feature.

_____ 2. The cumulative feature allows a preferred stockholder to accumulate his votes and cast them for one or more directors.

_____ 3. Preferred stockholders do not ordinarily share in the residual earnings of a company.

_____ 4. Sinking-fund arrangements are more commonly found with preferred stock issues than with corporate bonds.

_____ 5. Unlike a common stock dividend, preferred stock dividends carry a legal obligation and must be paid or the company will default.

_____ 6. The par value of common stock has little economic significance.

_____ 7. The book value and the market value of common stock are usually the same.

_____ 8. A "raider" buys a company's preferred stock, converts it into common stock, and makes a profit.

_____ 9. Corporate directors who act in a manner that results in personal gain may be subject to a derivative suit.

_____ 10. Proxy contests usually result in the victory of the dissatisfied stockholders.

_____ 11. A preemptive right entitles the common and preferred stockholders to maintain their proportional ownership in the corporation.

Multiple Choice

1. Some empirical studies have shown that the listing of a stock from the over-the-counter market to the New York Stock Exchange results in the following:
   a. It increases the value of the stock.
   b. No change in value occurs.
   c. The value of the stock increases but then decreases.
   d. The value decreases at first and then increases.

2. A participating feature allows preferred stockholders to:
   a. Participate in the election of the corporate board of directors.
   b. Convert their preferred stock into common stock.
   c. Receive some residual earnings of the corporation.

3. Which of the following features is (are) common to both preferred stock and corporate bond financing?
   a. Call feature.
   b. A sinking fund.
   c. A convertibility privilege.
   d. All of the above.
   e. a and c.

4. Which of the following values is most important to the investor in the secondary market?
   a. The par value of the stock.
   b. The book value of the stock.
   c. The market value of the stock.
   d. The liquidating value of the stock.

24 Convertible Securities and Warrants

Orientation: The purpose of this chapter is to explain options that enable one to obtain common stock. The options are convertible securities and warrants.

I. A convertible security is a bond or preferred stock that can be exchanged for a stated number of common shares at the option of the holder.

    A. The conversion ratio is the stated number of shares that the security can be converted into.

    B. The conversion price is the face value of the security divided by the conversion ratio.

    C. The conversion value equals the conversion ratio times the market price of the stock when one converts.

    D. The conversion premium is the difference between the price paid for the convertible security and its conversion value at time of issuance.

    E. The call price of a convertible is the price at which a company can redeem the issue prior to its maturity.

    F. Conversion of the security results in a dilution of earnings per share because the total number of shares outstanding increases while there is a reduction in deductible interest expense. The reduction in interest has a positive effect on earnings per share but, in general, this is more than offset by the increase in the number of shares outstanding.

G. The use of convertibles is sometimes used as a method of delayed common stock financing.

   1. No dilution of earnings occurs at time of issuance.

   2. Companies expect them to be converted sometime in the future.

   3. Less dilution of earnings occurs in the future because the conversion price is greater than common stock price at time of issuance.

H. Convertible securities can be sold with a lower interest or dividend rate because of the attractiveness of the conversion feature to investors.

I. A 20% premium of conversion value over call price is usually considered large enough to force conversion into common stock with a call.

Example I

Suppose a convertible debenture (1,000 face) can be called and redeemed by the company for $1,100. The conversion ratio is 16.5 shares. The current market price for common is $80 per share.

$$\text{Conversion price} = \frac{1,100}{16.5} = \$66.67$$

$(X)(66.67) + \$66.67 = \$80.00$ conversion value per share

Thus $X = 0.20$

or $80 \times 16.5 = \$1,320$

$(X)(\$1,100) + \$1,100 = \$1,320$ required conversion value per debenture

Thus $X = 0.20$

So a call would provide a 20% cushion here; hence, the firm could be relatively certain that a call would force conversion.

J. There are two ways in which a company can stimulate conversion:

   1. Include an acceleration clause, which periodically increases the conversion price and results in a lower conversion ratio over time.

   2. Increase dividend payments to common stockholders.

K. An overhanging issue is one that never forces conversion, or entices it, because the price of common does not rise high enough.

L. The value of the security is twofold:

1. The value of the common stock when one converts is the first component.

2. The value of the bond or preferred stock provides a cushion or a floor value in case the stock does not rise significantly.

$$\text{bond value} = B = \sum_{T=1}^{n} \frac{I}{(1+i)^T} + \frac{F}{(1+i)^n}$$

where I = annual interest payment (in dollars)
   i = market yield to maturity on straight bond of same company
   n = number of years to maturity
   F = face value of bond

Example II

Suppose that a company had a convertible outstanding (face $1,000) with 20 years to maturity at an 8% rate. If they wanted to issue a straight bond 20 years to maturity, a 10% yield would be required to attract investors. What is the current floor value or market price of the bond?

$$B = \sum_{T=1}^{20} \frac{\$80}{(1.10)^T} + \frac{\$1,000}{(1.10)^{20}}$$

$$= \$80(8.5136) + \$1,000(0.14864) = \$829.73$$

M. The market price of a convertible security is frequently above its conversion value, and this difference is called the premium-over-conversion value.

N. Unless the conversion feature is considered worthless, the security will sell for a premium-over-bond value (i.e., above the value of the security solely as a bond).

O. In comparing the two premiums, one finds an inverse relationship between them. In the extremes the security is selling either as a common stock or a bond equivalent.

II. Warrants are a "sweetener" added to a bond or debt issue, which entitle the holder to purchase a specified number of shares of stock at a stated price.

A. The exercise price can be either fixed or "stepped up" over time.

B. They generally have a fixed expiration date.

C. A detachable warrant can be sold separately in the marketplace.

D. A nondetachable warrant can only be exercised by the bondholder and cannot be sold on its own.

E. The theoretical value of a warrant is $NP_S - O$, where N is the number of shares that can be purchased with one warrant, P_S the market price of one share, and O the option price for N shares.

Example III

Suppose that one warrant entitles you to purchase three shares of stock at $20 per share. The current market price is $25.

$$\text{Theoretical value} - (3)(25) - 60 = \$15$$

STUDY PROBLEMS

1. Corporation X is about to issue a convertible bond at face value of $1,000. The conversion ratio is 20. The current market price of the common stock is $35. The coupon rate of this bond will be 10%. If Corporation X had chosen to finance a straight bond instead, the effective yield to investors would have been 12%. The number of years to maturity of the convertible is 20 years. What is the premium-over-bond value and what is the premium-over-conversion value?

$$(20)(35) = \$700 \text{ conversion value}$$
$$\$1,000 - 700 = \$300 \text{ premium-over-conversion value}$$

$$B = \sum_{T=1}^{20} \frac{\$100}{(1.12)^T} + \frac{\$1,000}{(1.12)^{20}}$$

$$= \$100(7.4694) + \$1,000(0.56743)$$
$$= \$74.69 + \$567.43 = \$642.12$$
$$= \$1,000 - \$642.12 = \underline{\$357.88} \text{ premium-over-bond value}$$

2. Compute the theoretical value of each of the following warrants, where N is the number of shares that can be purchased with one warrant, O the option price associated with the purchase of N shares, and P_S the market price of one share of stock.

	N	O	P_S
(a)	1	$ 25	$ 30
(b)	3	155	50
(c)	1.5	27	20
(d)	4.3	400	100

Solution:

$$TV = NP_S - O$$

(a) $TV = 1(30) - 25 = \$5$
(b) $TV = 3(50) - 155 = -5.00$, or zero
(c) $TV = (1.5)(20) - 27 = \$3$
(d) $TV = (4.3)(100) - 400 = \$30$

3. Suppose that you are considering buying one of two warrants. Both warrants entitle you to buy one share of common at $19 and $10, respectively. The common stock for both warrants is currently selling for $20. Further, you anticipate that both stocks will rise 20%. What are the warrants' theoretical values and which one provides the greatest leverage?

$$W_1: \quad 20 - 19 = \underline{\underline{\$1}} \text{ theoretical value}$$

$$W_2: \quad 20 - 10 = \underline{\underline{\$10}} \text{ theoretical value}$$

If stock rises to $25:

(a) W_1: increase value from $1 to $6, a gain of *600%*.

(b) W_2: increase value from $10 to $15, a gain of *50%*.

So warrant 1 provides the greatest leverage.

SELF-TESTS

True-False

_____ 1. The provision that protects holders of convertible securities in case of stock splits is called an antidilution clause.

_____ 2. At time of issuance, a convertible security will always be priced lower than its conversion value.

_____ 3. The greater the growth potential of the company's stock, the higher the premium the company can demand over its conversion value at the time of issuance.

_____ 4. As the conversion premium increases, investors are likely to demand higher coupon rates.

_____ 5. An overhanging issue increases the firm's financial flexibility.

_____ 6. Warrants usually sell for less than their theoretical values.

_____ 7. The value of a convertible is determined by its value as a straight bond or preferred stock and its conversion value into common stock.

_____ 8. Warrants always sell for their theoretical value.

_____ 9. A company can, at any time during the life of a convertible security, call the issue and force conversion.

_____ 10. Investors rarely exercise their conversion option.

Multiple Choice

1. Convertible bonds:
   a. Prohibit the issuance of more common stock.
   b. Can never be called.
   c. Are often an indirect way of selling common stock.
   d. Have no advantages to the investor over straight debt.

2. If a warrant carries a right to one share of common stock, and is exercisable at $20 per common share while the market price of a share is $30, the theoretical value of a share is:
   a. $10.00.
   b. $5.00.
   c. $1.00.
   d. Cannot be determined.

3. A convertible's floor value:
   a. Will equal its face value.
   b. Changes with interest-rate movement and changes in financial risk.
   c. Will remain constant.
   d. None of the above.

4. The call price of a convertible security is:
   a. The net proceeds received by the issuing company at time of issuance.
   b. Always greater than the face of the bond.
   c. Equal to the conversion value.
   d. None of the above.

5. Nondetachable warrants:
   a. Sell for more than detachable warrants in the market.
   b. Sell for less than detachable warrants in the market.
   c. Can never be sold alone in the market.
   d. None of the above.

25 *Mergers and Acquisitions*

Orientation: There are two principal ways by which a firm may grow: (1) internally, through the acquisition of specific assets which are financed by the retention of earnings and/or external financing; or (2) externally, through the acquisition of another company. We discussed internal growth in Chapters 13 and 14; we turn now to a discussion of external growth through mergers with, and acquisitions of, other firms.

I. Reasons for combinations

    A. Operating economies of scale are often realized through a merger or an acquisition. This comes about because of duplicate sales or production efforts.

        1. This type of economy is best realized through horizontal merger.

        2. Vertical mergers provide better control over distribution channels and purchasing.

    B. Management acquisition provides a firm facing a management vacuum with the ability to acquire aggressive management.

    C. Growth through acquisition or merger is faster than internal growth and may afford lower risk. The important parameter to examine is the effect on earnings per share via the price paid to acquire a firm.

D. Financing a rapidly growing firm may be made easier by merger with a "cash-rich" firm.

E. Tax considerations may play a role in merger decisions, especially with regard to the tax-loss carry-forward provision.

F. Diversification through acquisition may lead to a lower variability in firm earnings thus a reduction in firm risk.

G. Personal reasons of the owners may also affect the decision to merge.

II. Analyzing the impact of the terms of merger

    A. Of crucial importance is the effect of the merger on EPS of the surviving firm.

        1. The effect is dependent upon the price paid for the acquired firm. Anytime the price/earnings ratio (P/E) for a company exceeds the P/E of the acquiring company, dilution of earnings will occur.

        2. The price paid will of course depend upon anticipated earnings of the acquired firm.

    B. Book value per share becomes important only when it is significantly above market value and when the acquisition is made to gain liquidity.

III. Negotiation of a merger

    A. The acquiring firm must provide the firm it wishes to purchase with adequate incentive to sell.

    B. Often a contingent payment plan is developed to provide incentive to the management of the acquired firm.

    C. Tender offers, whereby the acquiring firm bypasses the management of proposed acquisition, are made directly to the shareholders.

IV. Holding companies

    A. A holding company has sufficient voting stock to have a controlling interest in one or more corporations.

        1. The advantage to the holding company accrues through the control of the associated firms with an investment smaller than the total value of the controlled firm's equity.

        2. The disadvantage of the holding company is the tax that must be paid on the dividends realized from its investments.

V. Acquisitions and capital budgeting

    A. The acquiring firm will want to view the acqusition of another firm in the same manner as it would any capital-budgeting problem. This involves discounting estimated future cash flows from the acquisition and comparing that stream to the present value of outflows.

    B. Estimation of cash flows is usually easier for a going concern than for a new project; therefore, there is a lower risk associated with these estimates.

VI. Procedural aspects involved in mergers

    A. The process of consolidation begins with discussion between the board of directors of the companies and ends with approval by the shareholders.

    B. The combination can be treated either as a purchase or as a pooling of interest from the accounting viewpoint.

        1. In a purchase arrangement the purchase price paid over net worth is considered goodwill and is amortized over future earnings.

        2. In the pooling of interest the balance sheets of the two firms are aggregated and goodwill is not shown.

    C. A firm may purchase the assets of a company or the stock of that company.

        1. If the assets of a firm are purchased, the acquired firm still exists; however, its only asset is cash or stock from the sale of its other assets.

        2. When stock is purchased, the purchased company is merged into the acquiring firm.

    D. If a dissenting stockholder does not feel the merger is proper, he may go to court to have a fair market price determined for his stock.

STUDY PROBLEMS

1. Assume the following data to be representative of the situation that exists after an acquisition.

			Year		
	1	*2*	*3*	*4*	*5*
After-tax annual cash flow	$1,000	$1,200	$1,100	$1,400	$1,600
Net investment	200	200	200	200	200
Cash flow after taxes	$ 800	$1,000	$ 900	$1,200	$1,400

Assume a discount rate of 12%. What is the maximum price that the firm should pay to acquire this firm?

Solution:

$$\text{Value} = \$800\ \frac{1}{1.12} + \$1,000\ \frac{1}{1.12^2} + \$900\ \frac{1}{1.12^3}$$

$$+ \$1,200\ \frac{1}{1.12^4} + \$1,400\ \frac{1}{1.12^5}$$

$$= \$800(0.893) + \$1,000(0.797) + \$900(0.712)$$

$$+ \$1,200(0.636) + \$1,400(0.567)$$

$$= \underline{\$3,709.20}$$

2. Company A is considering the acquisition of Company B. Company A must realize a return of 15% on its equity. The cash flows from Company B are expected to grow at a rate of 9% annually from its current level of $12 million. What is the maximum price Company A should pay for Company B?

Solution:

$$\text{Price} = \frac{\text{cash flow}}{\text{required return} - \text{growth rate}}$$

$$\frac{\$12,000,000}{0.15 - 0.09} = \underline{\underline{\$200,000,000}}$$

SELF-TESTS

True-False

_____ 1. The concept of synergism is the state wherein the whole is greater than the sum of the parts.

_____ 2. The higher the P/E ratio of the acquiring company in relation to that of the company being acquired and the larger the earnings of the acquired company in relation to those of the acquiring company, the greater the increase in earnings per share of the acquiring company.

_____ 3. A higher-than-normal ratio of exchange is not justified, even for a stock that promises high future earnings.

_____ 4. It is wrong to examine the effect on EPS of an acquisition alone as the basis for analyzing the merger, since the effects of synergism may play an important role in determining the attractiveness of the proposed acquisition.

_____ 5. In efficient markets it is expected that the P/E ratio after acquisition would approach a weighted average of the two firms' previous P/E ratios.

_____ 6. Contingent payments are most useful after new management takes over following an acquisition.

_____ 7. When considering an acquisition as an investment (capital budgeting), the main concern is with cash flows, not with prospective net income after financial charges.

_____ 8. Goodwill is usually capitalized during the current accounting period and not amortized, since there is no way to allocate the percentage of goodwill used each period.

_____ 9. Debt, common stock, and commercial paper are all instruments used in a pooling of interest.

_____ 10. Following a purchase of assets there still exists the corporate shell of the firm whose assets were acquired.

Multiple Choice

1. A combination of two corporations wherein one loses its corporate existence is:
   a. Statutory consolidation.
   b. Statutory merger.
   c. A tender offer.
   d. A corporate spinoff.

2. In a horizontal merger:
   a. Channels of distribution and production material acquisitions are realized.
   b. Common stock is traded for the common stock of the acquired firm.
   c. Two companies combine to eliminate duplicity of facilities.
   d. The directorates of two firms simply interlock.

3. Assume two companies with the following information:

	A	B
Present earnings (per share)	$25	$ 6
Shares (millions)	5	2
Earnings per share	$ 5	$ 3
Price of stock	$80	$30
P/E ratio	13	10

B has offered to sell its stock at a price of $33 to be paid for with A's stock. What is the earnings per share after acquisition?

a. $4.87.

b. $5.25.

c. $5.32.

d. $4.76.

4. Given the information in question 3 but changing the offer of A to purchase B from $33 to $35, what is the effect on EPS?

a. $5.27.

b. $4.95.

c. $4.83.

d. $5.00.

26

Growth through Multinational Operations

Orientation: The multinational firm is a relatively recent development in our business atmosphere. Its search for new markets and investment opportunities is accompanied by a host of problems: risk considerations, tax aspects, political problems, as well as financing difficulties. Each of these must be analyzed to determine whether entry into such new markets justifies the returns and risk generated.

I. Introduction

    A. A multinational enterprise is a firm having investment and sales in two or more countries.

    B. The United States has encountered significant growth in its international trade.

    C. Financial management of a multinational versus a domestic firm:

        1. In principle, the concepts of financial management are no different for multinational firms than for domestic business.

        2. The difference between the two organizations comes in the environment in which they operate.

II. Foreign investment

    A. Although more difficult to quantify, the decision to invest capital abroad should be analyzed similiarly to a domestic investment, with risk and expected return being the key factors to analyze.

1. Risk considerations

    a. The returns on investment for projects in different countries tend to be less correlated than projects in the same country, thereby increasing the company's opportunities for efficient diversification.

    b. In order for such diversification to be of benefit to the company's stockholders, the capital markets within the respective countries must be segmented from each other.

    c. If international capital markets are segmented, the acquisition of a foreign firm may be of particular benefit to the acquiring firm's stockholders.

2. Return considerations: The objective is to earn excess returns, resulting from the following:

    a. Expansion in the organization's markets.

    b. More efficient production.

    c. The acquisition of necessary raw materials.

B. Considerations in investing abroad

1. Taxation dissimilarities

    a. Taxation by the U.S. government

        (1) If international business is maintained through a foreign subsidiary, as opposed to a branch or division, the income generally is not taxed in the United States until distributed to the parent in the form of dividends.

        (2) In order to prevent excessive accumulation of earnings in tax havens, the income of certain foreign subsidiaries may be subject to the U.S. taxation prior to the actual remission of dividends.

        (3) Dividends received by U.S. corporations from a foreign subsidiary are not subject to the 85% dividend exemption.

        (4) The United States provides favorable tax treatment for certain types of operations.

            (a) A Western Hemisphere Trade Corporation (a domestic operation conducting business solely in the Western Hemisphere and receiving at least 95% of its gross income outside the United States) has a lower marginal tax rate, 34%.

   (b) A Domestic International Sales Corporation (DISC) is permitted to defer taxes on one-half of its income until such income is distributed to the stockholders.

 b. Taxation by foreign governments

  (1) Most industrial countries impose taxes on corporate income similiar to the taxes incurred in the United States.

  (2) Less-developed countries frequently have lower taxes and provide tax incentives in order to encourage foreign investment.

  (3) A value-added tax, encountered in some foreign countries, is a tax on the added value of a product at each stage of production.

  (4) In order for a company to avoid being subject to taxation by two different countries on the same income, the United States gives a federal income tax credit for foreign taxes paid by a U.S. corporation.

2. Political risk

 a. The political risks facing a multinational corporation vary from mild interference to complete confiscation (expropriation) of assets.

 b. The assessment of political risk requires forecasting political instability.

 c. If a company does decide to invest abroad, steps should be taken for self-preservation.

  (1) Cooperation with the host country is essential.

  (2) Protection against political action in less-developed countries may be possible by insurance offered through the Overseas Private Investment Corporation.

3. Foreign exchange risk

 a. This risk involves one of the following:

  (1) A devaluation of the currency of a country relative to the dollar.

  (2) A decline in the market price of a currency relative to the dollar.

  (3) Restrictions in convertibility from a currency to the dollar.

b. If devaluation in a currency does occur, the U.S. parent company incurs a loss in the value of cash and in the assets payable in the currency.

Example:

(1) The Pipes Corporation has £100,000 in a British bank.

(2) The current exchange ratio is $2.11 : £1.

(3) The British pound is devalued by 10%, with the new exchange ratio being $1.90 : £1.

(4) The currency loss would be $21,000:

Dollar value of British currency before devaluation: ($2.11 times £100,000)	$211,000
Value of the currency after devaluation: ($1.90 times £100,000)	190,000
Currency loss	$ 21,000

c. In addition to the immediate currency loss, a devaluation has possible long-run consequences, affecting future sales, costs, and remittances.

d. Protection against foreign exchange risk may possibly be achieved.

(1) A devaluation works to the advantage of a net debtor and to the disadvantage of a net creditor. Thus, a firm may *hedge* against devaluation by offsetting monetary assets and receivables against monetary liabilities.

(2) Management may contract for the purchase of a currency at a future time at a specified exchange ratio.

(3) A foreign currency swap arrangement may be established between two parties to exchange one currency for another at a specified future time and at a specified exchange ratio.

(4) Management may alter the transfer of funds between two subsidiaries in which a devaluation or revaluation is expected in one of the respective currencies.

C. Government restrictions: In the past, the U.S. government has imposed a number of constraints on foreign investments.

1. The purpose of such controls has been to reduce the outflow of capital from the United States.

2. In general, the controls restricted investment to a specified percentage of the corporation's foreign investments in a "base" year.

III. Multinational financing

    A. Internal sources

        1. Types of sources

            a. Direct investments from the U.S. parent.

            b. Retained earnings, depreciation, and depletion allowances.

        2. Seventy percent of the total financing of U.S.-owned foreign affiliates comes from internal sources, with approximately three-fourths of the internal sources being retained earnings, depreciation, and depletion allowances.

    B. External sources of financing

        1. Commercial bank loans

            a. The nature of the loan

                (1) The maturity structures of commercial bank loans in Europe are generally longer than bank loans in the United States.

                (2) The loans tend to be on a overdraft basis.

            b. A significant growth in international banking has occurred in conjunction with the growth in multinational companies.

        2. The discounting of trade bills is a common method of short-term financing.

        3. Eurodollar and Eurobond financing

            a. Eurodollar

                (1) Definition: A dollar deposit held in a bank outside the United States, typically of large denominations.

                (2) The banks receiving the deposits make dollar loans to prime borrowers.

                (3) The nature of the loans

                    (a) All loans are unsecured.

                    (b) The loans are short-term in nature and are generally used for working-capital requirements.

(c) The rate on a Eurodollar loan exceeds the prime rate and is more volatile.

(d) No compensating balances are required.

b. Eurobond

(1) Definition: A bond issued abroad which is denominated in dollars.

(2) In concept, a Eurobond is the same as a Eurodollar loan, except for a longer-term maturity.

(3) The use of Eurobonds has been sensitive to the capital restraints on foreign investment imposed by the U.S. government.

4. Development banks: In order to support economic development within a country, a number of countries have development banks for the purpose of making intermediate- and long-term loans. Examples would include the Export-Import Bank and the Agency for International Development.

5. The World Bank group is composed of three financial insitutions.

a. The International Bank for Reconstruction and Development (World Bank) makes loans to finance economic development.

b. The International Finance Corporation (IFC) makes loans to private enterprises in developing countries.

c. The International Development Association (IDA) makes loans on "soft" terms to countries with limited capacity to service debt.

IV. Financing international trade

A. Reasons for differences between foreign trade and domestic trade

1. The seller is generally unable to obtain as accurate credit information on the potential buyer.

2. Communication is more cumbersome.

3. Transportation of the goods is slower and less certain.

4. Legal settlement in case of default is more complicated and costly.

B. Documents involved in international trade

1. The *trade draft* (bill of exchange) is a written statement by the

exporter ordering the importer to pay a specific amount of money at a specific time.

    a. The draft may be either a sight draft or a time draft.

        (1) A *sight draft* is payable on presentation to the party to whom the draft is addressed.

        (2) A *time draft* is payable in a specified number of days subsequent to presenting the draft to the drawee.

    b. Features of the draft.

        (1) An unconditional order in writing signed by the drawee, the exporter.

        (2) Specifies the exact amount and time of payment.

        (3) Acceptance of the draft may be executed by either the drawee or a bank.

2. The *bill of lading* is a shipping document used in the transportation of goods from the exporter to the importer.

    a. The bill serves as a receipt from the transportation company to the exporter showing that certain goods have been received.

    b. The bill serves as a contract between the transportation company and the exporter to ship the goods and deliver them to a specific party at a designated point of destination.

    c. The bill serves as a document of title.

3. A *letter of credit* is issued by a bank, agreeing to honor a draft drawn on the importer provided that the bill of lading and other details are in order.

    a. Drafts drawn under an irrevocable letter must be honored by the issuing bank.

    b. A revocable letter of credit can be canceled or amended by the issuing bank.

STUDY PROBLEMS

1. Miller Shipping, an import dealer, purchased 50,000 francs from a firm in Paris, France. The value of the dollar in terms of the franc has been declining. The firm in Paris offers credit terms of 1/10, net 60. The 60-day future rate is $0.0257, whereas the spot rate is $0.0248.

(a) What is the dollar cost of paying the account within the discount period?

(b) What is the dollar cost of buying a future to close the account within 60 days?

(c) What is the effective cost of not taking the discount and the annual percentage cost of protection against devaluation?

Solution:

(a) $(50,000 \text{ f.})(1.00 - 0.01)(\$0.0248) = \$1,227.60$

(b) $(50,000 \text{ f.})(\$0.0257) = \$1,285.00$.

(c) Time value of money:

$$\frac{1}{99} \times \frac{360}{50} = 7.27\%$$

Cost of protection:

$$\frac{0.0257 - 0.0248}{0.0248} \times \frac{360}{60} = 21.8\%$$

2. The Banco a la Bolivia is currently paying 8% on its savings accounts. The Bolivian tax rate is 30%. John Wizard, an American investor, opens a savings account in the amount of $300,000. Mr. Wizard is in the 50% tax bracket.

(a) What taxes will be paid to the Bolivian government?

(b) What will be paid to the American government on the income from Bolivia?

Solution:

(a) $(\$300.000)(0.08)(0.30) = \$7,200$.

(b) $(\$300,000)(0.08)(0.50 - 0.30) = \$4,800$.

SELF-TESTS

True-False

_____ 1. One disadvantage of foreign investments is that the economic cycles of different countries tend not to be closely synchronized.

_____ 2. Taxation in less-developed countries is quite dissimilar to the U.S. system.

_____ 3. Subchapter S of the Internal Revenue Code is not intended to prevent the excessive accumulation of earnings in tax havens abroad and the resulting deferral of U.S. taxes.

4. The trade draft is a shipping document used in the transportation of goods from the exporter to the importer.

5. A bill of lading is where the bank agrees to honor a draft drawn on the importer provided that the bill of lading and other details are in order.

6. Eighty-five percent of the dividends received by a U.S. corporation from a foreign subsidiary are exempt from U.S. taxes.

7. The foreign value-added tax is a property tax wherein each addition to the value of a piece of property is taxed.

8. If a company believed that a nation was preparing to devalue its currency, the management of the business entity should reduce monetary assets and borrow extensively in the particular currency.

9. A foreign currency swap is simply an agreement between two parties to exchange one currency for another at a yet-to-be-determined future date but at a specified exchange ratio.

Multiple Choice

1. If a multinational firm combines investments in which the expected returns of the individual projects are negatively correlated with each other, risk will:
   a. Increase.
   b. Decrease.
   c. Remain unchanged.

2. Foreign exchange risk refers to:
   a. The risk that the currency of the United States is devalued *vis-à-vis* a foreign currency.
   b. The fact that the market price of the dollar declines relative to the foreign currency.
   c. The convertibility of a foreign currency is restricted.

3. Which of the following is *not* a hedge against foreign exchange risk?
   a. Balancing monetary assets and liabilities.
   b. Use of the spot market.
   c. Foreign currency swap.
   d. Adjustment of intracountry accounts.

4. Which of the following are internal sources of financing for the multinational firm?
   a. Retained earnings.
   b. Loans from parent.
   c. Depreciation.
   d. Depletion allowance.

e. None of the above.

f. All of the above.

5. The decision to invest capital abroad should be based upon considerations of expected return and risk. However, when investing abroad, many unique problems exist which can make quantifying the risk and return very difficult. Which of the following are *not* unique problems of the foreign environment?

a. Differences in currency exchange rates.

b. Differences in taxes.

c. Differences in accounting practices.

d. Differences in risk factors.

e. All of the above are special problems.

6. Which of the following is *not* a reason for investing abroad?

a. An increase in the positive correlation between a firm's investment projects may result.

b. Efficiency in production techniques may be gained.

c. Raw materials may be more abundant.

d. All of the above are reasons for investing abroad.

e. a and c.

7. Which of the following is *not* a form of foreign external financing?

a. Trade bills.

b. Eurobonds.

c. Eurodollars.

d. Commercial paper.

8. For many reasons a set of procedures has evolved for international trade which differ from those for domestic trade. Which of the following is *not* such a procedure?

a. An order to pay.

b. A bill of lading.

c. A comingling of risk account.

d. A letter of credit.

27

Failure and Reorganization

Orientation: Failure can be attributed to poor internal management as well as uncontrollable economic conditions. In this chapter, we will consider the alternatives open to an insolvent business. Specifically, the many liquidation procedures under both involuntary and voluntary settlements, as well as possible reorganization plans, will be discussed.

I. Voluntary settlements

    A. An *extension* is an agreement by which the creditors allow the debtor to extend the maturity of their obligations.

        1. Bypassing the ordinary legal procedures permits creditors to avoid the high legal expenses and possible shrinkage of their obligations.

        2. Those creditors who are not in favor of an extension being granted may receive the amounts owed them.

    B. A *composition* is a pro rata settlement of the creditors' claims in cash or in cash and promissory notes.

        1. The settlement must be agreed to by all creditors, although dissenting creditors are often paid in full because they have the power to force bankruptcy.

        2. A composition usually results in a more efficient settlement with lower legal expenses and fewer complications than a legal settlement.

    C. Creditors may agree to appoint a committee to control the operations of the company until the claims can be settled.

    D. When creditors feel that the company should not be preserved because of further possible financial deterioration, *liquidation* procedures are often started.

        1. Liquidation can be accomplished through *either* private settlement or through bankruptcy proceedings.

        2. In a private liquidation, the debtor assigns his assets to a trustee, who in turn liquidates the assets and distributes the proceeds to creditors on a pro rata basis.

II. Legal procedures—liquidation

    A. *The Bankruptcy Act of 1898,* as amended by the Chandler Act of 1938, allows the courts to take over the operation of an insolvent company and preserve the status quo until a decision is reached on whether to liquidate or reorganize the company.

        1. Bankruptcy proceedings may be either voluntary or involuntary.

           a. With a voluntary bankruptcy, the company files a petition of bankruptcy with a federal district court.

           b. An involuntary bankruptcy proceeding may be initiated by three or more creditors who have claims in excess of $500.

        2. In addition, the federal court will declare the company an involuntary bankrupt (firm) if it violates one of the six following acts.

           a. The debtor conceals some or all of its assets or it transfers its property, both with the intent of defrauding creditors.

           b. Cash or other assets are transferred to one creditor in preference to others.

           c. The insolvent debtor gives specific creditors a lien on its property.

           d. The debtor makes a general assignment for the benefit of creditors.

           e. The debtor, while insolvent, appoints a receiver or trustee to take charge of his property.

           f. The debtor admits in writing that he is unable to pay his debt and that he is willing to be judged a bankrupt (firm).

B. In the distribution of the proceeds of a liquidation, the *priority of claims* must be observed.

    1. The administrative and legal costs incurred during the bankruptcy settlement must be paid before creditors are entitled to receive any settlement.

    2. Secured creditors are next and are entitled to the proceeds realized from the liquidation of specific assets on which they have a lien.

C. When a trustee cannot be appointed quickly, the court appoints a receiver to manage the operation of the company and conserve its assets until a trustee can be selected.

III. Reorganization

A. A reorganization is an effort to keep a company alive by changing its capital structure, that is, reducing its fixed charges by substituting equity and limited-income securities for fixed-income securities.

B. A reorganization decision is usually chosen by creditors if the present value of the company as a going concern exceeds its liquidating value.

C. Most reorganizations occur under *Chapter X of the Bankruptcy Act,* and are initiated in a similar manner as a liquidation in bankruptcy.

D. The federal district court appoints a trustee to operate the debtor's business, and this trustee is responsible for drawing up an agreeable plan of reorganization.

E. To get court approval, the reorganization plan must be considered *fair, equitable,* and *feasible.*

    1. The fair and equitable standard means that all parties are treated according to their priority of claim.

    2. Feasibility refers to a workable plan with respect to earning power relative to the financial structure of the reorganized company.

    3. To be accepted, the plan must be approved by a *two-thirds* majority of each class of debt holders and by a simple majority of each class of stockholders.

F. The reorganization procedure for railroads is similar to other reorganizations, except that the Interstate Commerce Commission has a vote toward the approval or rejection of the proposed plan.

G. The difficult aspect of a reorganization is the recasting of the company's capital structure to reduce the amount of fixed charges.

   1. The first step of the reorganization plan is that of determining the total valuation of the company; this is projected from estimates of future earnings and an appropriate capitalization rate.

   2. The second step is the formulation of a new capital structure which will reduce fixed charges.

   3. The last step involves the valuation of old securities and their exchange for new securities.

      a. The exchange of new securities is usually proportioned on an *absolute priority* basis, which results in debenture holders receiving more favorable treatment than common stockholders.

      b. Under a *relative priority* basis, new securities are allocated on the basis of the relative market prices of the securities.

IV. Chapter XI procedures

   A. Chapter XI of the Bankruptcy Act permits a failing company to seek an arrangement, which, in essence, is a "legal" extension or composition.

      1. A court-appointed referee calls a meeting of the creditors to discuss the plan proposed by the debtor, which can be amended by the creditors.

      2. The arrangement applies only to the unsecured creditors, while the claims of the secured creditors must be met according to the terms of the obligation.

   B. At the time of this writing (Spring 1976), Congress was considering two major reform bills, one drafted by the Commission of the Bankruptcy Laws (H.R. 31), and the other by the National Conference of Bankruptcy Judges (H.R. 32).

   C. Under each bill, U.S. bankruptcy courts are established with judges appointed for 15-year terms.

      1. In the case of the commission bill, a separate administrative body is established in the executive branch of the government to administer the litigated estate.

      2. This administrative body will be staffed by permanent employees who will perform those duties presently under the control of

the referees, trustees, auctioneers, appraisers, accountants, and attorneys.

3. Under the second bill, H.R. 32, the present system of administration is largely retained and various outside parties are appointed by the court to administer the estate.

4. Under the commission bill, H.R. 32, the concept of an act of bankruptcy is abolished, and involuntary proceedings can be initiated by a creditor if the business ceases to pay its obligations.

   a. Under this bill, wages to employees and claims for contributions to employee benefit plans are given substantial priority, with the exception of administrative expenses which come first.

   b. Taxes accruing within 1 year prior to bankruptcy are next in priority, being followed by the claims of the general creditors.

D. The Commission Bill, H.R. 31, eliminates the overlap and confusion of Chapters X, XI, and XII, by consolidating them into one act.

1. When debts exceed $1 million or when there are more than 300 security holders, the court appoints a trustee to carry out the proceedings.

2. To eliminate the present infighting among different creditors and lawyers, a creditors' committee, composed of the seven largest creditors, is selected to represent all creditors in the bankruptcy proceedings.

   a. The *rule of absolute priority* is modified to allow participation by equity holders if they make contributions that are important to the operation of the reorganized company.

   b. The degree of participation is determined by their respective, appropriate contributions.

3. The final plans of the reorganization are submitted to the court, where each plan will be evaluated according to its feasibility, reasonableness of the valuation, and according to the fair and equitable criteria.

SELF-TEST

True-False

_____ 1. An extension usually results in large legal expenses and possible deterioration of assets.

_____ 2. In a composition, creditors receive a pro rata settlement in cash or in cash and treasury notes.

_____ 3. Creditors usually prefer a voluntary settlement instead of one brought forth by the court.

_____ 4. During a liquidation procedure, the referee has the responsibility of liquidating the assets and distributing the dividends to the creditors.

_____ 5. The company is declared a "debtor" in a reorganization as opposed to a "bankrupt" in a liquidation.

_____ 6. The absolute priority rule is fairest to the common stockholders.

_____ 7. An arrangement is a legal extension or composition applying only to secured creditors.

_____ 8. The bill being drafted by the Commission of the Bankruptcy Laws seeks more sweeping changes than the National Conference of Bankruptcy Judges bill.

_____ 9. Under the Commission Bill, the 15 judges are jointly appointed by the SEC and ICC.

_____ 10. The National Conference of Bankruptcy Judges bill suggests replacing the referees, trustees, auctioneers, appraisers, and attorneys with premanent staff employees.

_____ 11. Under the rule of absolute priority, preferred stockholders have priority over subordinated debenture holders.

_____ 12. Under the Commission bill, the creditors' committee is usually composed of the seven largest creditors.

Multiple Choice

1. The fair and equitable standard means:
   a. That assets are distributed according to creditors' priority of claim.
   b. That creditors are allowed to choose the trustee.
   c. That all creditors are to receive an equal proportion of the liquidated assets.

2. Railroad reorganizations occur under Section 77 of the Bankruptcy Act and:
   a. The Chandler Act of 1939.
   b. The Mahaffee Act of 1948.

    c. The Railroad Reorganization Act of 1943.

    d. The ICC Act of 1939.

3. A private liquidation is preferred over a public liquidation because it usually results in which of the following?

    a. Lower legal and administrative expenses.

    b. Faster liquidation of the assets.

    c. Less deterioration of the assets' value.

    d. Less disagreement among creditors.

4. Which of the following steps is taken first in a reorganization plan?

    a. Formulation of a new capital structure.

    b. Determination of the total valuation of the reorganized company.

    c. Determination of the total valuation of the old securities.

    d. Determination of a fair exchange of old securities and the new securities.

5. A reorganization and a composition are similar in that:

    a. The company's assets are not liquidated and the company's operations are continued.

    b. Creditors' claims are scaled down.

    c. Both are subject to Chapter X of the Bankruptcy Act.

Self-Teaching Supplement: Capital-Budgeting Techniques

I. NET PRESENT VALUE AND PROFITABILITY INDEX METHODS

In making investment decisions regarding fixed assets, the analyst compares the benefits of projects with their associated costs. Unfortunately, this comparison is complicated by the fact that the benefits and costs accruing from a given project usually do not occur in the same time period and thus are not directly comparable. This incomparability is a result of the time value of money (i.e., a dollar received today is worth more than a dollar received in the future). This comes about because a dollar today can be put into the bank and earn interest, resulting in a larger sum in the future. In economic terms we refer to the time value of money as its opportunity cost.

Using the Net Present Value and Profitability Index

In this section we compare the present value of a project's benefits with the present value of its cost. The difference in these present values is referred to as the net present value, and the ratio of benefits to cost is called the profitability index. Definitionally, then,

$$Net\ present\ value = \frac{\text{present value of future net cash flows} -}{\text{initial cash outlay}}$$

$$Profitability\ index = \frac{\text{present value of future net cash flows}}{\text{initial cash outlay}}$$

While both capital-budgeting techniques provide us with the same accept-reject decision, they may rank two or more projects differently. This difference results because net-present-value criteria measure the total dollar value of a project, while the profitability index measures its value relative to project cost. The decision criteria used in applying these decision tools are:

	NPV	*PI*
Accept	$\geqslant 0$	$\geqslant 1$
Reject	< 0	< 1

Solved Problems

Exercise 1:

The initial cash outlay of a project is $100; the present value of the cash flows is $75. Compute the project's net present value and its profitability index. Should it be accepted?

Solution:

$$\textit{Net present value} = \frac{\text{present value of future net cash flows} -}{\text{initial cash outlay}}$$

$$= \$75 - \$100 = \$-25$$

$$\textit{Profitability index} = \frac{\text{present value of future net cash flows}}{\text{initial cash outlay}}$$

$$= \frac{75}{100} = 0.75$$

Thus, the project should be rejected, as its net present value is negative and its profitability index is less than 1.

Exercise 2:

The present value of a project's future net cash flow is $580 and the initial cash outlay is $500. What is the project's net present value, its profitability index, and should the project be accepted?

Solution:

$$\text{NPV} = \$580 - \$500 = \$80$$

$$\text{PI} = \frac{\$580}{\$500} = 1.16$$

This project should be accepted, as the project's net present value is positive, and its profitability index is greater than 1.0.

Exercise 3:

A project's net present value is $300; the initial outlay is $500. What is the present value of the project's net cash flows?

Solution:

NPV = PV of project's net cash flows − initial outlay
$300 = PV of project's net cash flows − $500
$800 = PV of project's net cash flows

Exercise 4:

A project's profitability index is 1.5, and the present value of its net cash flows is $450. What is the project's initial cash outlay?

Solution:

$$PI = \frac{\text{present value of future net cash flows}}{\text{initial cash outlay}}$$

$$1.5 = \frac{\$450}{x}$$

$$x = \frac{\$450}{1.5}$$

$$= \$300$$

Exercise 5:

If either the net-present-value criteria or the profitability index give an accept signal, will the other criteria give a similar signal?

Solution:

Yes. The net present value and profitability index will always give similar accept-reject signals. Any time the present value of future net cash flows is greater than the initial outlay, the net-present-value criteria will be positive, signaling accept; and the profitability index will be greater than 1.0, signaling accept. However, because of size differences in projects, a small project, which is relatively more profitable than a project requiring a larger initial outlay, may have a smaller net present value. In this case, unless there is a limit on the amount of funds that is allocated, the net-present-value criteria should be used.

Compounding and Discounting: Single Cash Flows

To determine the present value of future cash flows, it is necessary to discount those cash flows back to the present. As demonstrated in Chapter 12 of the text, discounting cash flows back to the present is merely the reverse of compounding. For example, if we put $100 (X) in the bank, earning a rate of 10% (r) annually, at the end of 1 year (n) we would have $110 (TV):

$$TV = X(1 + r)^n$$
$$\$110 = \$100\ (1 + 0.10)$$

Correspondingly, at the end of 3 years we would have $133.10:

$$\$133.10 = \$100(1 + 0.10)^3$$

On the other hand, with an opportunity rate of 10%, the present value (PV) of $110 to be received in 1 year can be found as follows:

$$\$110 = PV(1 + 0.10)$$

$$PV = \$110\ \frac{1}{1 + 0.10}$$

$$= \$100$$

The present value of $133.10 to be received in 3 years is found similarly:

$$\$100 = \$133.10\ \frac{1}{(1 + 0.10)^3}$$

Solved Problems

Exercise 1:

What is the present value of $300 to be received in 3 years discounted at:

(a)   10% per annum?
(b)   5% per annum?
(c) 100% per annum?

Solution:

(a)
$$PV = X_n\ \frac{1}{(1 + k)^n}$$

$$= \$300\ \frac{1}{(1 + 0.10)^3}$$

$$= \frac{\$300}{1.331} = \$225.39$$

(b)
$$PV = \$300\ \frac{1}{(1 + 0.05)^3}$$

$$= \frac{\$300}{1.157625} = \$259.15$$

(c)
$$PV = \$300 \frac{1}{(1 + 1.0)^3}$$
$$= \frac{\$300}{8} = \$37.5$$

Exercise 2:

If the appropriate discount rate is 8%, what is the present value of $300 to be received in:

(a) 5 years?
(b) 10 years?
(c) 25 years?

Solution:

(a)
$$PV = X_n \frac{1}{(1 + k)^n}$$
$$= \$300 \frac{1}{(1 + 0.08)^5}$$
$$= \$300 \frac{1}{1.4693} = \$204.18$$

(b)
$$PV = \$300 \frac{1}{(1 + 0.08)^{10}}$$
$$= \$300 \frac{1}{2.1589}$$
$$= \$138.96$$

(c)
$$PV = \$300 \frac{1}{(1 + 0.08)^{25}}$$
$$= \$300 \frac{1}{6.8485}$$
$$= \$43.81$$

Fortunately, it is not necessary to do the individual calculations for $1/(1 + r)^n$ because in Table A-1 of the text the results of these calculations are presented for a large number of combinations of r and n. Thus, in order to determine the value of $1/(1 + 0.08)^5$ we need only look in the row of Table A-1 corresponding to the fifth period and the 8% column to find an appropriate value of 0.68058.

Self-Test 1

1. What is the present value of $250 to be received in 10 years if the appropriate discount rate is 8%?

2. How much must I put in the bank compounded annually at 6% to have $5,000 at the end of 10 years?

3. If a new machine costs $5,000 and will return $3,000 the first year, $4,000 the second year, $2,000 the third year, and my opportunity rate on money is 8%, what is the project's profitability index?

4. What is the NPV for the project in question 3? Should it be accepted?

5. If a new tractor costs $10,000 and will return $3,000 the first year, $5,000 the second year, and $4,000 the third year, calculate the net present value and profitability index using a 10% discount rate. Should the project be accepted?

6. Calculate the net present value and profitability index for the following:

Year	Benefit (+) or Cost (−)
0	$−8,000
1	+3,000
2	+6,000
3	+2,000
4	+1,000
5	−1,000

7. What is the net present value of a bond that pays $100 per year in interest at the end of each year for 10 years, and additionally at the end of 10 years will pay the $1,000 par value if the appropriate discount rate is 8% and the bond costs $1,093?

Compounding and Discounting: Annuities

Problem 7 of the Self-Test was actually an annuity problem. An annuity is simply a series of fixed payments for a specified number of years. This situation comes up quite frequently in finance, and in order to make the calculation of the present value of an annuity easier, you are provided with Table A-2 in the text, which gives present-value factors for an annuity. Now, in order to determine the present value of $1,000 received at the end of each year for five years, discounted back to present at 10%, you have two alternatives. You could use Table A-1 and discount each one of the five $1,000 flows individually as follows:

$$\$1,000 \; \frac{1}{1 + 0.10} = \$1,000(0.90909) = \$909.09$$

$$\$1,000 \; \frac{1}{1 + 0.10} = \$1,000(0.82645) = \$826.45$$

$$\$1,000 \; \frac{1}{1 + 0.10} = \$1,000(0.75131) = \$751.31$$

$$\$1,000 \; \frac{1}{1 + 0.10} = \$1,000(0.68301) = \$683.01$$

$$\$1,000 \; \frac{1}{1 + 0.10} = \$1,000(0.62092) = \underline{\$620.92}$$
$$\underline{\$3,790.78}$$

Alternatively, you could look up the annuity discount factor in Table A-2. The annuity factor for 5 years at 10% is 3.7908; multiplying this times $1,000 gives $3,790.80–the same answer you got using Table A-1. This is because you really only have one table, Table A-1, the values of which have been summed to form Table A-2. Thus, the annuity discount factor for 5 years at 10% in Table A-2 is equal to the sum of the discount factors for years 1 through 5 at 10% as found in Table A-1. Therefore, the annuity table value for n years at r percent is equal to

$$\begin{bmatrix} \text{Table A-2} \\ \text{n years} \\ \text{r\%} \end{bmatrix} = \sum_{t=1}^{n} \frac{1}{(1+r)^t} = \sum_{t=1}^{n} \begin{bmatrix} \text{Table A-1} \\ \text{n years} \\ \text{r\%} \end{bmatrix}$$

Solved Problems

Exercise 1:

Pick any number in Table A-2; note the number of years (call it n) and the discount rate (call it r). Now look in Table A-1 and add up the table values in the r discount-rate column for the first n years. What do you find?

Solution:

The value found in Table A-2 is equal to the value found from summing the values in Table A-1.

Exercise 2:

What is the present value of $50 to be received each year for 5 years if the appropriate discount rate is 8%? Solve this problem using Table A-1.

Solution:

Present value = $50(Table A-1; 1 year; 8%) + $50(Table A-1;
              2 years; 8%) + $50(Table A-1; 3 years; 8%)
              + $50(Table A-1; 4 years; 8%) + $50(Table A-1;
              5 years; 8%)
          = $50(0.92593) + $50(0.85734) + $50(0.79383)
              + $50(0.73503) + $50(0.68058)
          = $46.2965 + $42.867 + $39.6915 + $36.7515 + $34.029
          = $199.6355

Exercise 3:

Solve Exercise 2 using Table A-2.

Solution:

Present value = $50(Table A-2; 5 years; 8%) = $50(3.9927)
                                            = $199.635

Exercise 4:

What is the NPV of a bond that yields $80 per year in interest at the end
of each year for the next 15 years and matures in 15 years, at which time
it pays an additional $1,000 if it is currently selling for $800 and your
discount rate is 10%?

Solution:

NPV = $−800 + $80(Table A-2; 15 years; 10%) + $1,000(Table A-1;
      15 years; 10%)
    = $−800 + $80(7.6061) + $1,000(0.23939)
    = $−800 + $608.488 + $239.39
    = $47.88

Exercise 5:

What is the profitability index for the bond described in Exercise 4?

Solution:

$$PI = \frac{\$847.878}{\$800.00} = 1.0598$$

Exercise 6:

Given the following cash flows:

Year	Cash Flow
0	$-10,000
1	+5,000
2	+5,000
3	+5,000
4	+5,000
5	+5,000
6	+5,000
7	+10,000

what is the NPV of this project given an appropriate discount rate of

(a) 5%?
(b) 10%?
(c) 30%?

Solution:

(a)   NPV = $-10,000 + $5,000(Table A-2; 6 years; 5%)
                + $10,000(Table A-1; 7 years; 5%)
            = $-10,000 + $5,000(5.0757) + $10,000(0.71068)
            = $-10,000 + $25,378.50 + $7,106.8
            = $22,485.30

(b)   NPV = $-10,000 + $5,000(Table A-2; 6 years; 10%)
                + $10,000(Table A-1; 7 years; 10%)
            = $-10,000 + $5,000(4.3553) + $10,000(0.51316)
            = $-10,000 + $21,776.5 + $5,131.6
            = $16,908.10

(c)   NPV = $-10,000 + $5,000(Table A-2; 6 years; 30%)
                + $10,000(Table A-1; 7 years; 30%)
            = $-10,000 + $5,000(2.6427) + $10,000(0.15937)
            = $-10,000 + $13,213.50 + $1,593.7
            = $4,807.20

Self-Test 2

1. What is the NPV of the following cash flows if the appropriate discount
    rate is 20%?

Year	Cash Flow
0	$-15,000
1	+2,000
2	+2,000
3	+4,000
4	+5,000
5	+6,000

What is the profitability index should the project be accepted?

2. For how many years must $1,000 compound at 8% to accumulate to $2,000?

3. At what rate must $1,000 compound to accumulate to $3,000 in 7 years?

4. How much must you put in the bank compounded annually at 8% to accumulate to $3,000 at the end of 10 years?

5. What is the present value of $100 to be received at the end of each of the next 10 years discounted back to present at
    (a) 5%?
    (b) 10%?
    (c) 20%?
    (d) 30%?

6. How much is $50 worth if it is to be received at the end of 4 years if the appropriate discount rate is
    (a) 10%?
    (b) 20%?
    (c)   0%?
    (d) 100%?

7. What is the future value of $100 if it is placed in the bank for 5 years and compounded at 16%
    (a) Annually?
    (b) Semiannually?
    (c) Quarterly?

8. A company is examining a new machine to replace an existing machine that currently has a book value of $5,000 and can be sold for $2,000. The old machine has 5 years of expected life left, is being depreciated on a straight-line basis, and will have a salvage value of zero in 5 years. The new machine will perform the same task but more efficiently, resulting in cash benefits before depreciation and taxes of $10,000. The expected life of the new machine is 5 years; it costs $20,000 and can be sold for $5,000 at the end of the fifth year. Assuming straight-line depreciation, a 40% tax rate, and an appropriate discount rate of 14%, find the NPV and profitability index of the project.

II. THE INTERNAL-RATE-OF-RETURN METHOD

In the previous section we made capital-budgeting decisions through the use of the profitability index and net-present-value criteria, by comparing the present value of the benefits of the project with the present value of its costs either through division (determining the profitability index) or subtraction (determining a net present value). In each case you were supplied with an appropriate discount rate or cost of capital with which to determine the present value of future flows. You will now examine a method of evaluating projects that does *not* rely on an input discount rate but determines the discount rate that would make the project's NPV = 0, or, alternatively, makes its profitability index = 1.0. With the PI and NPV criteria we have a measure of the relative profitability and absolute profitability of the project, with all flows adjusted for the time value of money. The next criterion we examine, the internal rate of return, can be thought of as a rate of return or yield on the project. The decision rules on this criterion can be stated as follows: If the IRR is greater than or equal to the required rate of return or hurdle rate, the project should be accepted; otherwise, the project should be rejected. Although this seems quite straightforward and easy to understand, one finds that the solution process is often complex and time-consuming.

The Internal Rate of Return:
The Case of a Single Cash Inflow

The internal rate of return is defined as that rate, r, which equates the present value of a project's anticipated cash inflows with the present value of the relevant cash outflows. Where A_t is the cash flow for period t, whether it be positive (an inflow) or negative (an outflow), and n is the last period in which any cash flow is expected, the internal rate of return is represented by r in equation (A.1):

$$\sum_{t=0}^{n} \frac{A_t}{(1+r)^t} = 0 \qquad (A.1)$$

A solution to this problem becomes quite simple in the case in which the only outlay occurs in time period 0 (the present time period) and only one cash inflow occurs, say in time period t:

$$A_0 = \frac{A_t}{(1+r)^t}$$

$$\frac{A_0}{A_t} = \frac{1}{(1+r)^t}$$

Since you can determine a numerical value for A_0/A_t and you know that Table A-1 in the text gives you values for $1/(1+r)^t$, we can easily solve for r. All we have to do is look in Table A-1 in the tth row (corresponding to the number of years until the cash inflow) until we find the value A_0/A_t; the column that gives this value indicates the appropriate value of r.

Solved Problems

Exercise 1:

What is the internal rate of return on a project with an initial outlay of $6,000 which in the ninth year will produce one cash inflow of $18,000?

Solution:

$$\$6,000 = \frac{\$18,000}{(1+r)^9}$$

$$\frac{\$6,000}{\$18,000} = \frac{1}{(1+r)^9}$$

$$0.333 = \frac{1}{(1+r)^9}$$

The value of 0.333 is found in the 9-year row of Table A-1 in the 13% column; thus, 13% is the project's internal rate of return.

Exercise 2:

Given the following cash flows, what is the project's internal rate of return?

Year	Cash Flow
0	$-10,000
5	+40,000

Solution:

$$\frac{\$10,000}{\$40,000} \quad \frac{1}{(1+r)^5}$$

$$0.25 = \frac{1}{(1+r)^5}$$

Therefore, r = 32%.

Exercise 3:

If a project requires an initial outlay of $6,000 and will return $10,000 in year 13, what is its internal rate of return?

Solution:

$$\frac{\$6,000}{\$10,000} = \frac{1}{(1+r)^t}$$

$$0.6 = \frac{1}{(1+r)^{13}}$$

Therefore, r = 4%.

The accept-reject criteria for the internal-rate-of-return method states that if the project's internal rate of return is greater than or equal to the required rate of return or hurdle rate, the project should be accepted; otherwise, the project should be rejected. In other words,

IRR > required rate of return   Accept
IRR < required rate of return   Reject

Thus, if the required rate of return in Exercises 1 through 3 was 10%, the projects examined in Exercises 1 and 2 would be accepted, and the project in Exercise 3 would be rejected.

The Internal Rate of Return:
Multiple and Equal Cash Inflows

In the case where there is more than one cash inflow resulting from a project's acceptance, and the cash inflows form an annuity, a similar approach to that just outlined but using Table A-2 instead of Table A-1 will result in a correct solution. In this case the simplification proceeds as follows:

$$A_0 = \sum_{t=1}^{T} \frac{A_t}{(1+r)^t}$$

$$\frac{A_0}{A_t} = \sum_{t=1}^{T} \frac{1}{(1+r)^t}$$

If all the A_t values are equal and occur periodically (e.g., annually), we have an annuity. The value of the annuity discount factor, $\sum_{t=1}^{T} 1/(1+r)^t$, can be found in Table A-2. Since we know the term of the annuity, T years, when solving for r we need merely look in the T-year row until we find the value A_0/A_t; then looking to the column heading yields the internal rate of return.

Solved Problems

Exercise 1:

What is the internal rate of return on a project with an initial outlay of $24,000 which will produce cash inflows of $6,000 for each of the next 15 years?

Solution:

$$\$24,000 = \sum_{t=1}^{15} \frac{\$6,000}{(1+r)^t}$$

$$4.0 = \sum_{t=1}^{15} \frac{1}{(1+r)^t}$$

Therefore, r = 24%.

Exercise 2:

What is the internal rate of return on a project with an initial outlay of $18,000 which will produce cash inflows of $3,000 for each year for the next 9 years?

Solution:

$$\$18,000 = \sum_{t=1}^{9} \frac{\$3,000}{(1+r)^t}$$

$$6.0 = \sum_{t=1}^{9} \frac{1}{(1+r)^t}$$

Therefore, r = 9%.

Exercise 3:

Given the following cash flows, what is this project's internal rate of return?

Year	Cash Flow
0	$20,000
1	5,000
2	5,000
3	5,000
4	5,000
5	5,000

Solution:

$$\$20{,}000 = \sum_{t=1}^{5} \frac{\$5{,}000}{(1+r)^t}$$

$$4.0 = \sum_{t=1}^{5} \frac{1}{(1+r)^t}$$

Therefore, $r = 8\%$.

For Exercises 1 through 3, if the required rate of return was 10%, the project in Exercise 1 would be accepted while the projects in Exercises 2 and 3 would be rejected.

The Internal Rate of Return: Multiple and Unequal Cash Flows

Solution using the internal-rate-of-return criteria becomes most complex when there are unequal cash inflows resulting from a project's acceptance. In this case the solution can only be found by trial and error: first, arbitrarily picking a return and solving the problem; then, depending upon the result, raising or lowering that rate until the present value of the inflows equals the present value of the outflows.

Solved Problems:

Exercise 1:

What is the internal rate of return on a project that costs $20,000 and returns $3,000 per year for the first 4 years and $5,000 per year in years 5 through 8?

Solution:

$$\$20{,}000 = \sum_{t=1}^{4} \frac{\$3{,}000}{(1+r)^t} + \sum_{t=5}^{8} \frac{\$5{,}000}{(1+r)^t}$$

First, solve the problem using a discount rate picked arbitrarily. Try 20%. In this case this equation reduces to

$$\$20,000 = \$3,000(2.5887) + \$7,000(3.8372 - 2.5881)$$
$$= \$7,766.1 + \$8,739.5$$
$$\neq \$16,505.6$$

Thus, 20% is not this project's internal rate of return. If it were the internal rate of return, the present value of the inflows would equal the present value of the outflows; but the present value of the inflows is much less than the present value of the outflows. Since all the inflows occur in the future, the present value of these flows will increase as the discount rate is lowered, so here you should try a lower discount rate. If you try 13%, this equation becomes

$$\$20,000 = \$3,000(2.9745) + \$7,000(4.7988 - 2.9745)$$
$$= \$8,923.5 + \$12,770.1$$
$$\neq \$21,693.6$$

This time the present value of the inflows is greater than the present value of the outflows. In order to lower the present value of the outflows, the discount rate must be raised. This time try 15%:

$$\$20,000 = \$3,000(2.8550) + \$7,000(4.4873 - 2.8550)$$
$$= \$8,565.0 + \$11,426.1$$
$$\cong \$19,991.1$$

Now the present value of the inflows is approximately equal to the present value of the outflows using a discount rate of 15%; the project's internal rate of return is very close to 15%.

Exercise 2:

Given the following cash flows, what is the project's IRR?

Year	Cash Flow
0	$-12,000
1	+4,000
2	+4,000
3	+4,000
4	+4,000
5	+4,000
6	+2,000

Solution:

First, try 30%:

$$\$12,000 = \$4,000(2.4356) + \$2,000(0.20718)$$
$$= \$9,742.4 + \$414.36$$
$$\neq \$10,156.76$$

As the present value of the cash inflows is too low, you must lower the discount rate and try again. This time, try 25%:

$$\$12,000 = \$4,000(2.6893) + \$2,000(0.26214)$$
$$= \$10,757.2 + \$524.28$$
$$\neq \$11,281.48$$

Again, the present value of the cash inflows is too low, so again the discount rate is lowered and the problem is tried again. Next, try 20%:

$$\$12,000 = \$4,000(2.9906) + \$2,000(0.33490)$$
$$= \$11,962.4 + \$669.8$$
$$\neq \$12,632.2$$

Since the present value of the cash inflows is too high, the discount rate must be raised. We raised it to 23%:

$$\$12,000 = \$4,000(2.8035) + \$2,000(0.28878)$$
$$= \$11,214.0 + \$576.56$$
$$\neq \$11,790.56$$

This time the present value of the inflows is too low; thus, the discount rate is lowered. We now try 22%:

$$\$12,000 = \$4,000(2.8636) + \$2,000(0.30328)$$
$$= \$11,454.4 + \$606.56$$
$$\cong \$12,060.96$$

Thus, the IRR for this problem is between 22% and 23%, and closer to 22%.

Exercise 3:

What is the IRR associated with this project?

Year	Cash Flow
0	$-10,000
1	+3,000
2	+6,000
3	+9,000

Solution:

Try 20%:

$10,000 = $3,000(0.83333) + $6,000(0.69444) + $9,000(0.57870)
        = $2,499.99 + $4,166.64 + $5,208.3
        ≠ $11,874.93

The present value of the cash inflows is too large; therefore, the discount rate must be raised. Try 30%:

$10,000 = $3,000(0.76923) + $6,000(0.59172) + $9,000(0.45517)
        = $2,307.69 + $3,550.32 + $4,096.53
        ≠ $9,954.54

Now it is too small, so try 29%:

$10,000 = $3,000(0.77519) + $6,000(0.60093) + $9,000(0.46583)
        = $2,325.57 + $3,605.58 + $4,192.47
        ≠ $10,123.62

Thus, this project's IRR is just under 30%.

As you can see by now, calculating the IRR can become quite time-consuming when a trail-and-error search is necessitated. If it is necessary, remember the following guidelines:

(1) Always try a larger discount rate (or trial IRR) when the present value of the cash inflows is larger than the initial outlay.
(2) Always try a smaller discount rate (or trial IRR) when the present value of the cash inflows is smaller than the initial cash outlay.

Self-Test 3

1. What is the internal rate of return on a project that requires an initial outlay of $10,000 and returns $14,000 at the end of the fifth year?
2. What is the internal rate of return on a project that requires an initial outlay of $700 and returns $1,857 at the end of the twentieth year?
3. What is the internal rate of return on a project that requires a $30,000 outlay and returns $6,000 at the end of each of the next 10 years?
4. What is the internal rate of return on a project that requires an initial outlay of $20,000 and returns $3,928 at the end of each year for the next 15 years?

5. Given the following cash flows, determine an internal rate of return.

Year	Cash Flow
0	$-40,000
1	+10,000
2	+10,000
3	+10,000
4	+10,000
5	+10,000
6	+15,000

6. Given the following cash flows, determine an internal rate of return.

Year	Cash Flow
0	$-61,615
1	+10,000
2	+10,000
3	+10,000
4	+10,000
5	+10,000
6	+10,000
7	+70,000

7. Given the following cash flows, determine an internal rate of return.

Year	Cash Flow
0	$-2,992
1	+700
2	+1,400
3	+3,000

8. Given the following cash flows, determine an internal rate of return.

Year	Cash Flow
0	$5,490
1	2,000
2	2,000
3	4,000
4	3,000

9. What is the internal rate of return on a project that requires an initial outlay of $1,000 and returns $4,000 at the end of the second year?

Present-Value Tables

TABLE A · 1

Present Value of One Dollar Due at the End of N Years

N	1%	2%	3%	4%	5%	6%	7%	8%	9%	10%	N
01	0.99010	0.98039	0.97007	0.96154	0.95238	0.94340	0.93458	0.92593	0.91743	0.90909	01
02	.98030	.96117	.94260	.92456	.90703	.89000	.87344	.85734	.84168	.82645	02
03	.97059	.94232	.91514	.88900	.86384	.83962	.81630	.79383	.77218	.75131	03
04	.96098	.92385	.88849	.85480	.82270	.79209	.76290	.73503	.70843	.68301	04
05	.95147	.90573	.86261	.82193	.78353	.74726	.71299	.68058	.64993	.62092	05
06	.94204	.88797	.83748	.79031	.74622	.70496	.66634	.60317	.59627	.56447	06
07	.93272	.87056	.81309	.75992	.71068	.66506	.62275	.58349	.54703	.51316	07
08	.92348	.85349	.78941	.73069	.67684	.62741	.58201	.54027	.50187	.46651	08
09	.91434	.83675	.76642	.70259	.64461	.59190	.54393	.50025	.46043	.42410	09
10	.90529	.82035	.74409	.67556	.61391	.55839	.50835	.46319	.42241	.38554	10
11	.89632	.80426	.72242	.64958	.58468	.52679	.47509	.42888	.38753	.35049	11
12	.88745	.78849	.70138	.62460	.55684	.49697	.44401	.39711	.35553	.31863	12
13	.87866	.77303	.68095	.60057	.53032	.46884	.41496	.36770	.32618	.28966	13
14	.86996	.75787	.66112	.57747	.50507	.44230	.38782	.34046	.29925	.26333	14
15	.86135	.74301	.64186	.55526	.48102	.41726	.36245	.31524	.27454	.23939	15
16	.85282	.72845	.62317	.53391	.45811	.39365	.33873	.29189	.25187	.21763	16
17	.84438	.71416	.60502	.51337	.43630	.37136	.31657	.27027	.23107	.19784	17
18	.83602	.70016	.58739	.49363	.41552	.35034	.29586	.25025	.21199	.17986	18
19	.82774	.68643	.57029	.47464	.39573	.33051	.27651	.23171	.19449	.16351	19
20	.81954	.67297	.55367	.45639	.37689	.31180	.25842	.21455	.17843	.14864	20
21	.81143	.65978	.53755	.43883	.35894	.29415	.24151	.19866	.16370	.13513	21
22	.80340	.64684	.52189	.42195	.34185	.27750	.22571	.18394	.15018	.12285	22
23	.79544	.63416	.50669	.40573	.32557	.26180	.21095	.17031	.13778	.11168	23
24	.78757	.62172	.49193	.39012	.31007	.24698	.19715	.15770	.12640	.10153	24
25	.77977	.60953	.47760	.37512	.29530	.23300	.18425	.14602	.11597	.09230	25

Present Value of One Dollar Due at the End of N Years

N	11%	12%	13%	14%	15%	16%	17%	18%	19%	20%	N
01	0.90090	0.89286	0.88496	0.87719	0.86957	0.86207	0.85470	0.84746	0.84034	0.83333	01
02	.81162	.79719	.78315	.76947	.75614	.74316	.73051	.71818	.70616	.69444	02
03	.73119	.71178	.69305	.67497	.65752	.64066	.62437	.60863	.59342	.57870	03
04	.65873	.63552	.61332	.59208	.57175	.55229	.53365	.51579	.49867	.48225	04
05	.59345	.56743	.54276	.51937	.49718	.47611	.45611	.43711	.41905	.40188	05
06	.53464	.50663	.48032	.45559	.43233	.41044	.38984	.37043	.35214	.33490	06
07	.48166	.45235	.42506	.39964	.37594	.35383	.33320	.31392	.29592	.27908	07
08	.43393	.40388	.37616	.35056	.32690	.30503	.28478	.26604	.24867	.23257	08
09	.39092	.36061	.33288	.30751	.28426	.26295	.24340	.22546	.20897	.19381	09
10	.35218	.32197	.29459	.26974	.24718	.22668	.20804	.19106	.17560	.16151	10
11	.31728	.28748	.26070	.23662	.21494	.19542	.17781	.16192	.14756	.13459	11
12	.28584	.25667	.23071	.20756	.18691	.16846	.15197	.13722	.12400	.11216	12
13	.25751	.22917	.20416	.18207	.16253	.14523	.12989	.11629	.10420	.09346	13
14	.23199	.20462	.18068	.15971	.14133	.12520	.11102	.09855	.08757	.07789	14
15	.20900	.18270	.15989	.14010	.12289	.10793	.09489	.08352	.07359	.06491	15
16	.18829	.16312	.14150	.12289	.10686	.09304	.08110	.07078	.06184	.05409	16
17	.16963	.14564	.12522	.10780	.09293	.08021	.06932	.05998	.05196	.04507	17
18	.15282	.13004	.11081	.09456	.08080	.06914	.05925	.05083	.04367	.03756	18
19	.13768	.11611	.09806	.08295	.07026	.05961	.05064	.04308	.03669	.03130	19
20	.12403	.10367	.08678	.07276	.06110	.05139	.04328	.03651	.03084	.02608	20
21	.11174	.09256	.07680	.06383	.05313	.04430	.03699	.03094	.02591	.02174	21
22	.10067	.08264	.06796	.05599	.04620	.03819	.03162	.02622	.02178	.01811	22
23	.09069	.07379	.06014	.04911	.04017	.03292	.02702	.02222	.01830	.01509	23
24	.08170	.06588	.05322	.04308	.03493	.02838	.02310	.01883	.01538	.01258	24
25	.07361	.05882	.04710	.03779	.03038	.02447	.01974	.01596	.01292	.01048	25

TABLE A · 1

Present Value of One Dollar Due at the End of N Years

N	21%	22%	23%	24%	25%	26%	27%	28%	29%	30%	N
01	0.82645	0.81967	0.81301	0.80645	0.80000	0.79365	0.78740	0.78125	0.77519	0.76923	01
02	.68301	.67186	.66098	.65036	.64000	.62988	.62000	.61035	.60093	.59172	02
03	.56447	.55071	.53738	.52449	.51200	.49991	.48819	.47684	.46583	.45517	03
04	.46651	.45140	.43690	.42297	.40906	.39675	.38440	.37253	.36111	.35013	04
05	.38554	.37000	.35520	.34111	.32768	.31488	.30268	.29104	.27993	.26933	05
06	.31863	.30328	.28878	.27509	.26214	.24991	.23833	.22737	.21700	.20718	06
07	.26333	.24859	.23478	.22184	.20972	.19834	.18766	.17764	.16822	.15937	07
08	.21763	.20376	.19088	.17891	.16777	.15741	.14776	.13878	.13040	.12259	08
09	.17986	.16702	.15519	.14428	.13422	.12493	.11635	.10842	.10109	.09430	09
10	.14864	.13690	.12617	.11635	.10737	.09915	.09161	.08470	.07836	.07254	10
11	.12285	.11221	.10258	.09383	.08590	.07869	.07214	.06617	.06075	.05580	11
12	.10153	.09198	.08339	.07567	.06872	.06245	.05680	.05170	.04709	.04292	12
13	.08391	.07539	.06780	.06103	.05498	.04957	.04472	.04039	.03650	.03302	13
14	.06934	.06180	.05512	.04921	.04398	.03934	.03522	.03155	.02830	.02540	14
15	.05731	.05065	.04481	.03969	.03518	.03122	.02773	.02465	.02194	.01954	15
16	.04736	.04152	.03643	.03201	.02815	.02478	.02183	.01926	.01700	.01503	16
17	.03914	.03403	.02962	.02581	.02252	.01967	.01719	.01505	.01318	.01156	17
18	.03235	.02789	.02408	.02082	.01801	.01561	.01354	.01175	.01022	.00889	18
19	.02673	.02286	.01958	.01679	.01441	.01239	.01066	.00918	.00792	.00684	19
20	.02209	.01874	.01592	.01354	.01153	.00983	.00839	.00717	.00614	.00526	20
21	.01826	.01536	.01294	.01092	.00922	.00780	.00661	.00561	.00476	.00405	21
22	.01509	.01259	.01052	.00880	.00738	.00619	.00520	.00438	.00369	.00311	22
23	.01247	.01032	.00855	.00710	.00590	.00491	.00410	.00342	.00286	.00239	23
24	.01031	.00846	.00695	.00573	.00472	.00390	.00323	.00267	.00222	.00184	24
25	.00852	.00693	.00565	.00462	.00378	.00310	.00254	.00209	.00172	.00142	25

TABLE A · 1

Present Value of One Dollar Due at the End of N Years

N	31%	32%	33%	34%	35%	36%	37%	38%	39%	40%	N
01	0.76336	0.75758	0.75188	0.74627	0.74074	0.73529	0.72993	0.72464	0.71942	0.71429	01
02	.58272	.57392	.56532	.55692	.54870	.54066	.53279	.52510	.51757	.51020	02
03	.44482	.43479	.42505	.41561	.40644	.39754	.38890	.38051	.37235	.36443	03
04	.33956	.32939	.31959	.31016	.30107	.29231	.28387	.27573	.26788	.26031	04
05	.25920	.24953	.24029	.23146	.22301	.21493	.20720	.19980	.19272	.18593	05
06	.19787	.18904	.18067	.17273	.16520	.15804	.15124	.14479	.13865	.13281	06
07	.15104	.14321	.13584	.12890	.12237	.11621	.11040	.10492	.09975	.09486	07
08	.11530	.10849	.10214	.09620	.09064	.08545	.08058	.07603	.07176	.06776	08
09	.08802	.08219	.07680	.07179	.06714	.06283	.05882	.05509	.05163	.04840	09
10	.06719	.06227	.05774	.05357	.04973	.04620	.04293	.03992	.03714	.03457	10
11	.05129	.04717	.04341	.03998	.03684	.03397	.03134	.02893	.02672	.02469	11
12	.03915	.03574	.03264	.02984	.02729	.02498	.02287	.02096	.01922	.01764	12
13	.02989	.02707	.02454	.02227	.02021	.01837	.01670	.01519	.01383	.01260	13
14	.02281	.02051	.01845	.01662	.01497	.01350	.01219	.01101	.00995	.00900	14
15	.01742	.01554	.01387	.01240	.01109	.00993	.00890	.00798	.00716	.00643	15
16	.01329	.01177	.01043	.00925	.00822	.00730	.00649	.00578	.00515	.00459	16
17	.01015	.00892	.00784	.00691	.00609	.00537	.00474	.00419	.00370	.00328	17
18	.00775	.00676	.00590	.00515	.00451	.00395	.00346	.00304	.00267	.00234	18
19	.00591	.00512	.00443	.00385	.00334	.00290	.00253	.00220	.00192	.00167	19
20	.00451	.00388	.00333	.00287	.00247	.00213	.00184	.00159	.00138	.00120	20
21	.00345	.00294	.00251	.00214	.00183	.00157	.00135	.00115	.00099	.00085	21
22	.00263	.00223	.00188	.00160	.00136	.00115	.00098	.00084	.00071	.00061	22
23	.00201	.00169	.00142	.00119	.00101	.00085	.00072	.00061	.00051	.00044	23
24	.00153	.00128	.00107	.00089	.00074	.00062	.00052	.00044	.00037	.00031	24
25	.00117	.00097	.00080	.00066	.00055	.00046	.00038	.00032	.00027	.00022	25

Present-Value Tables

TABLE A · 2

Present Value of One Dollar Per Year. N Years at r%

Year	1%	2%	3%	4%	5%	6%	7%	8%	9%	10%	Year
1	0.9901	0.9804	0.9709	0.9615	0.9524	0.9434	0.9346	0.9259	0.9174	0.9091	1
2	1.9704	1.9416	1.9135	1.8861	1.8594	1.8334	1.8080	1.7833	1.7591	1.7355	2
3	2.9410	2.8839	2.8286	2.7751	2.7232	2.6730	2.6243	2.5771	2.5313	2.4868	3
4	3.9020	3.8077	3.7171	3.6299	3.5459	3.4651	3.3872	3.3121	3.2397	3.1699	4
5	4.8535	4.7134	4.5797	4.4518	4.3295	4.2123	4.1002	3.9927	3.8896	3.7908	5
6	5.7955	5.6014	5.4172	5.2421	5.0757	4.9173	4.7665	4.6229	4.4859	4.3553	6
7	6.7282	6.4720	6.2302	6.0020	5.7863	5.5824	5.3893	5.2064	5.0329	4.8684	7
8	7.6517	7.3254	7.0196	6.7327	6.4632	6.2098	5.9713	5.7466	5.5348	5.3349	8
9	8.5661	8.1622	7.7861	7.4353	7.1078	6.8017	6.5152	6.2469	5.9852	5.7590	9
10	9.4714	8.9825	8.5302	8.1109	7.7217	7.3601	7.0236	6.7101	6.4176	6.1446	10
11	10.3677	9.7868	9.2526	8.7604	8.3064	7.8868	7.4987	7.1389	6.8052	6.4951	11
12	11.2552	10.5753	9.9539	9.3850	8.8632	8.3838	7.9427	7.5361	7.1607	6.8137	12
13	12.1338	11.3483	10.6349	9.9856	9.3935	8.8527	8.3576	7.9038	7.4869	7.1034	13
14	13.0038	12.1062	11.2960	10.5631	9.8986	9.2950	8.7454	8.2442	7.7861	7.3667	14
15	13.8651	12.8492	11.9379	11.1183	10.3796	9.7122	9.1079	8.5595	8.0607	7.6061	15
16	14.7180	13.5777	12.5610	11.6522	10.8377	10.1059	9.4466	8.8514	8.3125	7.8237	16
17	15.5624	14.2918	13.1660	12.1656	11.2740	10.4772	9.7632	9.1216	8.5436	8.0215	17
18	16.3984	14.9920	13.7534	12.6592	11.6895	10.8276	10.0591	9.3719	8.7556	8.2014	18
19	17.2261	15.6784	14.3237	13.1339	12.0853	11.1581	10.3356	9.6036	8.9501	8.3649	19
20	18.0457	16.3514	14.8774	13.5903	12.4622	11.4699	10.5940	9.8181	9.1285	8.5136	20
21	18.8571	17.0111	15.4149	14.0291	12.8211	11.7640	10.8355	10.0168	9.2922	8.6487	21
22	19.6605	17.6580	15.9368	14.4511	13.1630	12.0416	11.0612	10.2007	9.4424	8.7715	22
23	20.4559	18.2921	16.4435	14.8568	13.4885	12.3033	11.2722	10.3710	9.5802	8.8832	23
24	21.2435	18.9139	16.9355	15.2469	13.7986	12.5503	11.4693	10.5287	9.7066	8.9847	24
25	22.0233	19.5234	17.4131	15.6220	14.0939	12.7833	11.6536	10.6748	9.8226	9.0770	25

TABLE A · 2

Present Value of One Dollar Per Year. N Years at r%

Year	11%	12%	13%	14%	15%	16%	17%	18%	19%	20%	Year
1	0.9009	0.8929	0.8850	0.8772	0.8696	0.8621	0.8547	0.8475	0.8403	0.8333	1
2	1.7125	1.6901	1.6681	1.6467	1.6257	1.6052	1.5852	1.5656	1.5465	1.5278	2
3	2.4437	2.4018	2.3612	2.3216	2.2832	2.2459	2.2096	2.1743	2.1399	2.1065	3
4	3.1024	3.0373	2.9745	2.9137	2.8550	2.7982	2.7432	2.6901	2.6386	2.5887	4
5	3.6959	3.6048	3.5172	3.4331	3.3522	3.2743	3.1993	3.1272	3.0576	2.9906	5
6	4.2305	4.1114	3.9976	3.8887	3.7845	3.6847	3.5892	3.4976	3.4098	3.3255	6
7	4.7122	4.5638	4.4226	4.2883	4.1604	4.0386	3.9224	3.8115	3.7057	3.6046	7
8	5.1461	4.9676	4.7988	4.6389	4.4873	4.3436	4.2072	4.0776	3.9544	3.8372	8
9	5.5370	5.3282	5.1317	4.9464	4.7716	4.6065	4.4506	4.3030	4.1633	4.0310	9
10	5.8892	5.6502	5.4262	5.2161	5.0188	4.8332	4.6586	4.4941	4.3389	4.1925	10
11	6.2065	5.9377	5.6869	5.4527	5.2337	5.0286	4.8364	4.6560	4.4865	4.3271	11
12	6.4924	6.1944	5.9176	5.6603	5.4206	5.1971	4.9884	4.7932	4.6105	4.4392	12
13	6.7499	6.4235	6.1218	5.8424	5.5831	5.3423	5.1183	4.9095	4.7147	4.5327	13
14	6.9819	6.6282	6.3025	6.0021	5.7245	5.4675	5.2293	5.0081	4.8023	4.6106	14
15	7.1909	6.8109	6.4624	6.1422	5.8474	5.5755	5.3242	5.0916	4.8759	4.6755	15
16	7.3792	6.9740	6.6039	6.2651	5.9542	5.6685	5.4053	5.1624	4.9377	4.7296	16
17	7.5488	7.1196	6.7291	6.3729	6.0472	5.7487	5.4746	5.2223	4.9897	4.7746	17
18	7.7016	7.2497	6.8399	6.4674	6.1280	5.8178	5.5339	5.2732	5.0333	4.8122	18
19	7.8393	7.3658	6.9380	6.5504	6.1982	5.8775	5.5845	5.3162	5.0700	4.8435	19
20	7.9633	7.4694	7.0248	6.6231	6.2593	5.9288	5.6278	5.3527	5.1009	4.8696	20
21	8.0751	7.5620	7.1016	6.6870	6.3125	5.9731	5.6648	5.3837	5.1268	4.8913	21
22	8.1757	7.6446	7.1695	6.7429	6.3587	6.0113	5.6964	5.4099	5.1486	4.9094	22
23	8.2664	7.7184	7.2297	6.7921	6.3988	6.0442	5.7234	5.4321	5.1668	4.9245	23
24	8.3481	7.7843	7.2829	6.8351	6.4338	6.0726	5.7465	5.4509	5.1822	4.9371	24
25	8.4217	7.8431	7.3300	6.8729	6.4641	6.0971	5.7662	5.4669	5.1951	4.9476	25

TABLE A · 2

Present Value of One Dollar Per Year. N Years at r%

Year	21%	22%	23%	24%	25%	26%	27%	28%	29%	30%	Year
1	0.8264	0.8197	0.8130	0.8065	0.8000	0.7937	0.7874	0.7813	0.7752	0.7692	1
2	1.5095	1.4915	1.4740	1.4568	1.4400	1.4235	1.4074	1.3916	1.3761	1.3609	2
3	2.0739	2.0422	2.0114	1.9813	1.9520	1.9234	1.8956	1.8684	1.8420	1.8161	3
4	2.5404	2.4936	2.4483	2.4043	2.3616	2.3202	2.2800	2.2410	2.2031	2.1662	4
5	2.9260	2.8636	2.8035	2.7454	2.6893	2.6351	2.5827	2.5320	2.4830	2.4356	5
6	3.2446	3.1669	3.0923	3.0205	2.9514	2.8850	2.8210	2.7594	2.7000	2.6427	6
7	3.5079	3.4155	3.3270	3.2423	3.1611	3.0833	3.0087	2.9370	2.8682	2.8021	7
8	3.7256	3.6193	3.5179	3.4212	3.3289	3.2407	3.1564	3.0758	2.9986	2.9247	8
9	3.9054	3.7863	3.6731	3.5655	3.4631	3.3657	3.2728	3.1842	3.0997	3.0190	9
10	4.0541	3.9232	3.7993	3.6819	3.5705	3.4648	3.3644	3.2689	3.1781	3.0915	10
11	4.1769	4.0354	3.9018	3.7757	3.6564	3.5435	3.4365	3.3351	3.2388	3.1473	11
12	4.2785	4.1274	3.9852	3.8514	3.7251	3.6060	3.4933	3.3868	3.2859	3.1903	12
13	4.3624	4.2028	4.0530	3.9124	3.7801	3.6555	3.6381	3.4272	3.3224	3.2233	13
14	4.4317	4.2646	4.1082	3.9616	3.8241	3.6949	3.5733	3.4587	3.3507	3.2487	14
15	4.4890	4.3152	4.1530	4.0013	3.8593	3.7261	3.6010	3.4834	3.3726	3.2682	15
16	4.5364	4.3567	4.1894	4.0333	3.8874	3.7509	3.6228	3.5026	3.3896	3.2832	16
17	4.5755	4.3908	4.2190	4.0591	3.9099	3.7705	3.6400	3.5177	3.4028	3.2948	17
18	4.6079	4.4187	4.2431	4.0799	3.9279	3.7861	3.6536	3.5294	3.4130	3.3037	18
19	4.6346	4.4415	4.2627	4.0967	3.9424	3.7985	3.6642	3.5386	3.4210	3.3105	19
20	4.6567	4.4603	4.2786	4.1103	3.9539	3.8083	3.6726	3.5458	3.4271	3.3158	20
21	4.6750	4.4756	4.2916	4.1212	3.9631	3.8161	3.6792	3.5514	3.4319	3.3198	21
22	4.6900	4.4882	4.3021	4.1300	3.9705	3.8223	3.6844	3.5558	3.4356	3.3230	22
23	4.7025	4.4985	4.3106	4.1371	3.9764	3.8273	3.6885	3.5592	3.4384	3.3254	23
24	4.7128	4.5070	4.3176	4.1428	3.9811	3.8312	3.6918	3.5619	3.4406	3.3272	24
25	4.7213	4.5139	4.3232	4.1474	3.9849	3.8342	3.6943	3.5640	3.4423	3.3286	25

TABLE A · 2

Present Value of One Dollar Per Year. N Years at r %

Year	31%	32%	33%	34%	35%	36%	37%	38%	39%	40%	Year
1	0.7634	0.7576	0.7519	0.7463	0.7407	0.7353	0.7299	0.7246	0.7194	0.7143	1
2	1.3461	1.3315	1.3172	1.3032	1.2894	1.2760	1.2627	1.2497	1.2370	1.2245	2
3	1.7909	1.7663	1.7423	1.7188	1.6959	1.6735	1.6516	1.6302	1.6093	1.5889	3
4	2.1305	2.0957	2.0618	2.0290	1.9969	1.9658	1.9355	1.9060	1.8772	1.8492	4
5	2.3897	2.3452	2.3021	2.2604	2.2200	2.1807	2.1427	2.1058	2.0699	2.0352	5
6	2.5875	2.5342	2.4828	2.4331	2.3852	2.3388	2.2939	2.2506	2.2086	2.1680	6
7	2.7386	2.6775	2.6187	2.5620	2.5075	2.4550	2.4043	2.3555	2.3083	2.2628	7
8	2.8539	2.7860	2.7208	2.6582	2.5982	2.5404	2.4849	2.4315	2.3801	2.3306	8
9	2.9419	2.8681	2.7976	2.7300	2.6653	2.6033	2.5437	2.4866	2.4317	2.3790	9
10	3.0091	2.9304	2.8553	2.7836	2.7150	2.6495	2.5867	2.5265	2.4689	2.4136	10
11	3.0604	2.9776	2.8987	2.8236	2.7519	2.6834	2.6180	2.5555	2.4956	2.4383	11
12	3.0995	3.0133	2.9314	2.8534	2.7792	2.7084	2.6409	2.5764	2.5148	2.4559	12
13	3.1294	3.0404	2.9559	2.8757	2.7994	2.7268	2.6576	2.5916	2.5286	2.4685	13
14	3.1522	3.0609	2.9744	2.8923	2.8144	2.7403	2.6698	2.6026	2.5386	2.4775	14
15	3.1696	3.0764	2.9883	2.9047	2.8255	2.7502	2.6787	2.6106	2.5457	2.4839	15
16	3.1829	3.0882	2.9987	2.9140	2.8337	2.7575	2.6852	2.6164	2.5509	2.4885	16
17	3.1931	3.0971	3.0065	2.9209	2.8398	2.7629	2.6899	2.6206	2.5546	2.4918	17
18	3.2008	3.1039	3.0124	2.9260	2.8443	2.7668	2.6934	2.6236	2.5573	2.4941	18
19	3.2067	3.1090	3.0169	2.9299	2.8476	2.7697	2.6959	2.6258	2.5592	2.4958	19
20	3.2112	3.1129	3.0202	2.9327	2.8501	2.7718	2.6977	2.6274	2.5606	2.4970	20
21	3.2147	3.1158	3.0227	2.9349	2.8519	2.7734	2.6991	2.6285	2.5616	2.4979	21
22	3.2173	3.1180	3.0246	2.9365	2.8533	2.7746	2.7000	2.6294	2.5623	2.4985	22
23	3.2193	3.1197	3.0260	2.9377	2.8543	2.7754	2.7008	2.6300	2.5628	2.4989	23
24	3.2209	3.1210	3.0271	2.9386	2.8550	2.7760	2.7013	2.6304	2.5632	2.4992	24
25	3.2220	3.1220	3.0279	2.9392	2.8556	2.7765	2.7017	2.6307	2.5634	2.4994	25

Answers to Self-Tests

CHAPTER 1	CHAPTER 2	CHAPTER 3	CHAPTER 4
True-False	**True-False**	**True-False**	**True-False**
1. F	1. F	1. T	1. T
2. T	2. F	2. T	2. T
3. F	3. F	3. T	3. F
4. T	4. F	4. F	4. T
5. T	5. F	5. T	5. T
6. F	6. T	6. F	6. F
7. T	7. F	7. T	7. T
8. F	8. T	8. F	8. F
9. T	9. F	9. T	9. F
10. F	10. T	10. T	10. F
Multiple Choice	**Multiple Choice**	**Multiple Choice**	**Multiple Choice**
1. d	1. e	1. c	1. e
2. e	2. a	2. d	2. c
3. e	3. e	3. d	3. e
4. e	4. e	4. c	4. e
5. d	5. d	5. d	5. c
6. d	6. b	6. a	6. d
7. d	7. e	7. f	7. f
8. a	8. e		8. e
	9. b		
	10. a		

CHAPTER 5

True-False

1. T
2. F
3. F
4. T
5. F
6. F
7. T
8. F
9. T
10. F

Multiple Choice

1. c
2. c
3. a
4. c
5. b
6. e
7. d

CHAPTER 6

True-False

1. F
2. F
3. F
4. T
5. F
6. F
7. T
8. T
9. T
10. T

Multiple Choice

1. d
2. b
3. d
4. d
5. b
6. c
7. a
8. c

CHAPTER 7

True-False

1. F
2. T
3. T
4. T
5. T
6. F
7. T
8. F
9. T
10. T

Multiple Choice

1. c
2. d
3. a
4. e
5. c
6. d

CHAPTER 8

True-False

1. T
2. T
3. T
4. F
5. F
6. T
7. T
8. F
9. F
10. F

Multiple Choice

1. a
2. b
3. b
4. d

CHAPTER 9

True-False

1. T
2. F
3. T
4. T
5. F
6. T
7. F
8. F
9. T

Multiple Choice

1. f
2. b
3. a
4. b
5. c
6. e
7. b
8. c

CHAPTER 10

True-False

1. F
2. T
3. T
4. F
5. T
6. F
7. F
8. F
9. T
10. F

Multiple Choice

1. a
2. c
3. b
4. d
5. e
6. b
7. a

CHAPTER 11

True-False

1. F
2. T
3. T
4. T
5. F
6. F
7. T
8. F
9. F
10. T
11. F
12. T

Multiple Choice

1. e
2. b
3. a
4. d
5. e
6. d
7. d

CHAPTER 12

True-False

1. F
2. F
3. T
4. T
5. T
6. T
7. F
8. T
9. F
10. F

Multiple Choice

1. d
2. d
3. c
4. a
5. c
6. d

CHAPTER 13	CHAPTER 15	CHAPTER 17	CHAPTER 19
True-False	**True-False**	**True-False**	**True-False**
1. T	1. F	1. F	1. T
2. T	2. T	2. F	2. F
3. T	3. F	3. T	3. F
4. T	4. T	4. F	4. F
5. T	5. F	5. T	5. T
6. F	6. T	6. F	6. F
7. F	7. T	7. T	7. T
8. F	8. F	8. F	8. F
9. T		9. T	9. T
10. T		10. T	10. T
Multiple Choice	**Multiple Choice**	**Multiple Choice**	**Multiple Choice**
1. c	1. c	1. d	1. b
2. e	2. a	2. a	2. d
3. a	3. e	3. c	3. b
4. c	4. e	4. d	4. c
5. e	5. d	5. both a and b	5. d
	6. c		6. c
			7. d
			8. e

CHAPTER 14	CHAPTER 16	CHAPTER 18	CHAPTER 20
True-False	**True-False**	**True-False**	**True-False**
1. F	1. F	1. F	1. F
2. T	2. T	2. F	2. F
3. F	3. F	3. T	3. T
4. F	4. F	4. F	4. F
5. T	5. T	5. T	5. F
6. F	6. F	6. T	6. T
7. T	7. F	7. F	7. F
8. T	8. T	8. T	8. T
9. T	9. F	9. T	9. F
10. T	10. T	10. F	10. F
Multiple Choice	**Multiple Choice**	**Multiple Choice**	**Multiple Choice**
1. b	1. d	1. d	1. c
2. c	2. a	2. d	2. d
3. a	3. b	3. d	3. d
4. b	4. c	4. b	4. d
5. b	5. c		5. c
	6. d		
	7. c		
	8. e		

CHAPTER 21

True-False

1. F
2. F
3. T
4. F
5. F
6. T
7. T
8. T
9. T
10. F

Multiple Choice

1. b
2. c
3. b
4. e
5. d
6. b
7. d

CHAPTER 22

True-False

1. F
2. F
3. F
4. F
5. F
6. F
7. F
8. F
9. F
10. T

Multiple Choice

1. d
2. a
3. f
4. d
5. d

CHAPTER 23

True-False

1. F
2. F
3. T
4. F
5. F
6. T
7. F
8. F
9. T
10. F
11. F

Multiple Choice

1. b
2. c
3. d
4. c

CHAPTER 24

True-False

1. T
2. F
3. T
4. T
5. F
6. F
7. T
8. F
9. F
10. F

Multiple Choice

1. c
2. a
3. b
4. b
5. c

CHAPTER 25

True-False

1. T
2. T
3. F
4. T
5. T
6. F
7. T
8. F
9. F
10. T

Multiple Choice

1. b
2. c
3. c
4. a

CHAPTER 26

True-False

1. F
2. T
3. T
4. F
5. F
6. F
7. F
8. T
9. F

Multiple Choice

1. b
2. c
3. b
4. f
5. e
6. a
7. d
8. c

CHAPTER 27

True-False

1. F
2. F
3. T
4. F
5. T
6. F
7. F
8. T
9. F
10. F
11. F
12. T

Multiple Choice

1. a
2. b
3. a
4. b
5. b

APPENDIX A

Self-Test 1

1. $250(Table A-1; 10 years; 8%)
   $250(0.46319) = $115.80

2. $5,000 = x(Table A-1; 10 years; 6%)
   = x(0.55839)
   $$x = \frac{\$5,000}{0.55839}$$
   = $895.43

3. $$PI = \frac{\text{present value of future net cash flows}}{\text{initial cash outlay}}$$
   Present value of future net cash flows
   = $3,000(Table A-1; 1 year; 8%) + $4,000(Table A-1; 2 years; 8%)
   + $2,000(Table A-1; 3 years; 8%)
   = $3,000(0.92593) + $4,000(0.85734) + $2,000(0.79383)
   = $2,777.79 + $3,429.36 + $1,587.66
   = $7,794.81
   $$PI = \frac{\$7,794.81}{\$5,000.00} = 1.5589$$

4. NPV = PV inflows − PV outflows
   = $7,794.81 − $5,000.00
   = $2,794.81
   Accept the project, as its NPV is positive and its PI is greater than 1.0.

5. NPV = $−10,000 + $3,000(Table A-1; 1 year; 10%) + $5,000(Table A-1;
   2 years; 10%) + $4,000(Table A-1; 3 years; 10%)
   = $−10,000 + $3,000(0.90909) + $5,000(0.82645)
   + $4,000(0.75131)
   = $−10,000 + $2,727.27 + $4,132.25 + $3,005.24
   = $−135.24
   $$PI = \frac{\$9,864.76}{\$10,000.00} = 0.9865$$
   Reject the project, as the NPV is negative and the PI is less than 1.0.

6. NPV = $-8,000 + $3,000(Table A-1; 1 year; 12%) + $6,000(Table A-1; 2 years; 12%) + $2,000(Table A-1; 3 years; 12%)
+ $1,000(Table A-1; 4 years; 12%) − $1,000(Table A-1; 5 years; 12%)

   = $-8,000 + $3,000(0.89286) + $6,000(0.79719) + $2,000(0.71178) + $1,000(0.63552) − $1,000(0.56743)

   = $-8,000 + $2,678.58 + $4,783.14 + $1,423.56 + $635.52 − $567.43

   = $953.37

   PI = $\dfrac{\$8,953.37}{\$8,000.00}$ = 1.1192

7. NPV = $-1,093.00
   + $100(Table A-1; 1 year; 8%) + $100(Table A-1; 2 years; 8%)
   + $100(Table A-1; 3 years; 8%) + $100(Table A-1; 4 years; 8%)
   + $100(Table A-1; 5 years; 8%) + $100(Table A-1; 6 years; 8%)
   + $100(Table A-1; 7 years; 8%) + $100(Table A-1; 9 years; 8%)
   + $1,100(Table A-1; 10 years; 8%)

   NPV = $-1,093.00 + $100(0.92593) + $100(0.85734) + $100(0.79383)
   + $100(0.73503) + $100(0.68958) + $100(0.63017)
   + $100(0.58349) + $100(0.54027) + $100(0.50025)
   + $1,100(0.46319)

   = $-1,093.00 + $92.593 + $85.784 + $79.383 + $73.503
   + $68.058 + $63.017 + $58.349 + $54.027 + $50.025
   + $509.509

   = $41.20

Self-Test 2

1. NPV = $-15,000 + $2,000 $\begin{bmatrix} \text{Table A-2} \\ \text{2 years} \\ 20\% \end{bmatrix}$ + $4,000 $\begin{bmatrix} \text{Table A-1} \\ \text{3 years} \\ 20\% \end{bmatrix}$

   + $5,000 $\begin{bmatrix} \text{Table A-1} \\ \text{4 years} \\ 20\% \end{bmatrix}$ + $6,000 $\begin{bmatrix} \text{Table A-1} \\ \text{5 years} \\ 20\% \end{bmatrix}$

   = $-15,000 + $2,000(1.5278) + $4,000(0.57870)
   + $5,000(0.48225) + $6,000(0.40188)

   = $-15,000 + $3,055.60 + $2,314.80 + $2,411.25 + $2,411.28

   = $-4,807.07

   PI = $\dfrac{\$10,192.93}{\$15,000.00}$ = 0.6795

The project should be rejected, as its NPV is negative and the PI is less than 1.0.

2. $1,000 = $2,000 $\begin{bmatrix} \text{Table A-1} \\ \text{? years} \\ 8\% \end{bmatrix}$

0.500 = $\begin{bmatrix} \text{Table A-1} \\ \text{? years} \\ 8\% \end{bmatrix}$

The table value in the 8% column comes closest to 0.500 in the 9-year row. Thus, it will take 9 years for $1,000 to accumulate to $2,000 if it is compounded at 8%.

3. $1,000 = $3,000 $\begin{bmatrix} \text{Table A-1} \\ \text{7 years} \\ ?\% \end{bmatrix}$

0.3333 = $\begin{bmatrix} \text{Table A-1} \\ \text{7 years} \\ ?\% \end{bmatrix}$

The table value in the 7-year row comes closest to 0.333 in the 17% column. Thus, it is necessary to compound $1,000 at 17% for 7 years in order to accumulate $3,000.

4.   X = $3,000 $\begin{bmatrix} \text{Table A-1} \\ \text{10 years} \\ 8\% \end{bmatrix}$

= $3,000(0.46319)

= $1,289.57

5. a. X = $100 $\begin{bmatrix} \text{Table A-2} \\ \text{10 years} \\ 5\% \end{bmatrix}$

= $100(7.7217)

= $772.17

b. X = $100 $\begin{bmatrix} \text{Table A-2} \\ \text{10 years} \\ 10\% \end{bmatrix}$

= $100(6.1446)

= $614.46

c. $X = \$100 \begin{bmatrix} \text{Table A-2} \\ \text{10 years} \\ 20\% \end{bmatrix}$

$= \$100(4.1925)$

$= \$419.25$

d. $X = \$100 \begin{bmatrix} \text{Table A-2} \\ \text{10 years} \\ 30\% \end{bmatrix}$

$= \$100(3.0915)$

$= \$309.15$

6. a. $X = \$50 \begin{bmatrix} \text{Table A-1} \\ \text{4 years} \\ 10\% \end{bmatrix}$

$= \$50(0.68301)$

$= \$34.15$

b. $X = \$50 \begin{bmatrix} \text{Table A-1} \\ \text{4 years} \\ 20\% \end{bmatrix}$

$= \$50(0.48225)$

$= \$24.11$

c. $X = \$50 \dfrac{1}{(1 + 0)^4}$

$= \$50 \left(\dfrac{1}{1}\right)$

$= \$50$

d. $X = \$50 \dfrac{1}{(1 + 1.0)^4}$

$= \$50 \left(\dfrac{1}{16}\right)$

$= \$3.125$

7. a. $\$100 = X \begin{bmatrix} \text{Table A-1} \\ \text{5 years} \\ 16\% \end{bmatrix}$

$= X(0.47611)$

$X = \$210.04$

b. $\$100 = X \begin{bmatrix} \text{Table A-1} \\ \text{10 periods} \\ 8\% \end{bmatrix}$

$= X(0.46319)$

$X = \$215.89$

c. $\$100 = X \begin{bmatrix} \text{Table A-1} \\ \text{20 periods} \\ 4\% \end{bmatrix}$

$= X(0.45639)$

$X = \$219.11$

8. a. Initial Outlay

New machine	$\$-20,000$
Sale of old machine	$+ 2,000$
Tax gain	
($5,000 - $2,000).4	$+ 1,200$
	$\$-16,800$

b. Annual Cash Flows

	Cash Method	Book Method
Savings	$10,000	$10,000
Change in depreciation		(3,000 − 1,000)
Taxable increase		8,000
Taxes	3,200	3,200
Annual net cash flow	$ 6,800	

c. Terminal flow:

Salvage value	$ 5,000
Annual cash flow	6,800
	$11,800

d. Cash-flow diagram:

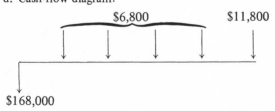

$6,800 $11,800

$168,000

e. $\text{NPV} = \$-16,800 = \$6,800 \begin{bmatrix} \text{Table A-2} \\ \text{4 years} \\ 14\% \end{bmatrix} + \$11,800 \begin{bmatrix} \text{Table A-1} \\ \text{5 years} \\ 14\% \end{bmatrix}$

$\phantom{e.\ \text{NPV}} = \$16,800 + \$6,800(2.9137) + \$11,800(0.51937)$

$\phantom{e.\ \text{NPV}} = \$-16,800 + \$19,813.16 + \$6,128.57$

$\phantom{e.\ \text{NPV}} = \$9,141.73$

$\text{PI} = \dfrac{\$25,941.73}{\$16,800} = 1.544$

Self-Test 3

1. $\$10,000 = \$14,000 \dfrac{1}{(1+r)^5}$

$0.71428 = \dfrac{1}{(1+r)^5}$

Therefore, IRR = 7%, as the Table A-1 value for 5 years closest to 0.71428 occurs in the 7% column (0.71299).

2. $\$700 = \$1,857 \dfrac{1}{(1+r)^{20}}$

$0.37695 = \dfrac{1}{(1+r)^{20}}$

Therefore, IRR = 5%.

3. $\$30,000 = \$6,000 \sum\limits_{t=1}^{10} \dfrac{1}{(1+r)^t}$

$5.0 = \sum\limits_{t=1}^{10} \dfrac{1}{(1+r)^t}$

Therefore, IRR = 15%.

4. $\$20,000 = \$3,928 \sum\limits_{t=1}^{15} \dfrac{1}{(1+r)^t}$

$5.0916 = \sum\limits_{t=1}^{15} \dfrac{1}{(1+r)^t}$

Therefore, IRR = 18%.

5. $40,000 = \$10,000 \sum_{t=1}^{5} \frac{1}{(1+r)^t} + \$15,000\frac{1}{(1+r)^6}$

Try 20%:

$40,000 = \$10,000(2.9906) + \$15,000(0.33490)$
$= \$29,906 + \$5,023.50$
$= \$34,929.50$

Try 15%:

$40,000 = \$10,000(3.3522) + \$15,000(0.43233)$
$= \$33,522.0 + \$6,484.95$
$= \$40,006.95$

Thus, 15% is the approximate IRR.

6. $61,615 = \$10,000 \sum_{t=1}^{6} \frac{1}{(1+r)^t} + \$70,000 \frac{1}{(1+r)^7}$

Try 20%:

$61,615.0 = \$10,000(3.3255) + \$70,000(0.27908)$
$= \$33,255 + \$19,535.6$
$= \$52,790.6$

Try 15%:

$61,615.0 = \$10,000(3.7845) + \$70,000(0.37594)$
$= \$37,845 + \$26,315.8$
$= \$64,160.8$

Try 16%:

$61,615.0 = \$100,000(3.6847) + \$70,000(0.35383)$
$= \$36,847 + \$24,768.10$
$= \$61,615.10$

7. $2,992 = \$700 \frac{1}{1+r} + \$1,400 \frac{1}{(1+r)^2} + \$3,000\frac{1}{(1+r)^3}$

Try 20%:

$2,992 = \$700(0.83333) + \$1,400(0.69444) + \$3,000(0.57870)$
$= \$583.33 + \$972.22 + \$1,736.10$
$= \$3,291.65$

Try 25%:

$2,992 = $700(0.8000) + $1,400(0.6400) + $3,000(0.51200)
    = $560 + $896 + $1,536
    = $2,992

Thus, the IRR = 25%.

8. $5,490 = $2,000 \sum_{t=1}^{2} \frac{1}{(1+r)^t} + $4,000 \frac{1}{(1+r)^3} + $3,000 \frac{1}{(1+r)^4}$

Try 20%:

$5,490 = $2,000(1.5278) + $4,000(0.57870) + $3,000(0.48225)
    = $3,055.60 + $2,314.8 + $1,446.75
    = $6,817.15

Try 30%:

$5,490 = $2,000(1.3609) $ $4,000(0.45517) + $3,000(0.35013)
    = $2,721.80 + $1,820.68 + $1,050.39
    = $5,592.87

Try 31%:

$5,490 = $2,000(1.3461) + $4,000(0.44482) + $3,000(0.33956)
    = $2,692.20 + $1,779.28 + $1,018.68
    = $5,490.16

Thus, 31% is this project's IRR.

9. $1,000 = $4,000 \frac{1}{(1+r)^2}$

   $(1+r)^2 = 4.0$
   $1 + r = \sqrt{4.0}$
   $1 + r = 2.0$
       $r = 1.0$, or IRR = 100%